Augustan Rome 44 BC *to* AD *14*

The Edinburgh History of Ancient Rome
General Editor: J. S. Richardson

Augustan Rome 44 BC to AD 14

The Restoration of the Republic and the Establishment of the Empire

J. S. Richardson

EDINBURGH
University Press

Edinburgh University Press Ltd
22 George Square, Edinburgh EH8 9LF

www.euppublishing.com

Typeset in Sabon
by Norman Tilley Graphics Ltd, Northampton,
and Printed and Bound in the United States of America
by Edwards Brothers, Inc .

A CIP record for this book is available from the
British Library

ISBN 978 0 7486 1954 2 (hardback)
ISBN 978 0 7486 1955 9 (paperback)
ISBN 978 0 7486 2904 6 (webready PDF)
ISBN 978 0 7486 5533 5 (epub)
ISBN 978 0 7486 5532 8 (Amazon ebook)

Published with the support of the Edinburgh University
Scholarly Publishing Initiatives Fund.

Contents

Illustrations

Series editor's preface

Rome, the city and its empire, stands at the centre of the history of Europe, of the Mediterranean, and of lands which we now call the Middle East. Its influence through the ages which followed its transformation into the Byzantine Empire down to modern times can be seen across the world. This series is designed to present for students and all who are interested in the history of western civilisation the changing shape of the entity that was Rome, through its earliest years, the development and extension of the republic, the shift into the Augustan Empire, the development of the imperial state which grew from that, and the differing patterns of that state which emerged in east and west in the fourth to sixth centuries. It covers not only the political and military history of that shifting and complex society but also the contributions of the economic and social history of the Roman world to that change and growth and the intellectual contexts of these developments. The team of contributors, all scholars at the forefront of research in archaeology and history in the English-speaking world, present in the eight volumes of the series an accessible and challenging account of Rome across a millennium and a half of its expansion and transformation. Each book stands on its own as a picture of the period it covers and together the series aims to answer the fundamental question: what was Rome, and how did a small city in central Italy become one of the most powerful and significant entities in the history of the world?

John Richardson, General Editor

Author's preface

The series of which this book is a part is intended to answer a deceptively simple question: what was Rome? As with all the best simple questions, the answer is far more complicated and, in the case of the history of ancient Rome, differs from period to period. This book deals with the years between the death of Julius Caesar in March 44 BC and that of Augustus in August AD 14. It was a time in which Rome changed radically and what Rome was also changed. Within the constitution of the city these changes seem at first glance strangely contradictory: when Julius Caesar was assassinated he was a dictator and had just been made a perpetual dictator, while at Augustus' death the claim was that the Republic had been restored over forty years earlier; on the other hand Julius had been a dictator within a still recognisable Republic, whereas Augustus was an unchallengeable monarch and had established a family-based dynasty. In this sense, Rome changed within this period from a republic into an empire: it had an emperor. Beyond that, and as part of a longer process, it was now that the Roman Empire began to become what it was to be for the next half-millennium, a territorial continuum with Rome, and then Rome and Constantinople, as its centre. Though it was to be another two centuries before all the free inhabitants of the empire were to be citizens of Rome, the elements were in place and the process under way. This volume in the series seeks to explain, through a narrative account of the period, how and (so far as is possible) why these remarkable changes came about.

I have many people to thank for help with the writing of this book. The idea for the series emerged from conversations with John Davey, then the Edinburgh University Press editor for classics and ancient history, and his continuing interest in the project has been always encouraging. Carol Macdonald, his successor at EUP, has been just as helpful and as sympathetic an editor as one could wish for. Among academic colleagues I would thank especially Michael Crawford and Jean-Louis Ferrary for their advice and assistance, and especially Jill Harries, who read the whole text and made acute and pertinent criticisms, some of which I have taken notice of. Last but not least, I would thank my wife, Joan, for her loving patience and persistence, without which this book would have taken even longer to complete.

Abbreviations

Appian
    B Civ.   *Bella civilia* (*Civil Wars*)
    Illyr.   *Illyrica* (*Illyrian Wars*)
    Praef.   *Praefatio* (Preface)
Apuleius
    Apol.   *Apologia* (*His Defence*)
Asconius
    In Scaur.   *In Scaurianum* (commentary on Cicero's speech *Pro Scauro*)
Aug.   Augustus
    RG   *Res Gestae Divi Augusti* (*Achievements of the Divine Augustus*)
Broughton, *MRR*   T. R. S. Broughton, *The Magistrates of the Roman Republic* (1951–86)

Caesar
    B Civ.   *Bellum Civile* (*The Civil War*)
    B Gall.   *Bellum Gallicum* (*The Gallic War*)
Censorinus
    DN   *De die natali* (*On Birthdays*)
Cic.   Cicero
    2 Verr.   *In Verrem, actio secunda* (second section of *Against Verres*)
    Ad Brut.   *Epistulae ad Brutum* (*Letters to Brutus*)
    Att.   *Epistulae ad Atticum* (*Letters to Atticus*)
    Fam.   *Epistulae ad familiares* (*Letters to his Friends*)
    Off.   *De officiis* (*On Duties*)
    Phil.   *Orationes Philippicae* (*Philippic Orations*)
    Q Fr.   *Epistulae ad Quintum fratrem* (*Letters to his Brother Quintus*)
    Vatin.   *In Vatinium* (*Against Vatinius*)
CIL   *Corpus Inscriptionum Latinarum*

Collatio	*Collatio legum Mosaicarum et Romanarum* (*Comparison of Mosaic and Roman Laws*)
Dig.	*Digesta* (*Digest* of Justinian)
Dio Cass.	Cassius Dio
Donatus	
Vit. Verg.	*Vita Vergilii* (*Life of Vergil*)
EJ	V. Ehrenberg and A. H. M. Jones (eds), *Documents Illustrating the Reigns of Augustus and Tiberius* (1976)
Fast. Amit.	*Fasti Amiterni* (list of magistrates from Amiternum)
Fast. Ant.	*Fasti Antiates* (calendar from Antium)
Fast. Ant. min.	*Fasti Antiates minores* (calendar of consuls from Antium)
Fast. Arv.	*Fasti Arvalium* (list of Roman magistrates, recorded by the priesthood of the *fratres arvales*)
Fast. Cap.	*Fasti consulares Capitolini* (list of consuls from Rome)
Fast. Cupr.	*Fasti Cuprenses* (list of consuls from Cupra Maritima)
Fast. Maff.	*Fasti Maffeani* (calendar of unknown provenance)
Fast. Ostiens.	*Fasti Ostienses* (list of consuls from Ostia)
Fast. Praenest.	*Fasti Praenestini* (calendar from Praeneste)
Fast. Val.	*Fasti Vallenses* (calendar of unknown college, from Rome)
Fast. Ven.	*Fasti Venusini* (calendar from Venusia)
Fast. Verul.	*Fasti Verulani* (calendar from Verulae)
Fer. Cum.	*Feriale Cumanum* (list of religious festival from Cumae)
Gaius	
Inst.	*Institutiones* (*Institutes*)
Gellius	Aulus Gellius
NA	*Noctes Atticae* (*Attic Nights*)
Hor.	Horace
Ars P.	*Ars poetica* (*Art of Poetry*)
Carm.	*Carmina* (*Odes*)
Epod.	*Epodi* (*Epodes*)
Epist.	*Epistulae* (*Letters*)
Sat.	*Satirae* or *Sermones* (*Satires*)

ILS	H. Dessau (ed.), *Inscriptiones Latinae Selectae* (1892–1916)
Inscr. Ital.	*Inscriptiones Italiae* (1931–)
Inst. Iust.	*Institutiones Iustiniani* (*Instututes of Justinian*)
Jerome	
Chron.	*Chronica* (*Chronicles*)
Josephus	
AJ	*Antiquitates Judaicae* (*Antiquities of the Jews*)
BJ	*Bellum Judaicum* (*The Jewish War*)
Julian	
Caes.	*Caesares* (*The Caesars*)
Juvenal	
Sat.	*Saturae* (*Satires*)
Livy	
Per.	*Periochae* (*Summaries*)
Praef.	*Praefatio* (*Preface*)
Macrobius	
Sat.	*Saturnalia*
MGH	*Monumenta Germaniae Historica*
Nic. Dam.	Nicolaus Damascenus
Vit. Aug.	*Vita Augusti* (Life of Augustus)
Ovid	
Am.	*Amores* (*Love Poems*)
Ars am.	*Ars amatoria* (*Art of Love*)
Fast.	*Fasti* (*The Calendar*)
Pont.	*Epistulae ex Ponto* (*Letters from Pontus*)
Tr.	*Tristia* (*Sorrows*)
Paulus	Iulius Paulus
Sent.	*Sententiae*
Pliny	Pliny (the Elder)
HN	*Naturalis historia* (*Natural History*)
Pliny	Pliny (the Younger)
Ep.	*Epistulae* (*Letters*)
Plut.	Plutarch
Alex.	*Alexander*
Ant.	*Antonius*
Brut.	*Brutus*
Caes.	*Caesar*
Cic.	*Cicero*

	Pomp.	*Pompeius*
	Reg. et imp.	*Regum et imperatorum apophthegmata*
	apophthegm.	*(Sayings of Kings and Generals)*
Prop.		Propertius
Quint.		Quintilian
	Decl. min.	*Declamationes minores (Lesser Declamations)*
	Inst.	*Institutio oratoria (Institutes of Oratory)*
RIC		H. Mattingly, E. A. Sydenham et al., *Roman Imperial Coinage* (1923–84)
RPC		A. Burnett et al., *Roman Provincial Coinage* (1992–)
RRC		M. H. Crawford, *Roman Republican Coinage* (1974)
Seneca		Seneca (the Elder)
	Controv.	*Controversiae (Controversies)*
	Suas.	*Suasoriae (Persuasions)*
Seneca		Seneca (the Younger)
	Ad Marc.	*Consolatio ad Marciam (Consolation to Marcia)*
	Ad Polyb.	*Ad Polybium de consolatione (To Polybius about Consolation)*
	Apocol.	*Apocolocyntosis (The Pumpkinification of the Deified Claudius)*
	Ben.	*De beneficiis (On Favours)*
	Brev. vit.	*De brevitate vitae (On the Shortness of Life)*
	Clem.	*De clementia (On Clemency)*
	Ep.	*Epistulae (Letters on Moral Issues)*
	Q Nat.	*Quaestiones naturales (Natural Questions)*
Suet.		Suetonius
	Aug.	*Divus Augustus*
	Calig.	*Gaius Caligula*
	Claud.	*Divus Claudius*
	Iul.	*Divus Iulius*
	Tib.	*Tiberius*
	Vita Hor.	*Vita Horatii (Life of Horace)*
Tacitus		
	Ann.	*Annales (Annals)*
Tib.		Tibullus

Ulpian
    Tit.   *Tituli (Abbreviated Extracts)*
Val. Max.   Valerius Maximus
Vell. Pat.   Velleius Paterculus
Verg.   Vergil
    Aen.   *Aeneid*
    Ecl.   *Eclogae (Eclogues)*
    G.   *Georgica (Georgics)*

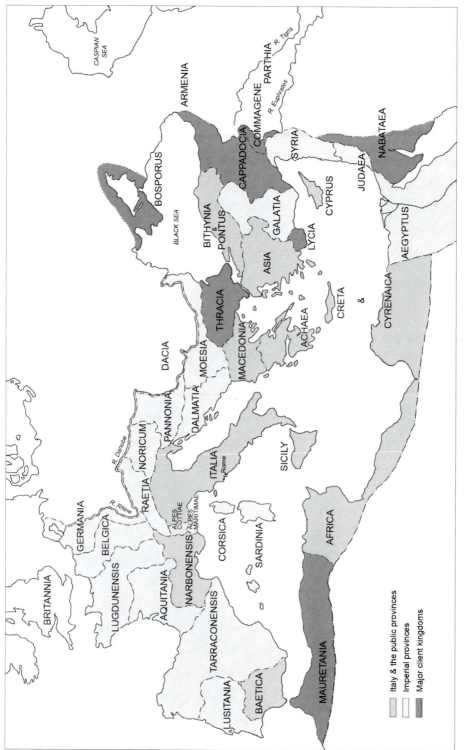

Map of the Roman Empire, *c.* AD 14 (map drawn by Donna Bilak)

CHAPTER 1

Setting the scene

In the Musée des Beaux Arts in Dijon there hangs a painted panel, showing a curious scene.[1] Two figures stand looking up into the sky: on the right, a woman, dressed in a heavy blue gown with a gem-encrusted gold circlet on her head, pointing upwards with her right hand; and on the left, a man, wearing a magnificent fur-lined red velvet robe, patterned in gold, and a crown, enclosing an exotic red cap with protruding flaps, which extend in front of and behind the crown, who shields his eyes at the brightness of a vision in the gold-painted sky. The woman is a prophet, the Sibyl of Tibur, and the man the emperor Augustus. The panel was painted by Konrad Witz as part of an altar-piece, commissioned for the church of St Leonard in Basel in 1435, which shows events from the Old Testament and from Roman history which parallel and foretell stories from the New Testament, demonstrating the significance for the whole human race of the salvation brought by Christ. The panel of Augustus and the Sibyl shows the story, told in the thirteenth-century chronicle of popes and emperors by Martinus Polonus,[2] that the emperor, having been urged by the senators to accept worship as a divinity, called the Sibyl to him for consultation in Rome; and that she, after three days, told him that a king would come from heaven. The emperor then saw a vision of the heavens being opened and, amidst a brilliant light, a beautiful virgin, standing on an altar, holding in her arms a young child; and he heard a voice proclaiming that this place was the altar of the son of God. Martinus goes on to say that the room in which Augustus received this vision became the church of Sta Maria on the Capitol, which is still called the Aracoeli (the Altar of Heaven).

For Konrad Witz, as for Martinus Polonus, Augustus was a figure

1. Musée des Beaux Arts Dijon, inv. D 161 A.
2. Martinus Polonus, *Chronicon pontificum et imperatorum* (ed. L. Weiland, *MGH* 22, Hanover 1872), 443.

Figure 1 Konrad Witz, *The Emperor Augustus and the Sibyl of Tibur* (© Musée des Beaux Arts Dijon, photo François Jay)

of immense significance, not only because he was the emperor of Rome but because he stood at a hinge in the history of the human race, the moment of the incarnation of the Christ. Secular historians have also seen him as an individual who marked a fundamental change in the structure of the world, as can be seen from the titles of books about him: Ronald Syme controversially entitled his classic work *The Roman Revolution*, while a recent more journalistic biography is called *Augustus: Godfather of Europe*.[3] Whether their focus is the salvation of humanity, the history of the Roman Empire or modern political structures, scholars, historians and artists through the ages have repeatedly seen Augustus as a man who was the author of, or at least a participant in, some of the most significant changes in European and world history. He is, for all that, a difficult man to pin down: in the fourth century AD, the emperor Julian, in a satire on earlier emperors, described him as entering a Saturnalia banquet organised by the gods, changing colour like a chameleon, from yellow to red to black.[4] The problem with Augustus, to which Julian's caricature draws attention, lies in the apparent discrepancy between the youth who seized control of the troops loyal to his assassinated great-uncle, Julius Caesar, in 44 BC and in the following year, in collaboration with Marcus Antonius and Lepidus, drew up lists of political opponents to be exterminated, and the self-proclaimed 'leader of Italy' who fought the battle of Actium against that same Antonius and Cleopatra in 31; to say nothing of the *princeps* of the Roman senate and people, who was honoured with the title of father of his country in 2 BC, and who presented himself in his own account of his achievements, the *Res Gestae Divi Augusti* (completed shortly before he died) as sharing power with others as the custom of the ancestors demanded, bringing peace and security to the Roman world and prosperity and reconstruction to the Roman people and its city. The historian Tacitus, writing a century later, presents a picture of differing views held by people at the time of Augustus' death:[5] some held, as Augustus claimed in the *Res Gestae*, that he had only used unconstitutional means when forced to by the conditions of civil war, and that he had brought peace and security to the nation and the world; but others that he had acted out of lust for power and used deceit and military force to achieve it. Tacitus' own view, set out in the opening chapters of his *Annales*, was clearly closer to the second opinion than the first, but it is notable that, when he came to represent the opposing views of those at the time, the debate centres on the fifteen years before Actium.

3. R. Syme, *The Roman Revolution*, Oxford: Oxford University Press, 1939; R. Holland, *Augustus: Godfather of Europe*, Stroud: Sutton, 2004.
4. Julian, *Caes.* 4. Syme commented that Julian was right to describe Augustus as a chameleon: 'colour changed, but not substance' (*Roman Revolution*, 2).
5. Tacitus, *Ann.* 1.8–10. See below, p. 219.

This book is not a biography of Augustus, much less an attempt to resolve the differences of view which Tacitus gives. Its intention is to give an account of what the entity we call 'Rome' was at the turn of the first centuries BC and AD, the ways in which it had changed from what went before and the processes which brought that change about. Inevitably, given the overwhelming importance of Augustus in the Roman world in this period, much of the focus will be on this individual, who brought about such great change and yet claimed to have altered so little; but in such a period in which the shape and structures of Rome shifted and altered, it must be remembered that Augustus himself was not unaffected. He was changed over these years, not simply an executor of change.

Caesar's heir: the background

Gaius Octavius (as Augustus was known for the first eighteen years of his life) was born shortly before daybreak on 23 September 63 BC, in the consulship of Marcus Tullius Cicero and Gaius Antonius, a day on which his father, also called Gaius Octavius, was present at a meeting of the senate where the conspiracy of Catiline was being discussed. Suetonius writes that Octavius was late in attending the meeting because of his wife's confinement. Though there have been since antiquity debates about the significance of the date of the birth of the young Octavius, not least among astrologers,[6] the undoubted fact that he was born in the year of Cicero's consulship and of the conspiracy of Catiline carries with it its own historical symbolism. The year 63 BC was, not least in Cicero's opinion, of crucial significance to the Roman Republic. From Cicero's standpoint, the suppression of Catiline and his supporters saved the Republic; but, even excepting that, the year was full of remembrances of the turbulent recent history of the state and foreshadowings of what was to come. At the beginning of a year the tribune of the plebs (the citizen inhabitants of the city), Publius Servilius Rullus, proposed an agrarian bill, echoing on a far larger scale the measures of the Gracchi and the distributions made to veteran soldiers by Marius and Sulla; later in the year, an elaborate show-trial was arranged, on the motion of another tribune, Titus Labienus, of a member of the equestrian

---

6. Suet. *Aug.* 5.1 and 94.5. On the astrology, see recently the discussion by Tamsyn Barton, 'Augustus and Capricorn: polyvalency and imperial rhetoric', *Journal of Roman Studies* 85 (1995), 33–51.

order, Publius Rabirius, for the murder of the radical tribune Lucius Appuleius Saturninus in 100 BC. This trial came to a farcical end, being abandoned after a red flag on the Janiculum hill was lowered, allegedly announcing an imminent attack on the city, but not before Cicero had appeared for the defence. Later still, at the time of the elections for the consulships of 62 at which Catiline ran unsuccessfully, Lucius Licinius Lucullus was allowed to celebrate his triumph over Mithridates and Tigranes, three years after he had returned to Rome, an event for which Cicero himself later claimed credit.[7] At the same time, in Syria Pompeius had been completing his reorganisation of the former Hellenistic kingdom into a Roman province, had heard of the death of Mithridates of Pontus and was preparing to return home; and in Rome Gaius Julius Caesar had not only been elected to the praetorship for the following year but had also been chosen for the most prestigious religious appointment in the city, that of high priest (*pontifex maximus*), against fierce competition from other far senior candidates. The struggles and preoccupations of the past half-century were still being played out in 63, even as the political and military powers which were to bring the Republic to an end were beginning to appear.

The young Octavius was born into this late Republican world, and was very much part of it. His father's family came from Velitrae, some twenty-five miles south-east of Rome, on the southern edge of the Alban hills, a Volscian town which had been Roman since 338 BC. His grandfather had been a member of the equestrian order, and so a wealthy and important man in Velitrae, but his father was the first member of his branch of the Octavii to enter the Roman senate, being elected as praetor for 61 and holding the province of Macedonia *pro consule* (i.e. with the power or *imperium* of a consul) in the two following years. There he won some military successes, enough at least for him to have been acclaimed as *imperator* (a recognition of a successful commander), on his return to Rome and subsequent progress to the consulship. In the event, he died while on his way back from Macedonia. He left, in addition to the young Gaius Octavius, two daughters, both called Octavia, the first the child of his first wife, Ancharia, and the second, young Octavius' sister, by his second wife, Atia. Through his mother, young Octavius was linked to the Julii Caesares, since her mother, Julia, was the sister of Julius Caesar. When Octavius was eleven years old he

7. Cic. *Lucullus* 3.

delivered a funeral oration for his grandmother (Suet. *Aug.* 8). He was probably her only surviving male descendant, but his appearance on this occasion will have underlined his relationship to Julius Caesar, then (in 53 and 52 BC) engaged in dealing with fresh revolts in the east and north of his newly conquered Gallic province. These were times of great turmoil within the political life of Rome: in 55, Pompeius and Marcus Licinius Crassus, who had formed in 60 an informal political alliance with Julius Caesar, had been elected consuls in January of their year of office after a violent interregnum, and they passed a law for the prolongation of Caesar's Gallic command for five more years, while they themselves were voted five-year commands in Spain and Syria respectively by another law. The elections in the following year were delayed through scandals involving both the consuls, and their successors for 53 did not enter office until July. The death of Crassus at the battle of Carrhae against the Parthians in 53 and of Julia, Pompeius' wife and Julius Caesar's daughter, in 54 inevitably put strains on the connection between the two remaining members of the pact concluded in 60, while further rioting at the elections in 53 led to the year 52 beginning once again with no consuls in office. The murder in January 52 of the populist agitator Publius Clodius Pulcher at the hands of the supporters of his adversary Titus Annius Milo, who was one of the candidates for the consulship, resulted in still further chaos and the election of Pompeius to the extraordinary post of sole consul three months into the year. In such a context the funeral oration by the eleven-year-old Octavius might seem almost a political manifesto, but in the complex world of the late Republic matters were less simple. Octavius' mother, Atia, had remarried, shortly after the elder Octavius' death in 59, and her new husband, young Octavius' stepfather, was Lucius Marcius Philippus, who was elected consul for 56 along with Cn. Cornelius Lentulus Marcellinus. The latter proved a strong opponent of Caesar, Pompeius and Crassus, refusing the candidacy for the consulship of the latter two in November 56, when they presented themselves late, and being responsible for the further delay in the elections until he was out of office the following year; as for Philippus, he seems to have played a more cautious role, not hindering his colleague (according to Cicero) when the latter was opposing measures promoted by Caesar earlier in the year; and when the moment of decision came in January 49, when Caesar crossed the Rubicon and advanced towards Rome, Philippus withdrew from the city to a more distant neutrality, apparently with Caesar's approval.[8] If Philippus was lukewarm towards his stepson's great-uncle in the late 50s, the same could not be said of Gaius Claudius Marcellus, who had married Octavia, the sister of young Octavius, by the mid 50s.[9] Elected consul for the year 50, it was Marcellus who late in the year belaboured the senate with stories of Caesar's imminent march across the Alps and into Italy, and, when he failed to get senatorial support for moves to have Caesar declared a public enemy, went (on his own authority as consul) to Pompeius, placed a sword in his hands and instructed him to raise forces to defend the Republic.[10] Despite this, Marcellus failed to follow Pompeius to Greece and in due course accepted Caesar's overtures,[11] remaining quietly out of the limelight until his death in 40.

The young Octavius thus was connected to a series of families with complicated relationships to the man who became the most powerful individual in the Roman world, Julius Caesar. His own relationship with his great-uncle seems to have been cemented by his presence with Caesar in the campaigns against the sons of Pompeius in Spain in 45; and Caesar drew up his final will after his return to Rome from Spain. In it he named the grandson of his younger sister, Gaius Octavius, and Lucius Pinarius and Quintus Pedius, probably the children of his elder sister, as his heirs, but left three-quarters of his estate to Octavius, with the remaining quarter to be shared between the other two. Moreover, at the end of the will Octavius was required as heir to take Caesar's name.[12]

This document was to prove immensely significant, not only for Octavius but for the history of Rome. It did not, of course, make him successor to Caesar's position in the state, which was not in the gift even of a dictator, the post which Caesar held continuously from at least April 46 until he was named as *dictator perpetuo* in February 44. It did, however, mark Octavius, now to be called Gaius Julius Caesar, as his principal heir. Why Caesar preferred Octavius to his other two relatives in this way is by no means certain. Certainly Pedius, and probably Pinarius too, were older than Octavius, who

8. Cic. *Q Fr.* 2.5.2 (consul est egregius Lentulus non impediente collega); *Att.* 9.15.4; 10.4.10.

9. Caesar attempted to persuade Pompeius to marry her after the death of Julia, though she was already married to Marcellus by that time (Suet. *Iul.* 27.1).

10. Appian, *B Civ.* 2.31; Dio Cass. 40.64; Plut. *Pomp.* 58–9.

11. Cic. *Att.* 10.15.3.

12. Suet. *Iul.* 83.1–2. The will was made on 13 September 45 BC. Suetonius says that Pedius and Pinarius were the grandsons of Caesar's sister, but this seems improbable, given their ages (see Syme, *Roman Revolution*, 128 n.4).

was approaching his eighteenth birthday when the will was made, and Pedius had served as a subordinate commander (*legatus*) with Caesar in Gaul in 58 and 57 BC, and in 48 as praetor was involved in a military action in which a revolt by Milo, Clodius' old enemy, was crushed and Milo killed;[13] in 45, he was a legate of Caesar's in the final campaigns against the Pompeians and was allowed to celebrate a triumph (illegally, since his command was not an independent one) on 13 December 45.[14] Of Pinarius, nothing else is known. It may simply be that Caesar thought better of Octavius than of the other two, and Octavius was made a member of the prestigious priestly college of *pontifices* and was later enrolled into previously hereditary ranks of the patricians by Caesar.[15] If Caesar was looking to one of his sisters' descendants for an heir, he might have thought that Octavius was better connected with the major families of Rome. For all the subsequent significance of this will, it must be remembered that there is no reason to believe that Caesar attached as much importance to it when he made it in September 45. He did not expect to be murdered the following March, and indeed Suetonius says that he left instructions for the appointment of guardians to his son, should one be born (Suet. *Iul.* 83.2), in which case those named in the will would not have inherited. In the 50s he had made Pompeius his heir, and after that Marcus Antonius, whom he would also have required to take his name, as was the case with Octavius.[16] Of course, to be the heir to such a man was a role of great consequence, but chiefly for the inheritance of Caesar's immense wealth and the continuance of his family; and in principle, though Caesar's heir might hope and expect to retain the political support of those who had been the supporters of his adoptive father, his extraordinary position in the Republic did not belong to the family. On the other hand, Rome had never seen a political or military figure with the power that Julius Caesar exercised in his last years, power which his being denominated *dictator perpetuo* showed

---

13. Caesar, *B Gall.* 2.1.1, 11.3; *B Civ.* 3.22.
14. Dio Cass. 43.31.1, 43.42.1; *Inscr. Ital.* 13.1.86–7. Another proconsular legate, Q. Fabius Maximus, also triumphed from Spain on 13 December 45, having entered office as suffect consul on 1 October. Fabius died on 31 December.
15. Nic, Dam. *Vit. Aug.* 4 says he succeeded L. Domitius Ahenobarbus, who had been killed fighting on the Pompeian side at Pharsalus in 48. On the patriciate, see Nic. Dam. *Vit. Aug.* 15. Caesar had been given the right of enrolling plebeians into the patriciate by the *lex Cassia*, probably late in 45 or in 44 (Suet. *Iul.* 41.1; Tacitus, *Ann.* 11.25; Dio Cass. 43.47.3).
16. Suet. *Iul.* 83.1; Cic. *Phil.* 2.71.

he had no intention of giving up. The very fact that such power had been created and wielded meant that, should anything happen to him, there would be others who would attempt to take his place, as well as those who would be determined that no one else would ever do so. In such a context, the bearer of Caesar's name would be in a hitherto unparalleled position.

Note: the naming of Caesar in this book

As will become clear, the use by the young Octavius of the name of 'Caesar', following the requirement by Julius Caesar in his will, played a crucial role in his establishment of himself as a force to be reckoned with in the power struggles in the years to come. For this reason in this book I have called him 'Caesar' down to the year 27 BC, when he was given the name 'Augustus'. It was common practice for an adopted son to use the name of his birth-family with the suffix '-ianus' as an additional name (so that the son of Lucius Aemilius Paullus, adopted into the family of the Cornelii Scipiones, became Publius Cornelius Scipio Aemilianus), and many modern historians use the name 'Octavianus' or 'Octavian' for the young Caesar, to avoid the danger of confusing him with his adoptive father; but it should be noted that, so far as we know, he never used this name himself, and indeed in the ancient sources it is only in the letters of Cicero, who had his own reasons for wanting to dissociate the young man from the dead dictator, that the name occurs until much later.[17] In an attempt to retain the name by which the young Caesar was known (and wished to be known), while avoiding confusion with his father, I have called the latter 'Julius Caesar' in those places where the distinction might not be clear.

17. Cic. *Fam.* 10.33.3 and 4, 12.23.4, 12.25.4; *Att.* 15.12.2, 16.8.1, 16.9.1, 16.11.1, 16.14.1; *Ad Brut.* 5.2. The name occurs once in Tacitus (*Ann.* 13.6), in a comparison of the youth of the emperor Nero at the beginning of his reign with others from earlier ages; but otherwise both Greek and Latin sources refer to him only as 'Caesar' or 'Augustus' until the fourth century AD.

CHAPTER 2

The assassination of Julius Caesar and its aftermath, 44–41 BC

The assassination of Julius Caesar on the Ides of March 44 threw the political world of Rome into disarray. It was true that he had many enemies: he himself had said, when Cicero had been kept waiting to present a petition shortly before, 'How can I doubt that I am deeply hated when Marcus Cicero is sitting there and can not meet me at his own convenience. If anyone is easy-going, he is; yet I have no doubt that he hates me strongly.'[1] Cicero, reporting this story, does not deny the charge. When Caesar had, illegally and absurdly, organised a snap election to replace Q. Fabius Maximus, the suffect consul, who died on the last day of the year, at which Gaius Caninius Rebilus was elected to serve for the rest of the day, Cicero wrote to his friend Manius Curius, a businessman living in Greece, that nobody had dinner in Rebilus' consulship, no crime was committed and such was the vigilance of the consul that he never slept. 'This seems to be a joke, because you weren't there. If you had seen it, you could not have held back your tears.'[2] Cicero goes on to say that there are innumerable instances of the same sort of thing happening, and other sources indicate that it was this flouting of the processes and proprieties of the business of the Republic which most offended his contemporaries.[3] Although modern scholars have been particularly interested to know whether Caesar did or did not see himself as a king or a god, it seems that the greatest offence (at least among the senatorial classes) was caused by his failure to rise to his feet when the entire senate in procession came to him, as he sat in front of the partially built temple of Venus Genetrix in the Forum Iulium, carrying their most recent decrees, granting him extraordinary honours.[4] When after this, before 15 February, he was appointed *dictator*

1. Cic. *Att.* 14.1.2.
2. Cic. *Fam.* 7.30.1–2.
3. See especially Suet. *Iul.* 76–9.

perpetuo it was clear that he intended to remain the ruler of Rome for life. Moreover, he was about to leave Rome to undertake an immense campaign against the Parthians, involving sixteen legions and ten thousand cavalry, of which he had already sent six legions and their auxiliaries across the Adriatic to Apollonia in southern Illyricum.[5] He was given the right to choose the magistrates for the next three years before he left.[6]

In retrospect, the assassination seems almost inevitable, given the hatred Caesar had provoked and the short time for the conspirators before he was due to leave.[7] Their number is disputed in our sources, some giving as many as sixty or eighty; but there is general agreement that Caesar's body bore twenty-three stab wounds, and, as Plutarch states that each assassin was to participate in the deed by striking a blow, the number of active participants will not have been more than twenty-three.[8] The larger numbers may be no more than estimates of those who supported the conspiracy, not all of whom need have been senators. The leaders were Gaius Cassius Longinus and Marcus Iunius Brutus, who had been on the Pompeian side in the civil war and subsequently pardoned by Caesar, but others included some of his long-term supporters, such as Decimus Iunius Brutus Albinus and Gaius Trebonius, of whom the former was named as a secondary heir in Caesar's will and the latter had been a suffect consul in 45. The setting of the murder in the senate and the pact that all should be involved in striking Caesar down point up the desire of the conspirators to show that they were engaged in the removal of an enemy of the constituted state, and their subsequent denomination of themselves as 'Liberators' confirms this. There may well have been private grudges, but Caesar's killers presented themselves and believed in themselves as restorers of Rome as it had been and should be.[9]

However inevitable the assassination may seem in hindsight, in 44 none but the conspirators themselves foresaw it, and they cannot

---

4. Suet. *Iul.* 78; Dio Cass. 44.8.
5. Appian, *B Civ.* 2.110; 3.24.
6. Dio Cass. 43.51.2–9. Dio says that in theory Caesar could only appoint half the magistrates, but that in practice he named all of them, though only the consuls and tribunes for the third year.
7. Appian, *B Civ.* 2.111, says he was due to depart four days after the Ides.
8. Nic. Dam. *Vit. Aug.* 19 (over eighty conspirators); Suet. *Iul.* 80.4 (over sixty); Plut. *Caes.* 66.11. (Nicolaus says there were thirty-five wounds (*Vit. Aug.* 24).)
9. See the contemporary analysis of Nic. Dam. *Vit. Aug.* 19, and the later perspective of Dio Cass. 44.1–2.

have predicted the chaotic and confused aftermath. It is far from clear that they had much idea of what to do next. Although Decimus Brutus had assembled a group of gladiators nearby in case of attempts to prevent the killing, the city was full of veteran soldiers from Caesar's armies and Marcus Aemilius Lepidus, who as master of horse (*magister equitum*) was the dictator's second-in-command, had a legion under arms outside the city boundary. Immediately after Caesar's death, Marcus Brutus apparently attempted to address the horrified senators, but they all rushed away from the scene, leaving three slaves to carry the body of the murdered man back to his house on a litter. The conspirators, accompanied by others who had not been involved hitherto but now wanted to be identified with the deed, withdrew to the Capitol, calling out to the people around that liberty had been restored. In the afternoon, Cassius and Marcus Brutus came down to the Forum to address those gathered there, who seem to have been too stunned by what had happened to react. The consul Antonius, meanwhile, had retreated to his house, afraid that his life was also in danger. That evening the conspirators were visited by several persons sympathetic to what they had done, including Cicero, whose name Marcus Brutus had cried out as he stood with his bloody dagger over Caesar's corpse, and Publius Cornelius Dolabella, whom Caesar had named as suffect consul to take over when he left for the Parthian campaign, and who now appeared in consular regalia, supporting the 'Liberators'. Cicero urged the conspirators to summon the senate to meet on the Capitol, but this came to nothing, and instead they asked Cicero to go to Antonius to persuade him to defend the state (the *res publica*, literally 'the property of the Roman people'); this he refused, arguing (as he later wrote) that while the consul was so terrified he would promise anything.[10] Nonetheless a deputation did go to Antonius and Lepidus to ask for a meeting on the Capitol to discuss the future state of affairs in the city, only to be told that they would have an answer in the morning.[11] By the morning, Antonius was ready: the troops of Lepidus were in possession of the Forum, and (in some ways still more important) Calpurnia, Caesar's widow, had sent her dead husband's papers and the money that he kept in the house to Antonius for safe keeping.

10. Cic. *Att.* 14.10.1, 15.11.2; *Phil.* 2.89.
11. Nic. Dam. *Vit. Aug.* 27.

The initiative was with the Caesarians. At a council held (according to Nicolaus of Damascus) by Antonius, Lepidus wanted to use it to avenge Caesar by warring against his murderers, while Aulus Hirtius, who had served as an officer with Caesar since the mid-50s and had been designated as consul for the following year, argued that they should negotiate with the conspirators.[12] Antonius followed Hirtius' advice, and summoned the senate to meet on the following day (17 March), at the temple of Tellus, close to his own house on the Esquiline hill. At the meeting, which took place with both Lepidus' troops and Caesar's veterans outside, many of the senators were favourable to the assassins and wanted them to be brought under safe escort to join their senatorial colleagues. Antonius, knowing that they would not come, agreed to this. The debate centred on the question of whether the 'Liberators' should be honoured as tyrannicides or granted an amnesty. Advocates of the former argued that Caesar's body should be thrown into the river Tiber and his acts annulled; but, as the consul Antonius pointed out, the annulment of Caesar's acts would not only cause major disruption and uncertainty throughout the Roman world but would also deprive many members of the senate of the magistracies they held and of provincial commands to which they had been assigned in the arrangements Caesar had made. Moreover it was not just these senators who might be alarmed; the veterans and soldiers in the city streets also depended on Caesar's acts for lands in the *coloniae* and other allotments that had been planned and established in Italy and other parts of the empire; and such men, many still bearing arms, would not take kindly to the body of their dead leader being dragged through the streets to the banks of the Tiber. On Cicero's motion, the amnesty was approved, and Caesar's acts were ratified and a public funeral decreed for him.

That evening, with the sons of Antonius and Lepidus acting as hostages for their safety, Marcus Brutus and Cassius came down from the Capitol and dined with the consul and the *magister equitum*. Antonius had succeeded in defusing the situation without large-scale bloodshed, but, as Cicero saw shortly afterwards, he had done better than that, at least from his own point of view. Little more than a month later, Cicero, writing to his friend Atticus, laments that all Brutus had achieved on the Ides of March was the establishment of all Caesar's actions, writings, words, promises and

12. Nic. Dam. *Vit. Aug.* 27.

plans for the future, more in force since his death than when he had been alive.[13] The one opportunity to rid Rome of the control of the tyrant had been lost when the senate had not been summoned immediately after the assassination and Caesar declared a public enemy. That, of course, had been Cicero's own plan; but instead Antonius had enmeshed the senators, and even the 'Liberators', in the organisational details of Caesar's own devising by their acknowledgement that he was a properly appointed magistrate of the city. The agreement of the senators to a public funeral, though a logical consequence of their refusal to disavow his legitimacy, provided for a further demonstration of the weakness of the 'Liberators' and their supporters. Within a few days of the meeting on 17 March, the body of the deceased dictator was brought down into the Forum by the magistrates and former magistrates of Rome and placed on the *rostra*, on which speakers stood, in a gilded model of the temple of Venus Genetrix, with the bloodstained clothing he was wearing when he was killed hung on a pillar beside it. There Antonius, as consul, gave a funeral oration, which consisted (according to Suetonius' account[14]) of a reading of the decree of the senate which had given Caesar divine honours and of the oath that they made to protect his personal safety, to which Antonius himself added only a few words of his own. Rapidly the whole scene got out of hand. The intention had been to take the body to the Campus Martius, outside the city walls, where a pyre had been prepared near the tomb of Caesar's daughter, Julia, where it was to be cremated. Instead the crowd set fire to the bier, heaping onto it dry branches and the benches on which those attending the law courts sat, while veteran soldiers and other bystanders threw armour, clothing and jewels as offerings. The fire burned all night, while an angry mob attempted to set fire to the houses of Marcus Brutus and of Cassius, and, having failed to do so, seized and killed a tribune of the plebs, Gaius Helvius Cinna, mistaking him for the praetor, Lucius Cornelius Cinna, who had spoken in support of the assassins. In the Forum, an altar was set up by a demagogic leader who claimed to be a grandson of the great Gaius Marius, and thus a relative of Caesar, where a cult of the dead dictator was conducted at the place where his body had been burned. In the meantime Brutus and Cassius fled the city.

13. Cic. *Att.* 14.10.1, written on 19 April.
14. Suet. *Iul.* 84. Appian, *B Civ.* 2.144–6 and Dio Cass. 44.35–50 give Antonius a much longer oration, and Cic. *Phil.* 2.90–1 blames him for having made an inflammatory speech at the funeral.

One reason for the violent outburst of grief for the dead Caesar was the reading of his will, which took place just before the day of the funeral. On the insistence of Lucius Piso, the father of Caesar's widow, Calpurnia, the will was unsealed and read in the house of Antonius and revealed not only that Gaius Octavius was, as noted above,[15] to be his main heir but that Caesar had left his gardens in Rome to be used by the people and also a bequest of 300 sesterces to each citizen. If this was planned by Antonius to stir up the resentment of the people in the streets of Rome against those who had killed their benefactor, it was highly successful; but the reading of the will was also bound to bring to the attention of all the individual who was named as Caesar's heir: the young Octavius.

Caesar had intended Octavius, despite his youth, to be his *magister equitum* for the campaigns against the Dacians and the Parthians in place of Lepidus, once the latter had set off for the province of Gallia Narbonensis and Hispania Citerior to which Caesar had assigned him,[16] and had sent him to Apollonia in Illyria, at the western end of the *via Egnatia*, close to the point at which legions were gathering in preparation for the campaigns. There Octavius, who was spending the time studying philosophy as well as training with the soldiers, received a letter from his mother, Atia, informing him of Caesar's murder. He consulted with friends who were with him, including Marcus Vipsanius Agrippa and Quintus Salvidienus Rufus, both of whom were to be of major significance in the years which followed, and promptly took ship across the Adriatic to Brundisium. He landed first at Lupiae (modern Lecce) rather than Brundisium itself, where troops were assembled, ready to cross to join the other forces being prepared for Caesar's intended campaigns. At Lupiae, Octavius heard more details of the assassination and also of Caesar's will and his own adoption. Learning that it was safe for him to enter Brundisium, he arrived there to a welcome from the Caesarian troops and found letters awaiting him from his mother and from his stepfather, Marcius Philippus.[17] The latter certainly was opposed to Octavius taking the bequest, no

---

15. See above, pp. 7–9.
16. *Fast. Cap.* (*Inscr. Ital.* 13.1.58–9 and 134); Appian, *B Civ.* 3.30; Dio Cass. 43.51.7. It appears from *Fast. Cap.* and Dio that this appointment was for one year, and that Octavius was to be replaced by Cn. Domitius Calenus in the year following.
17. Nic. Dam. *Vit. Aug.* 18; Suet. *Aug.* 3 (cf. Vell. Pat. 60.1; App. *B Civ.* 3.10.34 and 11.36).

doubt displaying the same caution that had kept him out of trouble through the turmoil of the struggle between Caesar and Pompeius; but Octavius clearly intended to do everything he could not only to secure his inheritance and his new name but also to prepare his military and political position for the turbulence which was bound to follow, and from which he intended to profit. His only strengths lay in his relationship with the dead dictator; in the financial resources that his now adoptive father had left him, which were very large but not immediately accessible; and in his influence as Caesar's heir over his former supporters, in the senate (which the dictator had increased in size to nine hundred by the addition of three hundred senators), in the upper classes (including several wealthy bankers), among the ordinary people of the lower classes (whose affection for Caesar had been evident in Rome after the Ides of March) and above all among the soldiers and the veterans who had fought in Gaul and in the wars against Pompeius and the Republicans. His opponents were likely to be not only Caesar's assassins and their supporters, not least in the senate, but also those at the head of what might be called the Caesarian establishment, of whom the most prominent were Marcus Antonius, currently consul and effectively leading events in the capital, and Marcus Aemilius Lepidus, still Caesar's *magister equitum* at the time of the assassination, and since the spring of 44 proconsular commander of the provinces of Gallia Narbonensis and Hispania Citerior. These men not only drew their power from the same sources that Octavius might hope to exploit but were also (as a result of Caesar's own arrangements of the offices of state) holders of magistracies and pro-magistracies which gave them *imperium* within the structures of Rome, which Octavius, a youth of eighteen, would have no hope of reaching in normal times for over a decade.

Octavius' actions on arriving in Brundisium relate precisely to the strengths and weaknesses of his position. His welcome by the troops Caesar had sent there en route for the campaigns in Dacia and the east will have confirmed his expectation (if that were necessary) that Caesar's soldiers would be well disposed to Caesar's heir; but more than goodwill would be needed. Both for preparing and provisioning troops and for securing their loyalty with rewards, cash was indispensable. According to Nicolaus he sent to Asia for the transfer of the monies that Caesar had collected there in preparation for the Parthian war, and later received that and also one year's taxation, which he later handed back to the public treasury.[18] Also, and crucially, it was at this point that, in anticipation of the ratification of Julius Caesar's will, he began to use the name Gaius Julius Caesar.

It was then as Caesar that he left Brundisium for Campania, to visit his stepfather and his mother, and to consult with other possible supporters, including Lucius Cornelius Balbus, the immensely rich Spaniard from Gades (modern Cadiz) who had acted as an agent for the dictator. He also called on Cicero, who was living in Puteoli at the villa next door to that in which Philippus was staying, and who was flattered and reassured by his respectful demeanour, while being suspicious of his intentions. Cicero also noted that while those with him addressed him as Caesar, Philippus did not; nor did Cicero.[19] For Caesar, however, this was his trump card, the one thing that separated him from the other Caesarian leaders, and he was not going to throw it away. Shortly afterwards, he set off for Rome, receiving encouragement on the way from veteran settlers who were angry with Antonius' failure to avenge the dictator's assassination. On his arrival he presented himself for the formal acceptance of his adoption to Gaius Antonius, the consul's brother, who was one of the praetors of the year and was acting as *praetor urbanus* in charge of the courts of the city in place of Marcus Brutus, since the latter's withdrawal from Rome after the granting of an amnesty to the 'Liberators'. Caesar was also introduced to an informal assembly of the people, apparently by another brother of Marcus Antonius, Lucius, tribune of the plebs in 44, and made a speech, the tone of which Cicero disliked.[20]

Marcus Antonius himself had been away from Rome, travelling through Campania to secure the allegiance of the veterans settled there by persuading them to swear to uphold the acts of Julius Caesar and urging them to be prepared to fight when needed. In his absence, Dolabella had, much to Cicero's delight, suppressed the cult which had been set up in the Forum at the place where the dictator's body had been burned, and executed those who had been responsible for it.[21] Antonius now returned to Rome, bringing with him a large number of veterans, who he claimed needed to be there to hear

18. Nic. Dam. *Vit. Aug.* 18. Appian, *B Civ.* 3.11, says that soldiers came to him from Macedonia, bringing supplies and money from Macedonia and other provinces.
19. On the young Caesar in Campania, see Cic. *Att.* 14.10.3, 12.2. He had arrived in Naples on 18 April (Cic. *Att.* 14.10.3).
20. Cic. *Att.* 14.20.5; 15.2.3.
21. Cic. *Att.* 14.15, 16.2, 17A, 19.4–5.

about arrangements he would be making to their benefit, but who would certainly be able to provide support against his opponents. Some were said to be proposing to reinstate the altar which Dolabella had removed.[22] Once Antonius was back in Rome, the young Caesar called upon him for help in acquiring the funds which the dictator had left in the temple of Ops ('Wealth') in Rome, in order to pay out the bequest to the people. According to Appian, who gives a full account of the meeting, with speeches (written of course by Appian), Antonius refused the request, arguing that the money in the temple of Ops belonged to the public treasury, and in any case had largely been exhausted.[23] Indeed both Antonius and Dolabella had been drawing on these funds, and no doubt intended to continue to do so. Antonius also managed to delay the process in the ancient assembly called the *comitia curiata*, which was needed to formalise the adoption of the young Caesar into his adoptive father's family.[24] Although our sources represent the young man as being surprised by Antonius' lack of cooperation, it is clear from his actions that his intention was to seize the initiative as the defender and proponent of the memory of the assassinated dictator and that Antonius was determined to prevent this. At the same time, Antonius was securing his position. Before he had left for Campania, he had announced that he would convene a meeting of the senate on 1 June, and the expectation was that he would use this to change the allocations of provinces.[25] In April, after Marcus Brutus and Cassius had removed themselves from the city, Antonius had won over Dolabella, after his election to the consulship, by assuring him of his support for the passing of a law to transfer to him the province of Syria (and thus the command of the armies which Julius Caesar had intended to lead against the Parthians); and Antonius immediately persuaded the senate to allot Macedonia to himself.[26] In the meantime, Decimus Brutus had already removed himself from Rome to avoid the hostility against the 'Liberators', and had taken up his command in the province of Cisalpine Gaul, to which he had been appointed by the dictator. Cicero at least, writing to Atticus in late

---

22. Cic. *Fam.* 11.2 (a letter from Brutus and Cassius to Antonius); *Phil.* 2.100 and 108.
23. Appian, *B Civ.* 3.14–20.
24. Dio Cass. 45.5.3.
25. Cic. *Att.* 14.14.4.
26. Appian (*B Civ.* 3.2 and 7, 4.57) and Florus (2.17.4) mistakenly believe that Cassius had been allocated Syria and Marcus Brutus Macedonia by Caesar; but see Cic. *Phil.* 11.12.27–30 and *Att.* 15.9.1.

May, feared that Antonius' intention was to take the Cisalpine province for himself, and that this would mean the end of any compromise between the consul and the 'Liberators', and was bound to lead to full-scale civil war.[27] In the event, the meeting of the senate on 1 June achieved nothing (perhaps because many senators, afraid of the potential violence of Antonius' veterans, brought from Campania, failed to appear). Instead, the consul had a law proposed, rapidly and unconstitutionally, by a tribune, which extended the tenure of the provinces that the consuls were to hold to five years and gave Antonius the province of Cisalpine Gaul and also of Transalpine Gaul.[28] This left Marcus Brutus and Cassius, to whom, as to the other praetors, provinces had not been allotted, dangerously unoccupied and in Italy; and on 5 June the senate decreed that for the time being they should be placed in control of the grain supplies to Rome from Asia and Sicily, and that provinces would be allotted to them along with the other praetors. This did not please either, as Cicero heard at a meeting of the two and their friends and family a few days later, and Cassius threatened to leave to go to Greece and Brutus to Asia.[29] In the event, they both stayed in Italy, collecting together a fleet, which could at least appear to be part of the role allotted to them by the senate. Early in August, Cassius was assigned to the province of Cyrene, in north Africa, and Brutus to Crete.

Meanwhile in July, two sets of games took place in Rome. On 7 July the traditional *ludi Apollinares* were celebrated. These were the responsibility of the urban praetor, but Marcus Brutus remained outside the city for fear of his life, and the games were presided over by Gaius Antonius in his stead. Brutus provided the necessary cash and put on a lavish show, in the hope of winning over the populace, though he was upset that the official announcement described the date of the beginning of the games as the Nones of July (the name of the month as decreed by the senate after Julius Caesar had returned to Italy from Spain in 45) rather than the previous name of Quinctilis.[30] At the same time, the young Caesar was preparing for the celebration of games, the *ludi Veneris Genetricis* (founded by

27. Cic. *Att.* 15.4.1.
28. For a discussion of the sources on this matter (which are in many respects contradictory), see T. Rice Holmes, *The Architect of the Roman Empire*, Oxford: Oxford University Press, 1928, 1.192–6.
29. Cic. *Att.* 15.9 and 11.
30. Cic. *Att.* 15.12.1; 16.1.1, 4.1; Appian, *B Civ.* 3.23.

his adoptive father in September 46 to mark the dedication of the temple to Venus, the divine ancestor of the Julian family), and to use them to commemorate the victories of the murdered Caesar.[31] He raised funds for this by selling property which had come to him under Julius Caesar's will, and undertook this because those responsible for the celebration were unwilling to promote so potentially contentious an event.[32] A political statement, however, was precisely what the new holder of the name of Caesar wanted it to be. He had already demanded that the gilded chair which the senate had decreed that the dictator should use, and the diadem which Antonius had offered to him at the celebration of the feast of the Lupercalia in February, should be exhibited at an earlier festival in May, which Antonius had refused to countenance; and a similar attempt to produce the chair at the *ludi victoriae Caesaris*, as they came to be called, was thwarted now.[33] The games were marked as extraordinary nonetheless by the appearance of a comet, visible even in the late afternoon, on the last seven days of the festival. Though the appearance of comets was usually seen as an ill omen, young Caesar took it as a mark of the favour of the gods, and recorded in his autobiography (quoted by the elder Pliny) that the crowds believed it showed that his father had been taken up into the heavens as a god.[34] Caesar proceeded to have a statue of his father with a star above its head placed in the temple of Venus Genetrix; and, according to Pliny, secretly regarded the day of the comet's appearance as the day of his own birth. In one sense at least he was right. In the context of the power struggles that followed the assassination of Julius Caesar, the recognition not only of his status as the dictator's son but of the divinity of his father was fundamental to all that was to take place thereafter; and it is clear that the young Caesar, even at his age, could see its significance.

Antonius also realised the dangers to his position from the increased prominence that these events brought to this contender for pre-eminence in Rome, now that the new Caesar was showing himself as the inheritor not only of the late dictator's private fortune

---

31. On the relationship of the *ludi Veneris Genetricis* and the *ludi victoriae Caesaris*, and the significance of the games to the young Caesar, see J. T. Ramsey and A. L. Licht, *The Comet of 44 BC and Caesar's Funeral Games*, Atlanta: Scholars Press, 1997.
32. Suet. *Aug.* 10.1.
33. Cic. *Att.* 15.3.3; Appian, *B Civ.* 3.28; Dio Cass. 45.6.4–5.
34. Pliny, *HN* 2.93–4; Seneca, *Q Nat.* 7.17.2; Dio Cass. 45.17.1; Obsequens 68. On the ill omen of comets, see also Manilius 1.874–926.

but also of his political power. His popularity with the ordinary people in Rome was increasing, and also with the soldiers who had served under his father. In the aftermath of the games, Antonius and Caesar embarked on a series of mutual verbal onslaughts, which were brought to a (temporary) end by an appeal to the consul by officers of his own bodyguard, who insisted that they should be reconciled. The two met on the Capitol, and (after a certain amount of mutual criticism) declared themselves to be friends; Caesar was escorted home by a considerable number of Antonius' delighted soldiers.[35] Antonius was less delighted by the favour shown to the young man, whom he clearly saw as a rival, by members of his own force, and was more infuriated by Caesar's next actions. There was a story that he wanted to be elected to a vacant position as tribune of the plebs, a move that would be illegal both because of his age and because, whether as Octavius or as Caesar, he was a patrician and so ineligible to be an officer of the plebs. Antonius declared that he would punish Caesar if he ignored the law and, when the populace showed their displeasure, cancelled the election.[36] The inconsistencies of the path which Antonius had tried to follow since the Ides of March were showing the weaknesses in his position. Marcus Brutus and Cassius had put out an edict in July, stating that they were prepared to live in exile if that would bring harmony to the Republic, and were apparently hoping for further cooperation from the consul.[37] They did not get it: Antonius convened a meeting of the senate on 1 August which probably allocated to them the provinces of Crete and Cyrene, tasks which they ignored. Shortly after this, Brutus left Italy, to travel not to Crete but to Athens, where he was welcomed as a tyrannicide, and Cassius headed late in September for the province of Asia.

At the same meeting Antonius was attacked by Lucius Piso, the late dictator's father-in-law, and, though Piso was not supported by others, this showed a further weakening in the consul's position. He needed to show himself to be in control and the leader of the opposition to the 'Liberators', and part of this was shown by an attack he made upon Cicero in the senate at its meeting on 1 September. Cicero had been away from Rome since mid-June, attempting and

---

35. Nic. Dam. *Vit. Aug.* 29; Appian, *B Civ.* 3.28–30.
36. Appian, *B Civ.* 3.31 (cf. Plut. *Ant.* 16.1; Suet. *Aug.* 10.2; Dio Cass. 45.6.2–3).
37. See their letter of 4 August to Antonius (Cic. *Fam.* 11.3) and Cicero's to Atticus of 19 August (Cic. *Att.* 16.7); the terms of the edict of Brutus and Cassius are given by Vell. Pat. 2.62.2.

failing to sail to Greece, intending to stay there until the beginning
of the following year, when Antonius would no longer be consul and
his successors, Gaius Vibius Pansa and Aulus Hirtius, would be in
office. They had both served for many years under Caesar, but were
also friends of Cicero's and of a more moderate disposition than the
hated Antonius. Cicero had returned to Rome on the last day of
August, having met Marcus Brutus at Velia, on the coast south-east
of Naples, and discovered that his friends in Rome thought he was
deserting them. Antonius wanted Cicero to attend the senate on
1 September, but the latter refused, claiming that he was ill and tired
from the journey, despite threats from Antonius that he would force
him to come. The following day, however, he was in the senate in
Antonius' absence, and claimed that he had been unwilling to be
there when the main business before the house had been the consul's
proposal to institute thanksgivings (*supplicationes*) to the dead
Julius Caesar, on the model of those addressed to the gods following
a major military victory. This, Cicero claimed, would be tantamount
to recognising the assassinated dictator as divine.[38] Antonius seems
to have been intending to take to himself the role which young
Caesar had assumed in his interpretation of the comet at the *ludi
Veneris Genetricis* by associating Julius Caesar's divinity with Rome
rather than with his adopted son; and a month later he went further
by having the words *parenti optime merito* ('To father for his
outstanding benefactions') inscribed on a statue of Julius which
he had erected previously on the *rostra*.[39] No doubt this is why he
wanted Cicero to be present on 1 September, to associate him and
others who had favoured the 'Liberators' with a recognition of
the dead dictator which would also reduce the growing power of the
young Caesar. If so, it did not work. On 2 September, Cicero not
only explained his absence of the previous day by urging that Julius
Caesar should not be enrolled among the gods but also argued that
Antonius was acting and had acted illegally, contrary to the wishes
of the ordinary people and (most tellingly) contrary to the policies
and wishes of the dead dictator himself. Antonius was furious, and
in a speech on 19 September he lambasted Cicero, accusing him,
amongst other things, of having set Pompeius against Julius Caesar
and so causing the civil war, and of being behind the assassination
on the Ides of March. As Cicero realised well enough, this was

38. Cic. *Phil.* 1.11–13; Plut. *Cic.* 43.6.
39. Cic. *Fam.* 12.3 (written to Cassius in early October).

intended to set the veteran soldiers against him,[40] but it will also have had the equally useful function, from Antonius' point of view, of representing his opponent as the real enemy of the veterans' late commander and hero. The mutual loathing of the two men by this stage was no doubt real and personal, but it was also necessary for each in order to maintain their political positions. Once Cicero had completed, at the end of October, his brilliant, blistering and libellous response to Antonius, the Second *Philippic*, written as a speech to the senate but never delivered, their enmity had become literally lethal. Already on 2 October Antonius stated in a public meeting that while he lived there was no room in the *res publica* for Caesar's killers, and Cicero reckoned that that meant himself as well as the likes of Cassius.[41]

Antonius, of course, had other opponents than the rather elderly supporters of the 'Liberators' in the senate. Late in September or early in October, Antonius let it be known that the young Caesar had attempted to suborn some of the consul's bodyguard to assassinate him. Caesar denied it and, so Cicero says, the people in the city believed that Antonius had trumped up the charge to get his hands on Caesar's money and that the consul himself was so aware of his unpopularity that, having caught the would-be murderers, he refused to make the matter public.[42] Whatever the truth of the matter (and Cicero at least wrote that some 'intelligent and honest men' believed it), it was clear that the two contenders for the support of the Caesarian soldiers were once again at loggerheads. On 9 October, Antonius left Rome for Brundisium to join four legions which were to be transferred from Macedonia for use in his new Gallic province. War against Decimus Brutus, the only one of the 'Liberators' in possession of a sizeable army, was now inevitable.

Elsewhere in the Roman world matters were quiet but unstable. In Spain Sextus Pompeius, the great Pompeius' only surviving son, had escaped after the defeat of the Pompeian forces by Julius Caesar at Munda in 45, and in 44 inflicted a major defeat on Asinius Pollio, the commander in Hispania Ulterior. Lepidus, who arrived in Hispania Citerior in the summer of 44, engaged in negotiations with Sextus and came to an agreement with him that he should give up his hostilities and leave Spain in return for the restoration to him of

40. Cic. *Fam.* 12.2.1.
41. Cic. *Fam.* 12.3.2; 23.2.
42. Cic. *Fam.* 12.23.2; Nic. Dam. *Vit. Aug.* 30; Appian, *B Civ.* 3.39.

the property of his father. He did not withdraw immediately, but early in the following year was to be found at Massilia (modern Marseilles) with his army and fleet. In Transalpine Gaul was Lucius Munatius Plancus, who had served for many years under Julius Caesar as a *legatus* in Gaul and through the civil wars; he was designated consul for 42, but had supported the amnesty proposed by Antonius for the 'Liberators' after the Ides of March.[43] Like Decimus Brutus he been replaced by Antonius by the plebiscite of 2 June, and, although less likely than Decimus to resist by force, was something of an unknown quantity. And by this time Marcus Brutus and Cassius had both sailed to the eastern Mediterranean. It was against this background that Antonius, accompanied by his wife Fulvia, headed towards Brundisium.

Caesar reacted to this on two fronts. Given that Antonius had put about the story of the alleged plot on the eve of his departing to join the legions which had come across from Macedonia, Caesar concluded that he was in grave danger. Advised by a group of friends, which included Agrippa and Maecenas, he sent some of his agents to Brundisium with the message that the soldiers there should remember the wrong done to Julius Caesar and not desert his son; Caesar himself left for Campania, stirring up the veterans there to support him, with a combination of emotional appeals and a promise of 500 denarii a head.[44] Antonius meanwhile arrived at Brundisium to find that four of the expected five legions from Macedonia had arrived; and they were angry that he had not punished the assassins of Julius Caesar. When Antonius responded furiously that they should be glad that they had been brought back to Italy rather than being sent to Parthia, and promised them 100 denarii each for marching with him to Cisalpine Gaul, they were not impressed. Their laughter led to more fury from the consul and to a riot. Antonius ordered the execution of ringleaders, but he was not able to prevent Caesar's agents distributing leaflets urging the soldiers to desert the mean and cruel Antonius for the generosity of the son and heir of their assassinated former commander. Antonius, seeing the danger of a large-scale mutiny, promised more cash and expressed regret that he had had to execute a few trouble-makers. Having conciliated the legionaries, he sent them north, up the Adriatic coast to Ariminum (modern Rimini) to await his return, and

43. Plut. *Brut.* 19.1.
44. Nic. Dam. *Vit. Aug.* 31; Cic. *Att.* 16.8.1; Vell. Pat. 2.61.2.

he himself set off for Rome with his bodyguard.[45]

Caesar was marshalling all possible support against Antonius. In early November, he showered Cicero with daily letters, asking his advice on whether he should march on Rome with his veterans, and urging Cicero himself to come to the senate. Cicero was painfully uncertain what to do: he was delighted with Caesar's vigorous opposition to Antonius but could not forget that this young man, who had just passed his nineteenth birthday, was clearly proposing to make war on Antonius. Consequently he in turn wrote daily to Atticus in Rome, reporting his own movements and asking for advice.[46] Caesar, hearing that Antonius was marching towards Rome, accompanied by his bodyguard and another legion of soldiers, went himself to the city, where a tribune who was an enemy of the consul brought him to a public meeting. There Caesar was presented as a leader who could oppose Antonius, and gave a speech in which he attacked Antonius and promised to serve the country in all things and, with regard to the immediate situation, to confront Antonius. This open opposition to the consul disturbed his soldiers, who thought that they had come to protect Caesar, but not to be involved in a civil war, and Caesar had to allow some to return home, while moving the remainder out of Rome to Arretium, in northern Etruria. He also gave them all further gifts, and encouraged them to stand by him and honour his father's memory, and indeed many returned before long.[47] Antonius arrived in Rome, with his bodyguard but without the rumoured additional legion, and summoned a meeting of the senate for 24 November, issuing an edict that anyone who failed to attend would be regarded as an enemy; he apparently intended to denounce Caesar as an enemy of the state. In the event he failed to be there himself, probably because he had heard just before that one of the three legions he had sent to Ariminium, the *legio Martia*, had instead marched to Alba, south-east of the capital, and had gone over to Caesar. The senate meeting was called instead for 28 November, but a motion against Caesar was not put because Antonius received word that another legion, the Fourth, had also deserted him for Caesar. A thanksgiving was voted for Lepidus for having reconciled Sextus Pompeius with the senate, and Antonius left Rome in a rapid and desperate attempt to win

---

45. Appian, *B Civ.* 3.43–4; Dio Cass. 45.13.1–2.
46. Cic. *Att.* 16.8, 16.9, 16.10, 16.11, 16.12, 16.13, 16.14 and 16.15.
47. Cic. *Att.* 16.8.2; Appian, *B Civ.* 3.41–2.

back the *Martia*. He was repelled from Alba by a shower of missiles; and returned to the senate, which met (illegally) after nightfall, where provinces were distributed among the praetors, with Marcus Brutus and Cassius being stripped of Crete and Cyrene, and Gaius Trebonius, also one of the 'Liberators', stripped of Asia, to which he had been assigned as proconsul by Julius Caesar.[48] Antonius, escorted by many supporters from the senate, left Rome and proceeded to Ariminium to join his remaining troops. Thence he marched north to Cisalpine Gaul.

Antonius' main and first task was to deal with Decimus Brutus. All trace of amnesty for the 'Liberators' had now vanished, under pressure from a competitor for the loyalty of the legionaries and veterans of the late dictator who actually bore his name, was urging the punishment of his assassins and was aspiring (as he said in a public meeting in Rome when he arrived from Campania in early November) to the honours his father had held.[49] Ironically it was the young Caesar in whom supporters of the 'Liberators', led by Cicero himself, now put their hopes of controlling and defeating Antonius. It was crucial for Antonius to deal with Decimus Brutus, both to remove the military threat and to show himself as the true inheritor of Julius Caesar's political legacy.

On his arrival in Cisalpina, Antonius demanded that Decimus surrender the province to him. Unsurprisingly Decimus refused, stating in an edict that he would continue to hold it within the control of the senate and people of Rome. He then withdrew to the town of Mutina (modern Modena), stocking it with provisions from the surrounding countryside and with salted meat from the slaughter of his transport oxen.[50] He was preparing for a long siege. In Rome the tribunes of the plebs for the following year, who took office in December, called a meeting of the senate for 20 December to discuss the need for the incoming consuls, Gaius Vibius Pansa and Aulus Hirtius, to have a bodyguard on 1 January at the inauguration of the new consular year. Cicero addressed the senators in what was now his normal style, attacking Antonius, praising the young Caesar for his incredible wisdom and courage. He ended by moving that the consuls designate should ensure that the senate was able to meet safely on 1 January; that Decimus Brutus should be recognised

---

48. Cic. *Phil.* 3.19–27; Appian, *B Civ.* 3.45 (who conflates the two meetings of the senate).
49. Cic. *Att.* 16.15.2.
50. Cic. *Phil.* 3.8; Appian, *B Civ.* 3.49.

for his services to the *res publica* and confirmed in the province
assigned to him by Julius Caesar, as should all the other provincial
commanders, whose provinces had been reassigned by Antonius'
measures; and that Gaius Caesar, along with the veterans he had
gathered together and two legions that had joined him, the Fourth
and *Martia*, should be publicly thanked and honoured.[51] He then
went straight from the senate meeting to address the people in
the Forum, urging them to prepare to defend their liberties against
Antonius, who, he claimed, had in effect been declared a public
enemy by the senate's support of Caesar.

By the time of the senate meeting on 1 January, news had reached
Rome that Antonius was blockading Mutina, and also that Caesar
was marching north to assist Decimus Brutus. After the new consuls
had made the sacrifices which marked their entry to office, they
summoned the senate to discuss the situation in Cisalpine Gaul. The
debate which followed revealed the mixture of allegiances that the
events of the previous year had produced. The two consuls, Hirtius
and Pansa, had both served with Julius Caesar but were opposed
to the measures which Antonius had taken and to his current
campaign. Cicero supported the 'Liberators', but strongly favoured
young Caesar as a way of disposing of Antonius. The first consular
called on to speak was Quintus Fufius Calenus, like Hirtius a former
officer of Julius Caesar in Gaul and the father of Pansa's wife, but
strongly supportive of Antonius. He argued that, rather than treat-
ing Antonius as a public enemy, envoys should be sent to persuade
him to lay down his arms. Cicero responded that the senate had
already by implication determined that Antonius was a public
enemy, that all Antonius' legislation should be repealed and that
young Caesar and the legions which had deserted Antonius should
continue to receive their support. Lucius Piso, the father-in-law of
the dead dictator, who had opposed Antonius in the senate at the
meeting on 1 August, now argued that it was unconstitutional to
condemn him in his absence and that he should be summoned
to Rome to stand trial. The debate continued until nightfall, when
the meeting was adjourned. At meetings on the subsequent days the
proposal that Antonius should be declared an enemy was thwarted
by a tribune of the plebs named Salvius, whose veto prevented the
motion from being voted on; but the senate decreed that Caesar
should command the forces against Antonius along with the consuls

51. Cic. *Phil.* 3.37–9.

and hold *imperium pro praetore*, giving him the power of a praetor; that the donations that he had promised the to legions, the Fourth and the *Martia*, should be paid from the public treasury and that they should receive land allotments at the end of the campaign; and that Caesar should be allowed to stand for the consulship ten years earlier than permitted by law, which would not allow him to stand until he was thirty-two. In the end the senate, perhaps moved by the entreaties of Antonius' wife, mother and small son, refrained from declaring him a public enemy, but, following Calenus' proposal, sent an embassy, consisting of Lucius Piso, Lucius Marcius Philippus (young Caesar's former stepfather) and the ailing but distinguished lawyer Servius Sulpicius Rufus. They were to order Antonius to withdraw from the siege of Mutina and from the province of Cisalpine Gaul by coming south of the river Rubicon, but to keep at least 200 Roman miles away from Rome.[52] The antipathy of much of the senate to Antonius was, however, clear: not only was an agrarian law, passed by Antonius and Dolabella in July to provide land for the veterans, revoked but, shortly after the embassy had left, the two consuls were instructed to proceed on a war footing and to conduct a levy of troops in Italy.[53] Early in February, Piso and Philippus returned from their mission, Servius Sulpicius having died on the way north. Predictably Antonius had refused the ultimatum and had prevented the ambassadors from contacting Decimus Brutus. He had also presented demands of his own: that the legislation he had passed should all be reinstated and that Marcus Brutus and Cassius should be recalled from the provinces that they had occupied; if they refused to come back, he should be given the province of Transalpine Gaul, held by Munatius Plancus, and the six legions stationed there.

The result was inevitable. Although, to Cicero's disgust, Antonius was not declared a public enemy, the senate decreed that the consuls and Caesar (holding *imperium pro praetore*) should take care that the *res publica* should take no harm, the formula used to allow the holders of *imperium* to take such measures as they saw fit in times of extreme emergency.[54] At about the same time, news came from Hirtius, already in the north, that the whole of Cisapline Gaul, with the exception of the towns of Bononia (modern Bologna, which

52. Cic. *Phil.* 6.4–5; 7.26.
53. Cic. *Phil.* 6.11–13; Dio Cass. 46.29.5.
54. Cic. *Phil.* 8.6; Aug. *RG* 1.3.

Antonius was defending with a large force), Parma and Regium Lepidum, were supporting the senate. Cicero hoped that, if Decimus Brutus could break out from Mutina, the war would be over quickly.[55]

News from other fronts was (from Cicero's point of view) mixed. Letters from Marcus Brutus, who had left Italy for Athens the previous August, were received early in February. In Athens, Brutus had had an enthusiastic reception and, as well as attending lectures from philosophers, had gathered the support of young Romans studying there, including the poet Horace and Cicero's son Marcus.[56] Brutus gathered forces and finances and proceeded to the provinces of Macedonia and Illyricum, taking over the legions of Hortensius, the governor of Macedonia, who refused to hand over his province to Gaius Antonius[57] when he arrived at the end of 44 to replace him, and ceded control to Brutus. The governor of Illyricum, Publius Vatinius, resisted Antonius' attempt to take over his forces, but was compelled to yield to Brutus when his soldiers deserted him to join the 'Liberator'. Brutus had by this time assembled a considerable force, partly from veterans from the defeated Pompeian army after Pharsalus, who were still in the area, and also had large financial resources, contributed by Marcus Appuleius, the retiring pro-quaestor of Asia, and Gaius Antistius Vetus, quaestor in Syria, both of whom joined him, and private individuals such as Cicero's friend Atticus, who had provided 100,000 sesterces for Brutus when he was forced to leave Italy.[58] When Gaius Antonius arrived at Dyrrhachium, he found himself faced with Brutus' superior forces and was compelled to retire down the coast to Apollonia. Once the news of all this had reached the senate, a proposal was made by Marcus Antonius' supporter, Fufius Calenus, that Brutus should be deprived of his command, but the senate supported Cicero, who lambasted Calenus in a speech in which he proposed that the actions of Brutus should be approved and he himself legitimised as

---

55. Cic. *Fam.* 12.5.2.
56. Hor. *Epist.* 2.2.43–9; Plut. *Brut.* 24.
57. Gaius Antonius, as praetor in 44, had been appointed to Macedonia at the senate meeting on 28 November, on the eve of his brother Marcus' departure to Cisalpine Gaul to confront Decimus Brutus, and was removed from it at the senate meeting on 20 December.
58. Cic. *Phil.* 10.11–13, 11.27; Nepos, *Atticus* 8.6; Plut. *Brut.* 25–26; Appian, *B Civ.* 4.75; Dio Cass. 47.21.

proconsul in Achaea, Macedonia and Illyricum. Hortensius was confirmed in his *imperium*, under the general command of Brutus.[59]

Cicero was delighted, and wrote an optimistic letter to Cassius in Syria.[60] But by the end of the month, he heard news which horrified him. Dolabella, on his way to Syria to confront Cassius, had reached the province of Asia in January, where he had met Gaius Trebonius, one of the 'Liberators', with whom Cicero was also in correspondence. Trebonius assisted Dolabella, taking care to protect himself from harm. Dolabella, however, tricked Trebonius into believing that he was about to leave the province and then captured Smyrna (modern İzmir, in western Turkey), where the latter was ensconced. He arrested Trebonius and had him decapitated. According to Appian, the soldiers, who hated Trebonius for his part in the assassination of Julius Caesar, played with the head as though it were a ball, until it was smashed to pieces. In Rome, on the motion of Calenus, Dolabella was immediately declared a public enemy, but Cicero failed in his attempt to have Cassius' position in Syria legitimised as commander against him.[61]

Meanwhile the position in Cisalpine Gaul seems to have reached a stalemate, though one which was becoming increasingly dangerous to Decimus Brutus, besieged in Mutina. In March a proposal was put to the senate by Calenus and Lucius Piso that another embassy be sent to Marcus Antonius, a proposal which was rejected. Another, more difficult to ignore, came from Marcus Lepidus, who was in command of Gallia Narbonensis and Hispania Citerior, and from Lucius Munatius Plancus in Gallia Transalpina, urging peace with Antonius; and in the debate in the senate which followed on 20 March Cicero read and commented on a letter which Antonius had sent to Hirtius and Caesar in which he made clear that he had been in contact with both Lepidus and Plancus. Cicero was also in correspondence with both, and Plancus at least was keen to reassure him and the senate that he would be faithful to the *res publica*.[62] The senate rejected the proposal, and in the days before their meeting the consul Pansa had left with a newly recruited army to join his colleague Hirtius and young Caesar in the north.

On 14 April Antonius attempted to prevent Pansa and his forces

59. Cic. *Phil.* 10.
60. Cic. *Fam.* 12.5.
61. Cic. *Phil.* 11.5–8, 15–16; Vell. Pat. 2.69.1; Appian, *B Civ.* 3.26; Dio Cass. 47.29.1–4.
62. Cic. *Fam.* 10.6, 7, 8 and 27; *Phil.* 13.43.

from joining up with the others by confronting the four inexperienced legions with two of his own at the village of Forum Gallorum, about eight miles from Mutina down the *via Aemilia*. Hirtius, however, had sent the *legio Martia* to meet Pansa, and, when he heard the battle had started, backed them up with two more. Antonius was initially successful against the newly recruited legions and Pansa was severely wounded, but eventually Antonius was defeated with the loss of his legionary standards. A week later he risked battle at Mutina to avoid the siege being broken and was again defeated, though Hirtius was killed in the action. Shortly afterwards Pansa died of wounds he had received at Forum Gallorum.

News of the two engagements reached Rome on 20 and 26 April respectively and was received with acclaim. Decimus Brutus was awarded a triumph and Antonius was at last declared a public enemy; furthermore, Cassius' position in Syria was regularised and Sextus Pompeius, who had been approached by the senate for aid against Antonius, was appointed as prefect of the fleet and the sea-coast. The senate was less forthcoming in the case of Caesar: Cicero proposed that he should be given the lesser triumphal celebration of an *ovatio*, but this was refused, being opposed by friends of Marcus Brutus.[63] There was no mention of Caesar in the honorific decrees voted by the senate, the size of the donatives promised to his troops in January was reduced and he was instructed to hand over to Decimus Brutus all the forces that he commanded (including those which had been commanded by Hirtius and Pansa), so that Brutus could continue the war against Antonius. In consequence he was not best pleased with the senate, or with Cicero, who (as he had heard) had described him as a young man to be praised, honoured and discarded.[64]

Whatever the senate might order, Caesar and his soldiers had other ideas. Neither the Fourth nor the *Martia* legion nor Caesar himself was prepared to serve under Decimus Brutus, who was one of the assassins of Julius Caesar, and young Caesar kept command of these and the legions of the dead consuls. Antonius left Mutina shortly after his defeat and was joined by Publius Ventidius, one of the praetors of the year, who had recruited three legions of veteran soldiers in Picenum.[65] Decimus Brutus had appealed to Caesar for

63. Cic. *Ad Brut.* 23.9.
64. D. Brutus to Cicero (Cic. *Fam.* 11.20.1) on 24 May 43.
65. Ventidius had probably been sent to Picenum by Antonius at the end of November of the previous year before the latter left Rome (R. Syme, *The Roman Revolution*, Oxford: Oxford University Press, 1939, 126).

aid but received none, and was compelled to pursue Antonius with only the tattered remains of the troops he had had with him in Mutina. Antonius avoided him and reached Lepidus' province of Gallia Narbonensis in mid-May. Lepidus and Plancus had agreed to act together against Antonius, and Plancus moved his forces up to confront the new arrival. Lepidus, however, ordered him back, and met up with Antonius' army near Forum Voconii, some twenty-four miles west of Forum Iulii (modern Fréjus) on the banks of the river Argens. Lepidus wrote from here to Cicero, assuring him of his loyalty to the senate.[66] Whether this was genuine or not, before the end of May Lepidus had joined forces with Antonius. He wrote to the senate on 30 May to say that his army had refused to fight against Antonius to avoid the shedding of Roman blood, and it seems that fraternisation between the camps had led to this result. When the news reached Rome, Lepidus was declared a public enemy. Plancus meanwhile withdrew to his own province, where he was joined by Decimus Brutus, unable to challenge the combined armies with his weakened force. There Plancus appealed to Caesar to join them, but, despite assurances that he would, he never did.[67] He had other plans.

Towards the end of June, the senate, in an attempt to keep Caesar's soldiers under their own control, sent a commission to provide rewards for them, deliberately leaving Caesar himself out of the discussions. The soldiers would have none of it, and Caesar, to whom the senate had offered the opportunity of being a candidate for the praetorship, sent a deputation of centurions to Rome to demand that he be elected consul. The senate objected that he was far to young (he was still under twenty), and the soldiers returned north, but not before one of them had confronted the senate by grasping his sword and declaring that if they would not do it, this would. Caesar responded by marching on Rome with his whole army. The city was defended only by one of the legions of raw recruits that Pansa had raised and, despite false rumours that some of Caesar's legions had deserted him which raised short-lived hopes among the senators, was an easy conquest. Cicero fled the city, never to return. Caesar entered Rome in August to a rapturous welcome, and on 19 August was elected consul along with his relation and fellow heir of the dead dictator, Quintus Pedius, in place of Hirtius

66. Cic. *Fam.* 10.34.
67. Cic. *Fam.* 10.23.6, 24.4.

and Pansa.[68] Caesar's adoption by the will of Julius Caesar was confirmed by a law passed in the assembly of the people, the declaration of Dolabella as a public enemy was reversed, and a law in the name of Pedius set up a court to try the assassins of Julius Caesar. Caesar also paid his troops donatives from the public treasury.[69]

It was as consul that Caesar marched towards Cisalpine Gaul. To prepare the way for his meeting with Antonius and Lepidus, he had Pedius persuade the senate to revoke the declarations which had made the two men public enemies. There were, however, other more pressing problems that confronted him as he progressed north. Not only was he faced with the troops of Antonius and Lepidus but they had been joined by Gaius Asinius Pollio, the governor of Hispania Ulterior, who, despite earlier assurances to Cicero that he was loyal to the senate even though Antonius had attempted to subvert one of his three legions, discovered on arrival in Gallia Narbonensis with two of his legions that Antonius was fully in control, and not only joined him but persuaded Plancus to do the same, abandoning Decimus Brutus.[70] The latter tried to escape with his soldiers to the Rhine valley, but, deserted by his forces, was captured by a Gallic chieftain and put to death on the orders of Antonius. He had already by now been condemned under Pedius' law as one of the 'Liberators'. For Caesar this meant that the military resources of Antonius and his associates were far greater than those he had to hand, which made inevitable what he had probably had in mind for some time: an attempt to bring about a reconciliation with Antonius and Lepidus, reuniting the old and new Caesarians against the threat posed by the remaining 'Liberators'. As for Antonius and Lepidus, they could refuse to cooperate, but as Antonius at least was a declared avenger of the assassinated dictator he would have been cautious of a military confrontation with a young man who bore the name of Caesar, especially one who had shown that he commanded the loyalty of many of his adoptive father's former soldiers and now held the rank of consul. It was Antonius who had described young Caesar as owing everything to his name;[71] in the present context, that 'everything' meant a great deal. In terms of the power politics of late 43 BC, a conjunction of the three was likely to be beneficial to

68. Suet. *Aug.* 26.1; Appian, *B Civ.* 3.88–93; Dio Cass. 46.41–2.
69. Appian, *B Civ.* 3.94–5; Dio Cass. 46.46–8.
70. Cic. *Fam.* 10.31, 32 and 33; Appian, *B Civ.* 3.81 and 97.
71. Cic. *Phil.* 13.24.

each, however unlikely it might have seemed at the beginning of
the year.

The triumvirate for the establishment of the *res publica*: proscriptions and Philippi, 43–42 BC

The meeting took place on a small island in the midst of a river near
Bononia.[72] Each side was accompanied by five legions, a precaution
which proved unnecessary. In a meeting which lasted two full days,
they agreed that Caesar should stand down as consul, to be replaced
by Ventidius, and that they should together hold power as a board
of three for the establishment of the state (*triumviri reipublicae
constituendae*), holding consular *imperium* and appointing the
magistrates, for a period of five years. They divided the western
provinces between them, Lepidus taking both the Spanish provinces
in addition to Gallia Narbonensis, Antonius holding the remainder
of Gaul, and Caesar Sicily, Sardinia and Africa. Lepidus, who was to
be consul in the following year, was to remain in Rome, governing
his provinces by *legati* while the other two prosecuted the war
against Marcus Brutus and Cassius. They also named eighteen of the
richest cities of Italy whose territories were to supply land for their
soldiers; and, to provide cash for their needs as well as to dispose of
their enemies, agreed to institute an extensive proscription, in which
those whose names were placed on the list of the proscribed would
be hunted to their deaths and their property confiscated. To cement
the alliance Caesar, although already engaged to Servilia, daughter of
Servilius Isauricus (consul in 48), was to marry Claudia, the daughter of Antonius' wife Fulvia by her first husband, the radical tribune
of the 50s, Publius Clodius Pulcher.[73]

   The three commanders proceeded to march on Rome with one
legion each and their praetorian cohorts and entered the city one at
a time, Caesar leading.[74] Immediately one of the tribunes of the
plebs, Publius Titius, held an assembly of the people on 27 November at which he proposed and carried a law through which the
triumvirate was established as agreed at Bononia. The triumvirs also
instituted the proscriptions they had decided on then, with a list of
130 names of those to be killed being posted on the night following

72. Aug. *RG* 1 and 7; Plut. *Cic.* 46, *Ant.* 18–19; Suet. *Aug.* 96.1; Appian, *B Civ.* 4.2–3;
Dio Cass. 46.54–5.
73. Suet. *Aug.* 62.1.
74. Appian, *B Civ.* 4.2; Dio Cass. 47.2.

the passing of the *lex Titia*, to be followed shortly afterwards by another 150. The terror that this produced had already been fore-shadowed before the arrival of the three in Rome by their sending execution squads to deal with seventeen of the most important of their enemies, one of whom, so Appian writes, was Cicero. The result was panic in the city, which the consul Pedius attempted to allay by announcing the names of the seventeen, contrary to the intentions of Antonius, Lepidus and Caesar. One further death that resulted was that of Pedius himself, who died, worn out by the stress of what had happened, that night.[75]

The lists that appeared over the next days were prefaced by an edict from the triumvirs, which Appian reproduces, claiming he has translated it from the original Latin.[76] In this they stated that they were properly punishing those who had murdered Julius Caesar and those who had condoned and supported his murderers as well as those who had opposed and threatened themselves, and that, as they were about to embark on a campaign against the surviving assassins (by whom they meant Marcus Brutus and Cassius in the east), they would not leave such persons alive in Rome before they left; those on the lists of the proscribed were to be killed, as were any who attempted to protect them, and a reward of 25,000 denarii was promised to any free man who presented the head of one of the proscribed, and 10,000 and freedom to any slave. They made a direct comparison with the proscriptions that the dictator Sulla had carried out on his re-entry to Rome in 82 BC, while undertaking to be less severe than Sulla had been. In the event, again according to Appian, some 300 senators were sentenced to death and confiscation of their property, and about 2,000 members of the equestrian order.[77] Of the more prominent members of the senate, many fled from Italy to join Sextus Pompeius or Cassius and Brutus in the east. Cicero, who was at one of his villas at Tusculum when he heard of the proscriptions, had intended to sail to Macedonia, where Brutus held sway, but because of stormy weather had to land at Caieta, near another of his villas at Formiae. Here he was discovered by a detach-ment of soldiers as he made his way back to the coast and, having told his slaves not to resist, was killed. His head and hands were cut

75. Appian, *B Civ.* 4.6.
76. Appian, *B Civ.* 4.8–11.
77. Appian, *B Civ.* 4.5. Livy, *Per.* 120, puts the numbers at 130 senators and many equestrians; Dio declines to determine the exact number (Dio Cass. 47.13.1).

off and sent to Rome, where Antonius ordered that they be displayed on the *rostra* in the Forum.[78]

The death of Cicero marked (and, as Antonius' treatment of his dead body shows, was meant to mark) the end of senatorial opposition to the ambitions of Antonius himself and his colleagues in the triumvirate. Plutarch reports a story that the young Caesar initially resisted the inclusion of Cicero on the list of the proscribed but, after two days of argument, agreed that he should be killed on the insistence of Antonius and with the agreement of Lepidus, whose uncle and brother respectively were to be added to the list.[79] Whether that is true or not, Cicero was at the end of his life an iconic figure. Though his consulship in 63 BC and his suppression of Catiline's conspiracy were not as significant an event as he himself repeatedly claimed, and though through the 50s and during the dominance of Julius Caesar he was politically weak and often vacillating, so that the conspirators took care not to include him in their plans, it was Cicero's name that Brutus called out as he stood over the corpse of the dictator.[80] In what followed, Cicero emerged as a vigorous leader of the supporters of the 'Liberators' in the senate and it was as an opponent of Antonius that he came to place his hopes on the young Caesar. The last book that he wrote, during the months he was engaged in his battle of words with Antonius in late 44 and early 43, to his son Marcus, the *De officiis* (*On Duties*), expounding a moral and practical philosophy for a young man whom he hoped would play his part in a restored Republic, is set about both with condemnations of the tyranny with which the dead dictator had reduced a free people to slavery, and with observations that the leader of a state such as Rome could only lead by winning the trust and the love of its masses and of its elite, not by terrorising them. 'Fear,' he writes, 'is a bad guardian of permanence but benevolence a faithful one even to the end of time.'[81] This, in the context of Julius Caesar's assassination, was a lesson that the young Caesar, Cicero's protégé, learned well and applied when he had become master of the Roman world, though it is not, of course, clear that he needed Cicero's instruction; but his frequent and careful application of Republican precedent and the 'ways of the

---

78. Livy, fr. 120; Plut. *Cic.* 47–8; Appian, *B Civ.* 4.19–20.
79. Plut. *Cic.* 46.5.
80. Cic. *Phil.* 2.28 and 30, quoting Antonius' charge.
81. Cic. *Off.* 2.23: malus enim est custos diuturnitatis metus contraque benivolentia fidelis vel ad perpetuitatem.

ancestors' (*mos maiorum*) shows that he knew the value of respecting what Cicero held dear, even if he had been responsible for Cicero's murder.

Cicero was the only former consul to be killed; others escaped, including Lucius Caesar, the brother of Antonius' mother, who was initially protected by his sister and, when discovered at some point in the following year, was reluctantly pardoned by Antonius at her insistence, and Lepidus' brother, Lucius Aemilius Paullus, who was able to sail from Italy to Miletus.[82] In one aspect the flight of the likes of Lucius Paullus was for the triumvirs almost as satisfactory an outcome of proscription as execution: one part of the plan was undoubtedly to replenish their coffers from the forfeited estates of the proscribed, and this could be achieved as satisfactorily in their absence as in the event of their execution.

The triumvirs, however, were not able to accumulate enough cash by this process, not least because there were few who were prepared to buy the property of the proscribed and thus those who did purchase paid very low prices for the land they acquired. As a result, early in the following year the triumvirs instituted a range of new taxes based on the value of land and of slaves, and also demanded that 1,400 of the richest women submit valuations of their property and pay such taxes as were required of them. This last demand created an outcry from the women concerned, led by Hortensia, the daughter of Quintus Hortensius, the consul of 69 and one of the great orators of the late Republic. As a result the triumvirs backed down and reduced the number of women whose property was to be valued to 400, though they added further burdens on all males possessing 400,000 sesterces, the census requirement for membership of the equestrian order.[83]

The proscriptions, however successful or otherwise they were in raising the money the triumvirs needed to reward their troops and to pay for the forthcoming war against Brutus and Cassius, undoubtedly resulted in a reign of terror unknown in Rome since the series of political murders which had accompanied the struggle between Marius and Sulla forty years before. The stories of killings, betrayals and brutalities, and of remarkable loyalty and courage, which are recorded by Valerius Maximus, Appian, Dio Cassius

---

82. Appian, *B Civ.* 4.37; Dio Cass. 47.8.
83. Val. Max. 8.3.3; Plut. *Ant.* 21; Appian, *B Civ.* 431–4; Dio Cass. 47 14.2 and 16.5.

and others,[84] present a horrifying picture, paralleled by accounts of events in the twentieth century, such as those in Spain and Germany in the 1930s and in South America in the 1970s and 1980s. The historians are, not surprisingly, inclined to place the blame for these events on Antonius and Lepidus rather than on Caesar: history tends to exculpate the victors. This can be seen even in the most telling and earliest account, the famous inscription know as the *Laudatio Turiae*, erected by a grieving husband some thirty-five years after the proscriptions, in which he tells of the courage of his late wife in protecting him and insisting before a hostile Lepidus, who was consul in 42, on the validity of an exemption obtained from Caesar.[85] The husband is understandably grateful to the latter at the expense of Lepidus; but Caesar's part in the whole process cannot be underestimated. He, along with his colleagues, had agreed to the proscriptions at their meeting at Bononia. The overturning of the function of the government of the city to protect its citizens so that the autocrats who were empowered to establish the *res publica*, the common good, were enabled to use military force to murder their enemies was even more terrifying than the killings and confiscations themselves. Of course Antonius and Lepidus could (and did) claim that they were punishing those who had declared them as public enemies, and what could be a more appropriate response than the posting of lists of those who were now to be considered as public enemies? But the subversion of public power for private ends on such a scale was state-sponsored terrorism, directed against citizens, and resulted in panic and a breakdown of the norms of public life which had been the foundation of the Roman Republic. The extent of this disruption was merely emphasised when the senate voted the award of civic crowns, previously given to those who had saved the lives of citizens, to the triumvirs.[86]

The new year, 42 BC, began with the entry into the consulship of Marcus Lepidus and Lucius Munatius Plancus, both of whom had been nominated by Julius Caesar in the early months of 44. In pursuance of the policy they had adopted at Bononia, the triumvirs

---

84. Val. Max. 6.7.2–3, 8.5–7; Appian, *B Civ.* 4.17–29, 36–51; Dio Cass. 47.5–13. Appian notes that many books had been written by Roman historians, detailing stories of the proscriptions (*B Civ.* 4.16).
85. *Laudatio Turiae* II.21–34. On this and other accounts of the proscriptions, see now J. Osgood, *Caesar's Legacy: Civil War and the Emergence of the Roman Empire*, Cambridge: Cambridge University Press, 2006, 62–107.
86. Dio Cass. 47.13.3.

took a solemn oath on the first day of the year that they would maintain the late dictator's acts, and required all other senators to do the
same and that the same be done every subsequent year. The three
also saw to it, among many other honours instituted on that day,
that the senate and people included Julius Caesar among the gods,
so that he was thereafter to be called *Divus Iulius*, and a law was
passed that resulted in statues of the new god being set up in towns
throughout Italy.[87] The dominance of the new Caesarian autocrats
could not have been signalled more decisively.

Autocracy, however, does not mean omnipotence. While the
triumvirs held Spain, Gaul and Italy, Marcus Brutus and Cassius
dominated the eastern Mediterranean and thus the richest provinces
of the Roman world, while Sextus Pompeius, who discovered that
his name was on the list of the proscribed, had sailed with his fleet
to Sicily, which he effectively controlled. Brutus in Macedonia had
held Gaius Antonius, the triumvir's brother, in custody, despite his
attempts to foment mutiny among Brutus' troops, but when he heard
of Cicero's death in the proscriptions he had him executed.[88] Cassius
in Syria, whose tenure of the province had been legitimised probably
in April 43, had gathered together a substantial army from various
Roman commanders in the area and trapped Dolabella, now a
public enemy as a result of his murder of Trebonius, in the city of
Laodicea, the seaport of Antioch, and besieged him there. When
Cassius succeeded in entering the town, Dolabella committed
suicide.[89] Cassius intended to invade Egypt to punish Cleopatra, who
had been supporting Dolabella, but was urged by Brutus to meet him
in view of the impending threat they both faced from the armies of
the triumvirate. They met at Smyrna. There they decided to establish
their position in Asia and to replenish their funds by attacking those
who were supporters of the triumvirs before they had to face
the armies which Antonius and Caesar were preparing to lead
against them. Cassius moved against the island of Rhodes, where his
admiral, Staius Murcus, defeated the Rhodian fleet, which was
added to Cassius' ships, and an assault was launched on the island.
The city was taken and those who had led the resistance were put
to death. All the gold and silver, both privately owned and in the
treasuries of the temples, was seized, a garrison was installed, and

---

87. Dio Cass. 47.18–19; *ILS* 72, 73 and 73a.
88. Livy, *Per.* 121; Plut. *Brut.* 28.1–2.
89. Livy, *Per.* 121; Appian, *B Civ.* 4.60–2; Dio Cass. 47.30.

Cassius ordered that the cities of Asia should pay him as much tribute as would have been collected from the province in the next ten years. This was a crushing blow to an area which, although famously wealthy, had suffered from depredations by Dolabella, en route to Syria in the previous year. Cassius also deposed and executed Ariobarzanes, king of Cappadocia, and seized his treasury. Brutus meanwhile moved into Lycia. There many communities surrendered to him, but the main city, Xanthus, resisted. Brutus eventually took the place, but many of the inhabitants committed suicide. The treasury of the port town of Patara was plundered as were the possessions of its citizens, and Brutus added the Lycian fleet to his own before sailing to the Hellespont.[90] The two met again at Sardis before moving their troops to the Hellespont to cross into Europe. It was now the summer of 42, and the scene was being set for the 'Liberators' final confrontation with their opponents.

It took Antonius and Caesar rather longer to reach northern Greece. Caesar attempted to deal with Sextus Pompeius in Sicily, but a fleet he sent under his legate, Quintus Salvidienus, was defeated and Caesar was compelled to promise Pompeius, who had been gaining support from some of the towns in the south of Italy whose territory had been listed by the triumvirs to be allocated to their soldiers after the war, that he would remove the towns of Vibo and Rhegium from the list. Caesar then hurried to join Antonius at Brundisium, where he was being prevented from sailing across to Macedonia by Staius Murcus and a fleet of sixty ships. Although Murcus withdrew when Caesar's ships looked likely to entrap his own, thus allowing both Antonius and Caesar to get their forces across the Adriatic, he remained in the vicinity and, supplemented by more ships sent by Brutus and commanded by Gnaeus Domitius Ahenobarbus, caused ongoing problems for the triumvirs by interrupting their supply routes.[91] Already the triumvirs had sent advance forces under Lucius Decidius Saxa and Gaius Norbanus to prevent Brutus and Cassius from moving their army along the coast from the Hellespont, but their position was outflanked thanks to help that the 'Liberators' had from a local Thracian prince. Saxa and Norbanus were forced to withdraw and Brutus and Cassius established a strong position to the west of the city of Philippi. Here they were able to keep in touch with their fleet, which controlled

90. Plut. *Brut.* 28–33; Appian, *B Civ.* 4.65–81; Dio Cass. 47.32–4.
91. Livy, *Per.* 123; Appian, *B Civ.* 4.85–8; Dio Cass. 47.36.4–37.1.

the Aegean sea and protected their supply base on the island of Thasos.

Antonius arrived with his forces, having marched across Macedonia from Dyrrhachium, to be followed shortly after by Caesar, who, though ill, could not afford not to be there. A first battle was indecisive, with Brutus on the right wing defeating the Caesarians and capturing Caesar's camp, only to discover that he was not there. Cassius, however, was overwhelmed by Antonius, who broke into his camp. Cassius, unaware of Brutus' success, committed suicide. Brutus withdrew into his fortifications and refused battle for some three weeks. The triumvirs were short of supplies, and their situation was made worse by the destruction in the Adriatic by Murcus and Ahenobarbus of a fleet bringing them two further legions. In the end, on 23 October, Brutus was compelled by the taunts of his opponents and still more by the agitations of his soldiers and their officers to try battle again. The fighting was fierce and close, but the final outcome saw the defeat of Brutus and his army. Brutus committed suicide the following morning. The two sides had each lost some 20,000 men in the two battles. The numbers of Roman dead rank alongside the losses at Cannae and Arausio as the heaviest in the history of the Republic, and by far the worst in the period of the civil wars.[92] Antonius saw to the burial of Brutus, though Caesar had his head cut off to be sent to Rome and thrown down at the foot of his father's statue, a piece of vengeance that was thwarted by the loss of the head during a storm at sea. Such others of the already condemned 'Liberators' as were captured were killed or committed suicide. Caesar had prayed to Mars Ultor (Mars the Avenger) before the battle and promised to build a temple if he was victorious; the temple was not dedicated for another forty years, but the work of retribution was already in hand.[93] Those that escaped fled westwards to join up with Staius Murcus and Sextus Pompeius. Most of the soldiers who had fought under Brutus and Cassius simply transferred into the triumviral armies. Of the legions that had fought with them, Antonius and Caesar demobbed all those who had served their period of service, except for 8,000 who

---

92. Plut. *Brut.* 43–53; Appian, *B Civ.* 4.101–38; Dio Cass. 47.35–49. The date of the second battle is recorded in the Praeneste Calendar. On the numbers of dead, see P. A. Brunt, *Italian Manpower 225 BC–AD 14*, Oxford: Oxford University Press, 1971, 485–8.
93. Plut. *Brut.* 53.2; Suet. *Aug.* 13; Appian, *B Civ.* 4.135; Dio Cass. 47, 49. Vow to Mars Ultor: Ovid, *Fast.* 5.569–78; Suet. *Aug.* 29.2; on the dedication of the temple, see below, pp. 154–5.

stated that they wished to continue and were enrolled in the praetorian cohorts, which served the two triumvirs as bodyguards. The
remainder they divided between themselves before they left Macedonia to continue their programme of establishing their control of
the Roman world. Of the eleven legions at their disposal, Antonius
was to have six in order to take control of the eastern Mediterranean
provinces which had previously been held by the 'Liberators', and
Caesar handed over to him a further two, on the understanding that
these would be replaced by the two legions which Fufius Calenus
commanded in Italy on behalf of Antonius.

The allocation of provinces that Lepidus, Caesar and Antonius
had made at Bononia remained in place with some significant adjustments. There were rumours that Lepidus, in Rome and still consul
when the battles were fought at Philippi, had been negotiating
with Sextus Pompeius, and the other two triumvirs redivided his
provinces. Antonius was to keep Gallia Transalpina and take Narbonensis from Lepidus, while Cisalpina was added to Italy; Caesar
retained Africa, Sardinia and Sicily (currently controlled by Sextus
Pompeius) and when, having returned to Rome the following year,
he found that the rumours about Lepidus were false, he transferred
Africa to him while taking Spain. The one thing that is clear from
this manoeuvring is that Lepidus' position in the triumvirate was far
weaker than that of the other two. In the event, however, it was not
in the provinces that either Antonius or Caesar controlled that were
to be the focus of the events which followed.

The victory at Philippi meant the end of the 'Liberators' but not
the appearance of a successor to the dictator whom they had killed.
This did not, of course, mean that they had succeeded in restoring
the oligarchic control of Rome under the leadership of the senate.
Both the fact of what Julius Caesar had been and the extraordinary
position he had occupied, taken with the actions of the various
parties involved in the years between his assassination and Philippi,
made a return to the Rome of the Republic impossible. The events
of 44 and 43 showed clearly that the senate, composed as it was of
individuals of many different views, frequently failed to come to a
common decision and, even when a line of action was agreed, was
unable to divert the leading players, once they had an army behind
them, from their goal, which (as became increasingly clear) was in
each case to become the pre-eminent power in the state.

This is most obvious in the case of Antonius and of young Caesar
in the eighteen months following the Ides of March 44 BC. Although

he initially appears to have been wary of confronting the 'Liberators' directly in view of the support they had from some senators, Antonius moved to outright opposition once it became clear that the late dictator's soldiers were implacably hostile to them, and he proceeded to woo their loyalty, not only by donations and appeals to the memory of Julius Caesar but by such measures as his judicial law, passed in the first half of September 44, which provided for a third group of jurors for the law courts in addition to those of senators and equestrians, and made up of former soldiers.[94] This would have not only provided protection for Antonius, as champion of the veterans, against condemnation in the courts but also given prestige to the soldiers who had served under Julius Caesar in the wars of the past fifteen years. Antonius' success can be seen in his ability, once he had arrived with his army in Cisapline Gaul at the end of 44 BC, to ignore the posturing of the senate and their demands that he should end the siege of Decimus Brutus in Mutina and withdraw from his province. Young Caesar's aims were much the same, though he did not have the resources that were available to Antonius. The latter was consul and, along with Lepidus, seen by many as Julius Caesar's closest associates. Gaius Octavius, as he was when he arrived in Italy from Apollonia, was the late dictator's heir and, like Antonius, used this and the standing it gave him in the affection of the people and the soldiers to rally both to his support. It was no doubt because he lacked his rival's status in the political world of Rome that he spent time establishing himself with Cicero and his friends in the senate, though he was careful not to support the 'Liberators'. It was, however, after the raising of Caesarian veterans in Campania in October 44 at a time when he had no power within the constitution, and after the suborning of two of Antonius' legions that followed, that he was, on Cicero's motion, granted the *imperium* of a praetor in January 43. Though he was sent north to confront Antonius at Mutina with the two consuls at the behest of the senate, it was his control of the army that enabled him to march on Rome and demand the consulship to which he was elected in August 43. Given the ambitions of these two men and probably of Lepidus too, the triumvirate looks more like a marriage of convenience than a long-term relationship. The crucial problem that

94. Cic. *Phil.* 1.19–20; 5.8; 13.3 and 5. For this interpretation, see J. T. Ramsey, 'Mark Antony's judicial reform and its revival under the Triumvirs', *Journal of Roman Studies* 95 (2005), 20–37.

faced them all was the control that Cassius and Marcus Brutus were exercising with their armies over the wealthy provinces and kingdoms of the east. From this point of view the victory at Philippi marked not only the success of the triumvirs but also the removal of a main reason for their alliance. It is hardly surprising, therefore, that the years that followed were marked as much by wary hostility as by cooperation between them.

As for the 'Liberators', they too, whatever the intentions of the conspirators in March 44 BC, were by the time of the battles at Philippi engaged in a struggle to replace Julius Caesar rather than to abolish what he had been. Of the two leaders, Marcus Brutus, with his educated literary leanings[95] and his devotion to philosophy, was (and still is) regarded as the figurehead, but it was Cassius who was the more energetic, more competent and (from the viewpoint of the triumvirs) more dangerous. Both showed themselves determined and ruthless in exacting cash and loyalty from the cities and peoples of Asia Minor in their preparations for the final clash with Antonius and Caesar; but even before that Cassius' behaviour in the province of Syria in 43 and early 42 BC shows him acting as a conquering warlord rather than a provincial governor. The evidence of the Jewish historian Josephus, writing a century later, reveals that Judaea, properly an autonomous kingdom, though paying tribute to Rome, was required to pay the immense sum of 700 talents to Cassius; and that when, despite the efforts of Antipater, father of the future king Herod the Great, and his family, who switched their previous allegiance to Julius Caesar to the latest Roman general to arrive, four major cities failed to provide their share, Cassius sold their inhabitants into slavery.[96] What is particularly noticeable is that for Josephus and those about whom he was writing, Cassius was no different from the Roman commanders whom they had dealt with before, such as Pompeius and Julius Caesar and their representatives, or from those who would follow, notably Antonius and (after Actium) Augustus. Each made demands for loyalty and extracted funds and each took pains to ensure that those in control of the area would do as they were told, and the policy of Antipater and after him Herod was to attach themselves to whichever Roman held sway in the eastern Mediterranean and was thereby in a position

95. He is said to have spent the evening before the battle of Pharsalus in 48 BC working on an epitome of the historian Polybius (Plut. *Brut.* 4.7)
96. Josephus, *AJ* 14.271–6; *BJ* 1.220–2.

Figure 2 Denarius of Marcus Brutus, 43–42 BC (*RRC* 508.3) (© The Trustees of the British Museum)

to support them in the local context, which in Judaea, with its own internal political and religious complexities, was exceptionally unstable.[97] In this context, Cassius was one of a series of Roman warlords, not readily distinguishable from the others, each of whom was attempting to establish himself as the pre-eminent figure in the Roman world. Indeed it was not only the Jews who saw Cassius in this light. Plutarch records a letter sent by Marcus Brutus to Cassius while the latter was in Syria, calling him to the conference they held in Smyrna, to dissuade him from further expansion of his power in the region, reminding him that their aim was not to construct an empire for themselves but to bring freedom to their own fatherland.[98] This is what might be expected from Brutus, but it is worth remembering that he too at this time was not above representing himself as a figure standing out from the other members of the Roman elite, whose 'freedom' he had claimed to vindicate by the assassination of Julius Caesar. The coinage that the 'Liberators' minted as they made their preparations for the Philippi campaign included several coins which made explicit reference to *Libertas*, and one which showed a cap of liberty, two daggers and the inscription EID MAR ('the Ides of March'); but some (including that celebrating the Ides of March) showed the head of Brutus himself, in a style

97. For the situation in Judaea see E. M. Smallwood, *The Jews under Roman Rule from Pompey to Diocletian: A Study in Political Relations*, 2nd edn, Boston and Leiden: Brill, 2001, chs 2–4.
98. Plut. *Brut.* 28.3–5.

that echoed coins issued by the triumvirs a few months before.[99] This remarkable and ironic combination of images suggests that the liberty that was being fought for by Cassius and Marcus Brutus did not also mean equality, even among the upper classes at Rome. *Libertas* might mean 'liberty' but it did not exclude pre-eminence; what mattered, it appeared, was who was pre-eminent.

The battle of Philippi was a watershed just because it was a struggle between two groups of men, all of whom saw themselves, though in different ways, as successors to the position of leadership in the Roman world that Julius Caesar had occupied and perhaps created. The outcome was to remove two of them. The *triumviri*, the board of three for the establishment of the state, remained, and another contender, Sextus Pompeius, was in the wings, awaiting his opportunity. The next decade saw the struggle shift to one between these four, but the prize for the winner remained the same.

99. Coins of the 'Liberators': *RRC* 508.3 (Ides of March issue); 506.1, 507.1a, 508.3 (head of Brutus). Portrait coins of the triumvirs: *RRC* 492–4.

CHAPTER 3

The life and death of the triumvirate: from Philippi to Actium

Troubles in the triumvirate: war in Italy and Sicily, 41–36 BC

Early in 41 BC Antonius headed east from Philippi to ensure the security of the whole area which Brutus and Cassius had previously controlled. He proceeded to the province of Asia, where (unsurprisingly) he was welcomed as a god, and at Ephesus addressed the people of the whole province with a demand that they supply him with money on the same basis as they had supplied Brutus and Cassius. This was to provide money to reward the soldiers; he had undertaken with Caesar to raise this, Caesar agreeing to attend to the allocation of land in Italy. Antonius then moved through Asia Minor, rewarding those who, like the Rhodians and Lycians, had resisted Brutus and Cassius and installing a new king in Cappadocia. He also summoned Cleopatra from Egypt to explain why she had not provided support to him for the Philippi campaign. She arrived with more than an adequate account (she had, after all, tried to support Dolabella against Cassius), and Antonius not only accepted her story but saw to the murder of her sister, Arsinoe, whom Cleopatra saw as a threat to her tenure of the Egyptian throne and who was taking refuge in Ephesus. The ancient sources all see this as a result of Antonius' infatuation with Cleopatra, and there is no reason to doubt them; but it also needs to be noted that, whatever her physical attractions, Cleopatra was also a political power of great significance. She was the last of the great Hellenistic monarchs, who had dominated the region from the death of Alexander the Great until the coming of Rome, and even now was the most significant power in the eastern Mediterranean. For Antonius, who as the true victor of Philippi was the most powerful man in the Roman world, she represented a combination of political power and personal desirability. It is hardly surprising that, after settling various disputes in Syria, he joined her in Alexandria, spending the winter of 41/40 there.[1]

Meanwhile, Caesar, still unwell, returned to Italy at the end of 41 BC. He was sufficiently ill by the time he reached Brundisium for it to be rumoured that he had died. After arriving in Rome, where the senate had awarded a lengthy thanksgiving to the victors of Philippi, he produced letters from Antonius which confirmed the arrangements made after the battle, and set about the difficult task of confiscating land and assigning it to the veterans of his and Antonius' army. Although eighteen of the richest Italian cities had been selected at Bononia to reward the soldiers, these cities were quick to object that the burden should be shared more widely; and indeed two of them, Vibo and Rhegium, had already gained exemption as a result of Caesar's undertaking to Sextus Pompeius in the run-up to the Philippi campaign. While the Italians, particularly those in the wealthy regions of central and northern Italy, argued for change, the veterans rioted and, when they suspected that Caesar might attempt to modify the promises made to them, threatened his life. Grain shortages resulted from the activities of Sextus Pompeius, who cut off supplies and ravaged Bruttium in southern Italy. Worse was to come: one of the consuls of 41 was Antonius' brother Lucius, who, with the support of Antonius' energetic and turbulent wife Fulvia, mounted a two-pronged attack on Caesar, claiming both that he was attempting to rob Antonius of the credit for rewarding the soldiers he had led and that the Italian landowners were being robbed of their possessions. Caesar reacted by divorcing his wife, Fulvia's daughter, but allowed a role for Antonius' agents in the distribution of the land; that, however, was not enough for Lucius and Fulvia. They, it seems, were intent on discrediting and undermining Caesar, and relations deteriorated to a point at which war between the two sides seemed inevitable. Lucius had stationed himself at Praeneste, 37 kilometres south-east of Rome. Some of Caesar's soldiers who had previously served under Antonius urged that Caesar and Lucius should meet to resolve their disputes, and Gabii, half-way between Rome and Praeneste, was chosen as a suitable place. In the event, a clash between squadrons of cavalry on the two sides as Lucius approached the town led him to withdraw and to a final breakdown of relations. Manius, an agent of Marcus

---

1. Josephus, *AJ* 14.301–29; *BJ* 1.243–7; Plut. *Ant.* 23–9; Appian, *B Civ.* 5.4–11; Dio Cass. 48.24.

Antonius, produced letters, allegedly from Antonius himself, sanctioning war if his standing were to be damaged, and Lucius marched on Rome. Lepidus the triumvir, who was still in the capital, fled and Lucius was welcomed by the populace, no doubt in the expectation that Caesar would soon be overthrown.[2]

Of the two, Caesar was in the more difficult position. Lucius had hopes that he would gain reinforcement from his brother's supporters, notably Asinius Pollio, who was still in Cisalpine Gaul with seven legions, and Fufius Calenus and Ventidius, who were commanding large numbers in Gaul, which was Antonius' province. Caesar's only support was Savidienus, whom he had sent to Spain and who was still on the way there, having been obstructed by Pollio and Ventidius. Moreover the seas were controlled by Sextus Pompeius, based in Sicily, to whom some of Brutus' and Cassius' ships had gone, and the remainder of that fleet was still based in the Adriatic under Domitius Ahenobarbus. As Salvidienus made his way back, fighting broke out in Etruria. Lucius Antonius tried to break through to join up with Pollio and Ventidius, but Salvidienus and Caesar's troops, commanded by Vipsanius Agrippa, outmanoeuvred him, and he withdrew to the fortified city of Perusia (modern Perugia). Caesar set up a siege there, and then with Agrippa marched to confront Pollio and Ventidius. The latter pair seem to have been uncertain about what to do. Although Lucius claimed he was fighting on behalf of his brother, Caesar too claimed that he was acting in accord with his agreement with Antonius; and no word came from the man himself in the east. Ventidius and Pollio avoided a battle. Another hope for the increasingly desperate besieged in Perusia was Munatius Plancus, who had been establishing veterans on land near Beneventum; he enlisted troops when instructed to do so by Fulvia and, after defeating some forces of Caesar's, retreated to Spoletium, south of Perusia. When Ventidius and Pollio managed to join up with Plancus and move towards Perusia, they were confronted again, this time by Agrippa and Salvidienus, and, on Plancus' advice, again refused battle. They separated and went each his own way. In the early months of the following year, Lucius Antonius surrendered. He himself was spared by Caesar, who indeed sent him in some capacity to Spain later in the year, after which he disappears from the historical record. Fulvia fled eastwards to Antonius, as did Munatius Plancus. Ventidius collected together the

2. Appian, *B Civ.* 5.12–30; Dio Cass. 48.4–13.

forces abandoned by Plancus with his own, and was chosen by the soldiers as their commander. Pollio returned to the north, where at some point in the year he persuaded Domitius Ahenobarbus and his fleet to join the Antonian side. Meanwhile Caesar had put to death many senators and members of the equestrian order who had been with Lucius Antonius in Perusia, and also all but one of the town council, the exception being an individual who had served on the jury which had condemned the murderers of the dictator Caesar while a member of the court that had been set up in Rome. Some sources record that Caesar sacrificed three hundred senators and equestrians at an altar dedicated to Divus Julius on the Ides of March; all agree that the soldiers not only plundered the town but burnt it to the ground.[3]

Caesar and his associates, Agrippa and Salvidienus, had won; but the problems that had given Lucius Antonius a platform for his opposition remained. The distribution of land to the veterans continued to cause grief to those who were dispossessed, both to those who, like the poet Horace, had fought alongside Brutus and Cassius at Philippi and to Italians who had had no more involvement in the struggle than being owners of land which the triumvirs had identified as rewards for their soldiers. Inevitably the soldiers too seized as much land as they could, sometimes with little regard for the justice of their claims.[4] With these difficulties in Italy and the uncertainties about the attitude of Antonius, who had failed to support his brother throughout the siege of Perusia, Caesar had to try to strengthen his position. He was helped by the death of Fufius Calenus, Antonius' commander in Transalpine Gaul, at a time when he himself was in northern Italy, and he promptly seized control of the province and the eleven legions there, leaving Salvidienus in command. Lepidus was in Africa, having taken over the province allotted to him after struggles between the representatives of Antonius and Caesar. The other element in the confused picture was Sextus Pompeius. Several of the refugees from Perusia had fled to him, including Antonius' mother, whom Sextus sent to Antonius, who had moved from Alexandria to Athens, escorted by amongst

3. Suet. *Aug.* 15; Seneca, *Clem.* 1.11.1; Appian, *B Civ.* 5.48–9; Dio Cass. 48.14.
4. See Appian, *B Civ.* 5.12–13. Horace mentions the loss of his farm as forcing him to take up verse writing (*Epist.* 2.2.49–53). Vergil tells of the problems of the dispossessed in *Eclogues* 1 and 9. In general, see J. Osgood, *Caesar's Legacy: Civil War and the Emergence of the Roman Empire*, Cambridge: Cambridge University Press, 2006, 108–51.

others his father-in-law, Lucius Scribonius Libo. Libo suggested to Antonius that Antonius and Pompeius should join together against Caesar, and, so Appian writes, was told that he would do so if there was a war with Caesar, but that if Caesar stuck to his agreements with Antonius, the latter would attempt to bring Caesar and Pompeius together.[5] Caesar, having heard that Antonius was in Athens and realising that, although he had a large land army, he had no control of the seas, wrote to his friend and agent Maecenas to arrange a marriage between himself and Libo's sister, Scribonia, to which Libo assented and told his family to do so too.

This was the position when Antonius, having reached the Adriatic and joined up with Domitius Ahenobarbus and the fleet which he commanded, crossed to Brundisium, only to discover that the garrison which Caesar had placed there refused to give him entry. Antonius laid siege to the town, while Pompeius seized Sardinia and sailed to Italy, landing in the south and ravaging some of the territory. Caesar was now in real danger. He sent Agrippa to deal with Pompeius and with assaults Antonius was making on towns near Brundisium, and marched to relieve the siege on Brundisium itself. When he got there, he found he could do no more than camp outside the siege-works. While he waited, Antonius sent for further reinforcements from Macedonia; but Agrippa was having considerable success, both against Pompeius and in recapturing a town that Antonius had seized shortly before. It looked as though the final battle between the two triumvirs was imminent.

At this point the armies of the two men took a role in the impasse. Some of them had met, and after exchanging mutual recriminations about the wrongs that each of their leaders had done to the other, they determined to attempt to reconcile them. Just at this time news reached Brundisium that Antonius' wife, Fulvia, who had been instrumental in starting the trouble which led to the siege of Perusia, had died in Greece, and this too seems to have encouraged the soldiers to bring an end to the enmity between their generals. Another person who was keen to see the two reconciled was Lucius Cocceius Nerva, a friend of them both, whom Caesar had earlier sent as an envoy to Antonius and who had stayed with him. Nerva now persuaded Antonius to allow him to approach Caesar, not least because, as he discovered, Antonius' army was unwilling to fight. A negotiating committee, made up of Nerva, Asinius Pollio, on behalf

5. Appian, *B Civ.* 5.52.

of Antonius, and Maecenas, on behalf of Caesar, met. Antonius had already been persuaded to get Pompeius to return to Sicily and that Ahenobarbus, who was particularly suspected by Caesar's soldiers as a former supporter of the 'Liberators', should also retire from the scene. The three agreed that there should be peace between the two leaders, and that, to cement the agreement, Antonius should marry Caesar's sister Octavia, recently widowed by the death of her husband, Marcellus. The two triumvirs met and embraced as the soldiers cheered, and proceeded (as they had after Philippi) to divide the control of the Roman world between them, ignoring their colleague, Lepidus. This time a line of separation was established at Scodra (modern Shkodër, in northern Albania), just north of the boundary between the provinces of Illyricum and Macedonia: the provinces north and west of that line were to be Caesar's, those east of it Antonius'; Lepidus was to be left in charge of Africa and Sextus Pompeius held Sicily. Italy was to be Caesar's base, but it was agreed that both Caesar and Antonius should have the right to recruit soldiers there in equal numbers.[6] Once again, there was no mention of Lepidus. If there was any doubt after Philippi as to the ranking of the triumvirs, the agreement at Brundisium dispelled it. Antonius was the leading figure: he was the true victor of Philippi and was to now to take on the campaign against the Parthians which Julius Caesar had been about to lead when he was assassinated in March 44. Next came Caesar, still only twenty-three in September 40, the month in which the meeting at Brundisium took place, but now in charge of a sweep of provinces from Illyricum to Spain and, in all probability, of a war against Sextus Pompeius. Lepidus, not even consulted at Brundisium, was in a definite third place.

That is not to say that Antonius and Caesar, as they moved from Brundisium to Rome to celebrate the marriage of Antonius and Octavia, had no problems of their own. Antonius was confronted and almost lynched by soldiers at Brundisium before they left, demanding the cash payments which they had been promised, and which Antonius had agreed that he should raise. The money was not available, whether because (as the sources believe) he had been spending lavishly on Cleopatra or because of the funds that would be needed for his campaigns in the east.[7] Caesar had a different problem: Antonius, whether out of a frankness resulting from his

6. Plut. *Ant.* 30–1; Appian, *B Civ.* 5.65; Dio Cass. 48.28–9.
7. Dio Cass. 48.30.2–3.

reconciliation or in an attempt to break up the close circle which had surrounded Caesar, informed the latter that before the meeting at Brundisium he had been approached by Salvidienus, who had offered to join him against Caesar. Caesar summoned Salvidienus from Gaul and confronted him with the charge; Salvidienus committed suicide.[8]

There was another unresolved difficulty that faced both Antonius and Caesar. Sextus Pompeius, who had allied himself with Antonius before the meeting at Brundisium, was extremely dissatisfied with the outcome of the pact and resumed his attacks on the coast of Italy, keeping the merchants who would have brought the grain needed to feed the city of Rome from venturing near. In Rome the populace, who had welcomed the two triumvirs when they arrived from Brundisium, turned hostile and Caesar was pelted with stones by rioters and only rescued by the intervention of Antonius, who sent in some of his troops. The riot was quelled, but only with substantial loss of life. Antonius and Caesar decided that they had to negotiate and contacted Scribonius Libo to bring this about. Pompeius was uncertain and there was a division of opinion among his supporters: Staius Murcus wanted a reconciliation but Menodorus, Pompeius' most successful commander, who had succeeded in recapturing Sardinia, urged that famine in Rome would soon bring down their enemies. Pompeius had become suspicious of Murcus and, on Menodorus' advice, had him murdered. Early in 39, however, Pompeius agreed to a meeting and the three met at the seaside town of Baiae. Pompeius expected that he would be given a share in the triumvirate, in place of Lepidus, but Antonius and Caesar offered no more than a return from exile. The discussion came to an abrupt end. Behind the scenes, however, negotiation continued and eventually Pompeius was persuaded by his relatives, especially his wife Scribonia and his mother Mucia, to meet Antonius and Caesar again, this time at Misenum,[9] at the southern end of the bay of Baiae, and here an agreement was reached. Pompeius agreed to withdraw the troops he had in Italy and to end the raids, allowing grain to come to Rome from Sicily and Sardinia, of which, along with the other islands of the Mediterranean, he was acknowledged as controller. He was also given control of the

---

8. Livy, *Per.* 127; Suet. *Aug.* 66.2; Appian, *B Civ.* 5.66; Dio Cass. 48.33. Suetonius and Dio record that Caesar handed him over to the senate for condemnation.
9. Vell. Pat. 2.77.1; Plut. *Ant.* 32.1; Dio Cass. 48.36. Appian, *B Civ.* 5.72, places the meeting at Puteoli.

Peloponnese in southern Greece, and in Rome he was to be enrolled in the prestigious order of augurs and given the promise of a consulship in the years to come. Of the refugees who had fled to him during the past years, those who were among the proscribed were allowed to return so long as they had not been condemned as assassins of Julius Caesar, and were to receive one quarter of their property back. Slaves who had served with Pompeius were to be freed, and free men were to be treated in the same way as the veterans in the armies of the triumvirs. The agreement was sealed and sent to the temple of the Vestals in Rome for safe keeping, and on the following day Pompeius entertained Caesar and Antonius at a banquet on his warship. He ignored the suggestion of Menodorus that he should seize the opportunity and take them both prisoner.

Pompeius had gained all, or almost all, that he had set out to achieve. He was not formally a member of the triumvirate but was so effectively, and probably better placed than Lepidus. The extent to which Antonius and Caesar had been compelled to give way to Pompeius' demands demonstrates the leverage which, at least in the short term, he was able to exert, especially on Italy and Rome. As a sign of his new status, his daughter was betrothed to the three-year-old Marcellus, the son of Caesar's sister by her late husband and thus now Antonius' stepson. When arrangements were made about consuls for the next years, in addition to those who had been pre-appointed by Antonius and Caesar for 38 to 35 in view of the former's imminent departure for the war against the Parthians, further appointments were made for 34 to 31, which included Pompeius and his collaborator Domitius Ahenobarbus.

At Rome, there was jubilation at the news, and Caesar and Antonius proceeded to their own areas to undertake military operations. Antonius left for Greece, where, to Pompeius' irritation, he levied a tax before handing over the Peloponnese. He stayed on in Greece, spending the winter of 39/38 with Octavia in Athens, but sent Publius Ventidius to Syria to meet an invasion of the province by the Parthians, led by the Roman renegade Quintus Labienus, who in 42 had been sent by Brutus and Cassius to request aid from the Parthian king Pacorus, and who after Philippi remained with him. Ventidius defeated the Parthians and Labienus was killed. Caesar in the meantime went to Gaul, where Agrippa was in command, to quell unrest there, but returned to Italy on the report that pirates were once again at sea off the Italian coast and grain ships were not getting through to Rome. Caesar claimed that some of these men, when captured and tortured, admitted that they had been commissioned by Pompeius, but the latter, when confronted with this, denied it and in response complained of his treatment in the Peloponnese. Pompeius fell out with his admiral, Menodorus, who was holding Sardinia on Pompeius' behalf, and who early in 38 deserted to Caesar, handing over not only Sardinia but a fleet of sixty ships and three legions of soldiers. To add to all this, Caesar divorced Scribonia in the autumn of 39 and in January of the following year married Livia, the third and last of his wives, who already had a son by her husband, Tiberius Claudius Nero, and was pregnant with another. The enmity between Caesar and Pompeius could not be clearer. In an attempt to rally the triumvirate behind him, Caesar called a meeting at Brundisium to which Antonius came, but when he arrived there he found that neither Lepidus nor Caesar himself was there and immediately returned to Greece, writing to Caesar that he should not break the agreement made at Misenum.[10] This made no difference.

The first year of the war saw Caesar thwarted in an attempt to invade Sicily. Fleets led by Menodorus and Calvisius Sabinus, the consul of the previous year, were checked as they sailed down the coast and Caesar's own fleet was defeated in the straits of Messana. To make matters worse, both the Caesarian fleets were then wrecked in a storm. Caesar withdrew and spent the rest of the year and the winter which followed constructing ships and making preparations, for which purpose he recalled Agrippa, designated as consul for 37, to supervise the work. In Rome, the populace, again threatened by famine, grew increasingly restless. Caesar sent his friend Gaius Maecenas to Greece to secure assistance from Antonius, which was duly promised.[11]

Agrippa spent much of his consular year constructing a new fleet, and in the process built a canal which linked the deep fresh-water Lake Avernus, which lies behind Baiae, with the sea, in order to provide a safe harbourage and a training area for the twenty thousand slaves who were to man the new ships.[12] In the spring Antonius arrived at Tarentum with the promised ships, but Caesar, who had now decided to postpone further moves against Pompeius until his own preparations were complete, was unwilling to receive them,

10. Appian, *B Civ.* 5.78; Dio Cass. 48.46.
11. Appian, *B Civ.* 5.92–3.
12. Strabo, 5.4.5; Vell. Pat. 2.79.2; Suet. *Aug.* 16.1.

not least because Antonius was seeking in return troops to use in his campaigns against the Parthians, which, according to the agreement made at Brundisium three years before, he was entitled to levy in Italy. After further negotiations, undertaken particularly by Octavia between her brother and her husband, and yet another picturesque reconciliation between the two men, it was agreed that Caesar should have 120 ships, with a further ten lighter vessels which Octavia persuaded Antonius to provide, while Caesar promised four legions and added a thousand men from his own bodyguard.[13] The legions were in the event never sent, but for the time being the two men seemed in accord. At the same time they agreed to extend the period of the triumvirate for a further five years, backdating the renewal to the beginning of the year, since the first term had ended on 31 December 38.[14] All this was done without consulting Lepidus, and the distribution of provinces remained as previously agreed at Brundisium in 40. Antonius and Octavia returned across the Adriatic, but Octavia travelled no further than Corcyra, whence Antonius sent her back to Italy, on the grounds that she should not be exposed to the dangers of the war he was intending to fight against the Parthians.

Caesar continued his preparations for war against Sextus Pompeius. Menodorus, who had deserted Pompeius for Caesar in 38, now changed sides again, taking with him some six or seven ships, resenting the fact that he had been placed under the command of Calvisius Sabinus; and Sabinus was relieved of his post as a result, to be replaced by Agrippa.[15] It was not until the beginning of July 36 that the campaign began in earnest. The plan was for a three-fold attack on Sicily, with Caesar and Agrippa sailing from Puteoli, Lepidus from Africa and Statilius Taurus (who had been suffect consul in 37) from Tarentum, where he commanded the ships which had been left by Antonius. Despite the careful synchronisation on the first day of the month of July (named for his father, Julius Caesar in early 44) and the propitiatory rites which Caesar undertook to ensure good weather, the joint expedition was nearly ruined by a severe storm which blew up. Lepidus lost transport ships, but

13. Appian, *B Civ.* 5.95. Plutarch (*Ant.* 35) gives different figures, but Appian's are more likely to be correct (see C. B. R. Pelling, *Plutarch: Life of Antony*, Cambridge: Cambridge University Press, 1988, 215).
14. Appian, *B Civ.* 5.95; Dio Cass. 48.54.6. The date of the renewed tenure is given in the *Fasti Capitolini* at the head of the entry for the year 37.
15. Appian, *B Civ.* 5.96; Dio Cass. 48.54.7.

managed to land his forces and laid siege to Lilybaeum, where
Pompeius had posted a force to protect the western end of the island.
Taurus turned back to Tarentum, but Caesar and Agrippa suffered
major damage while attempting to sail from the bay of Naples round
the promontory of Sorrento. Caesar reached land, reordered his
forces and set about repairing his ships, while sending Maecenas to
Rome to prevent Pompeius' friends there from benefiting from his
problems. Pompeius himself had made his base at Messana in the
north-eastern corner of Sicily, where he kept the greater part of his
fleet. He attempted to disrupt the preparations on the mainland by
sending Menodorus to attack the shipyards, but after a successful onslaught Menodorus once again deserted Pompeius. Caesar
succeeded in landing on the Aeolian islands and left Agrippa on the
island of Hiera. From here he engaged with a Pompeian fleet, based
at Mylae, on the north coast of Sicily west of Messana, and defeated
it. Caesar, who had joined up with Statilius, crossed to attack
Tauromenium, on the east coast, not far from the volcanic Mount
Etna, while Pompeius was distracted by events at Mylae. Caesar
failed to capture the town and was in turn attacked by Pompeius,
losing a battle at sea of the coast. Caesar's land forces succeeded,
after a difficult march, in reaching Mylae, and once he had recovered
from his setback, he too joined up with Agrippa there. On 3 September a major sea-battle took place off Naulochus, a promontory to
the east of Mylae, where the Caesarian fleet, under Agrippa's
command, defeated Pompeius, who fled to Messana with seventeen
ships.[16] Thence he sailed eastwards, hoping to join Antonius in a war
against Caesar.

Meanwhile Agrippa led the Caesarian forces to Messana, where
he joined Lepidus in a blockade. The troops that Pompeius had
summoned from Lilybaeum in the west of the island offered to
surrender. Agrippa wanted to wait for Caesar to come from
Naulochus, but Lepidus took it upon himself not only to accept the
surrender but also to allow the Pompeians to join his own soldiers in
plundering Messana, and sent orders to the towns still occupied
by Pompeius' forces not to admit Caesar's soldiers. Caesar arrived
at Messana and confronted Lepidus, who in turn objected to his
treatment by the other two triumvirs and offered a new deal in the
division of the provinces. Lepidus was relying on the backing of his
now large army, but the soldiers he had brought from Africa were

16. Livy, *Per.* 129; Vell. Pat. 2.79.4–5; Appian, *B Civ.* 5.116–21; Dio Cass. 49.8–10.

angry at his favourable treatment of the Pompeians and neither group wanted another round of civil war. When Caesar, unknown to Lepidus, entered the latter's camp with a small guard, he was able to win over a considerable number to his side, and after a momentary uncertainty and some brawling, the whole army deserted Lepidus. Caesar, without consulting Antonius, deprived Lepidus of his command as triumvir and sent him back to Rome as a private citizen. The only position he was allowed to keep was that of *pontifex maximus*, the head of the college of priests, which he had held since his appointment in the months after the assassination of Julius Caesar in 44.

With Lepidus out of the way and Sextus Pompeius a fugitive, Caesar was in a very strong position; but he was faced by a threat from within his own army, who demanded rewards and demobilisation. They were not satisfied by Caesar's promise that he would not involve them in any more civil war and that he was intending to begin a campaign against the troublesome peoples of northern Illyricum, and, after a series of threats and promises, Caesar only managed to calm the mutiny by allowing those who had fought both at Mutina and at Philippi to be disbanded and given a cash payment and land, some of which was in Campania.[17] Only then could he proceed to Rome, which he entered on 13 November in celebration of an *ovatio*, the lesser form of triumph. The honours awarded by an appropriately grateful senate and people, however, were large, and included a golden statue in the Forum. Agrippa was awarded the very special honour of a naval crown for his outstanding part in the defeat of Pompeius.[18]

Caesar also seems to have taken the opportunity at this time of announcing that the civil wars were over and that the normal pattern of government would be restored, once Antonius returned from the war in Parthia. It is probably in this context that he was offered the sacrosanctity (*sacrosanctitas*) of a tribune of the plebs for life, and possibly the full power of a tribune (*tribunicia potestas*).[19] This would mark him out in a way that was unique, but nonetheless related to the venerable institutions of the Republic. In the meantime he set Calvisius Sabinus the task of dealing with banditry in Italy, a

17. Vell. Pat. 2.81.1–2; Appian, *B Civ.* 5.127–9; Dio Cass. 49.13–15.
18. Verg. *Aen.* 8.684; Vell. Pat. 2.81.3; Pliny, *HN* 16.7–8; Appian, *B Civ.* 5.130; Dio Cass. 49.1.4.
19. Appian, *B Civ.* 5.132 (office of tribune); Dio Cass. 49.15.6 (same protection as a tribune and a seat on the tribunes' bench).

move which also provided evidence of a return to normality after the turmoil of the past years.[20] For those in Rome and Italy at least, this was a moment of welcome restoration of peace and of hopes for better things to come.

The confrontation mounts: Antonius in the east, Caesar in the west, 36–32 BC

Caesar's promises, however, were dependent on Antonius' return and cooperation. The year 36 saw not only the defeat of Sextus Pompeius but also the beginning of Antonius' invasion of Parthia. Ventidius had repelled two Parthian invasions of Syria in 39 and 38, was replaced by Antonius himself and returned to Rome, where he celebrated a triumph. Antonius, on returning from his meeting with Caesar at Tarentum in 37, spent time establishing a series of kingdoms in Asia Minor and the eastern Mediterranean, including re-establishing Herod in Judaea, following the pattern of earlier Roman generals in the same area, most recently Cassius in 43. Antonius gave Cleopatra territories in Syria and the lucrative balsam groves near Jericho. Although these grants were not out of line with those made to other rulers, and Antonius did not also give her the rest of Herod's kingdom as Cleopatra apparently wished, they were accompanied by his acknowledgement of the twin son and daughter that she had borne to him, who were given the names of Alexander Helios ('the Sun') and Cleopatra Selene ('the Moon').[21] The following year she was to have another son by him who would be called Ptolemy Philadelphos. It may be too much to assume, as some scholars have done, that Antonius married Cleopatra at this point or indeed that he was setting up himself and her as rulers on the model of the Hellenistic kings; the distribution of territories to rulers was necessary to provide a secure basis for his forthcoming invasion of Parthia, and Cleopatra's share was not excessive. Moreover Egypt was far more significant in terms of wealth and prestige than the others, being the last of the kingdoms set up by the generals of Alexander the Great to survive. That said, it is obvious that his relationship with the queen of Egypt was on a different footing from that with the other rulers he had put in place. It was, according to Plutarch, Cleopatra who was with him up to the moment at which the

---

20. Appian, *B Civ.* 5.132; *ILS* 2488.
21. Plut. *Ant.* 36.

Parthian campaign began and whom he then sent back to Egypt.[22]

Antonius' plan of attack was to march not into Mesopotamia but northwards, up the course of the river Euphrates and then through the mountains to assault the city of Phraaspa, the capital of the king of Media, an important ally of Phraates, who had recently acceded to the throne of Parthia, following the abdication of his father, whom he promptly murdered. Antonius was supported by the king of Armenia, Artavasdes, who also promised substantial cavalry to supplement the huge army that Antonius had mustered. The long march caused problems and required the supply-train and the heavy siege engines to take a longer route, since the mountain tracks on which the main army marched were impassable for them. Parthian and Median cavalry was able to attack the supply-train, destroying two legions that accompanied it, and Artavasdes and his Armenian cavalry failed to appear. Antonius on his arrival at Phraaspa was in a difficult situation, and after a fruitless attempt to take the place set off back late in the season. After a slow and miserable march, beset by the wintry conditions and by harrying from the Parthians, the army reached Armenia, where, despite his anger with Artavasdes for having failed to support him, Antonius treated him with apparent respect in order to get through to Syria, where he was met by Cleopatra, who provided clothing for the exhausted troops and money.[23]

Antonius' retreat was not the total disaster that later hostile writers described, but it was nonetheless a complete failure. He had taken an army of immense size against Parthia,[24] with the intention of revenging the defeat of Crassus at Carrhae in 53 and carrying out the plans which Julius Caesar was about to undertake when he was assassinated in 44. Antonius lost one third of his forces and, more importantly, achieved nothing. The effect of this was seen when he reached Alexandria. Sextus Pompeius, having escaped from Messana, sailed to Mytilene, where he attracted considerable support. He intended to ally himself with Antonius against Caesar and sent an embassy to Alexandria to propose that they join forces,

22. Plut. *Ant.* 37.3.
23. Livy, *Per.* 130; Vell. Pat. 2.82.1–3; Plut. *Ant.* 37–51; Dio Cass. 49.23–31.
24. Antonius' army is reckoned at sixteen legions and ten thousand cavalry, to which should be added large numbers of other forces from the eastern provinces and the Armenian forces of Artavasdes. The Roman troops alone were more than twice as many as the troops Crassus had when he invaded Parthia in 53 (see A. N. Sherwin-White, *Roman Policy in the East, 168 BC to AD 1*, London: Duckworth, 1984, 311).

but when he heard what had happened to Antonius' expedition, he also sent envoys to the Parthian king. These were intercepted by Antonius, who, after bringing the two sets of envoys face to face, dispatched a fleet under Marcus Titius, who had served under Pompeius, to arrest Pompeius and prevent his attempts to seize parts of the provinces of Asia and Bithynia. Titius captured Pompeius and received his surrender. It is said that Antonius initially ordered Titius to execute him and then changed his mind, but the first letter, ordering execution, arrived after the second; and whatever the truth of this story, Pompeius was put to death by Titius. In Rome Caesar ordered games to celebrate the event and had a statue of Antonius riding in a chariot placed in the Forum. It looks as though Caesar was, at least publicly, maintaining good relations with Antonius, though in a way which emphasised the importance of his own victory over Pompeius in Sicily. The alteration in Pompeius' attitude to Antonius after his arrival at Mytilene demonstrated, however, the damage done to Antonius' reputation by his failure against the Parthians.[25]

The obvious and perhaps the only way for Antonius to restore his standing was to succeed where he had failed in 36. He was helped by the breakdown of relations between his adversaries. The king of Media quarrelled with Phraates, the Parthian king, and contacted Antonius to ask for an alliance. The latter was delighted, but his first concern was to deal with the king of Armenia, whom he blamed for the failure of his earlier campaign. He attempted to lure Artavasdes to Alexandria, but without success, and proceeded to rebuild his army for a further expedition. Caesar continued his policy of apparent friendship and cooperation with Antonius, while doing so in a way which emphasised the difficulties of his own position. Caesar sent Octavia with supplies for Antonius' army, a gift of money and two thousand legionaries to act as a bodyguard. This last was particularly galling to Antonius, since Caesar had undertaken when they had met at Tarentum in 37 to send four legions in return for the ships which Antonius provided for the war against Sextus Pompeius, a force which would have been more than ten times the size of the one he was now being provided with; and, of course, the entrusting of this mission to Octavia simply underlined the fact of Antonius' ever-closer relationship with Cleopatra. Antonius heard of Octavia's imminent arrival when she had reached Athens and, while accepting

25. Livy, *Per.* 131; Appian, *B Civ.* 5.136–45; Dio Cass. 49.17–18.

the supplies and the troops, wrote to tell her to return to Rome.[26]

Antonius' campaign began the following year. He was consul, but according to Dio resigned his office on the first day of the year, and was succeeded by the first of a series of suffect consuls who held the magistracy in 34.[27] Antonius had other matters on his mind. He invaded Armenia, having given out that he intended to attack the Parthians, and after various attempts to entice Artavasdes into his clutches, marched directly against the Armenian capital, Artaxata, while continuing negotiations with the king. There he arrested Artavasdes, eventually fettering him with silver chains in recognition of his royalty, and, leaving forces in occupation of Armenia, took him back to Alexandria. While in Armenia, Antonius betrothed his son, Alexander Helios, to the daughter of his ally, the king of Media, and when, on his return to Alexandria, he entered the city in a victorious procession, a still more overtly dynastic event took place. It is remarkable enough that he had arrived in the city in what looked suspiciously like an imitation of a Roman triumph;[28] but, apparently on the same occasion, he announced that Cleopatra was to be called queen of kings and that her son Ptolemy Caesarion was indeed the son of the late dictator Julius Caesar, and would be called king of kings. They were to rule Egypt and Cyprus, while Alexander Helios would rule over Armenia and the lands west of the Euphrates (including Parthia, which Antonius was hardly in a position to give); Cleopatra Selene would have Cyrenaica; and Ptolemy Philadelphos would have Syria and the whole of the territory west of the Euphrates as far as the Hellespont.[29] Whether all this happened in the spectacular style in which our two main sources, Plutarch and Dio, report it may be doubted, since it certainly suited Caesar's propaganda in the years which followed to represent Antonius as so besotted with Cleopatra that he had turned his back on Rome and his Roman wife and that his only intention was to establish an oriental dynasty. Velleius Paterculus certainly depicts Antonius in just such a way, and places his decision to attack Italy immediately after his capture of Artavasdes.[30] The motives of Antonius at this

---

26. Plut. *Ant.* 50–3; Dio Cass. 49.33. On the agreement at Tarentum, see above, p. 56.
27. Dio Cass. 49.39.1. See Broughton, *MRR* 2.410–11.
28. Plut. *Ant.* 50.6–7.
29. Plut. *Ant.* 54.4–9; Dio Cass. 49.41.1–3.
30. Vell. Pat. 2.82.3–4. See the discussion by A. J. Woodman, *Velleius Paterculus: The Caesarian and Augustan Narrative (2.41–93)*, Cambridge: Cambridge University Press, 1983, 211–13. Velleius also has Artavasdes fettered in golden chains.

Figure 3 Denarius of Marcus Antonius, 32 BC (*RRC* 543) (© The Trustees of the British Museum)

point are not recoverable, and later he does seem to have intended an invasion of Italy, which was never carried out; but there is no other indication that he meant to undertake an assault on Caesar's position in the west so early, and Velleius is probably predating it in line with later allegations from the Caesarian side. That does not mean, however, that the famous 'donations of Alexandria' are simply a fabrication, or even that they were really no more than an extension of Antonius' policy, seen in his preparations for the expedition against Parthia, of establishing a network of secure client-kingdoms. By 32 Antonius was advertising on his coinage a position very like that described by Plutarch and Dio: an issue of denarii showed on one side a head of Antonius, with an inscription that declared 'Armenia defeated', and on the other a head of Cleopatra, with an inscription describing her as 'queen of kings' and of her children as kings.[31]

In the meantime Caesar was also undertaking military activity which, if less ambitious than Antonius' onslaught on Parthia, was also more successful and gave the opportunity of building on the boost to his reputation as a successful general which the defeat of Sextus Pompeius had brought him. In 35, as Antonius prepared for his campaign against Armenia, Caesar turned his attention to Illyricum, the Roman name for the long stretch of land occupied by Illyrian tribes along the eastern side of the Adriatic, bordering Italy in the north-east and Macedonia in the south-west.[32] The immediate

31. *RRC* 543.
32. For Caesar's campaigns in Illyricum in 35 to 33, see Appian, *Illyr.* 16–28; Dio Cass. 49.34–8, 43.8.

reasons for his interest in this region are not obvious, though it had given trouble in the mid-40s and the Dalmatians, who occupied the southern section of the area, had defeated forces sent against them by Julius Caesar and, though subsequently subdued and made to pay tribute, had ceased to do so after the dictator's assassination.[33] One reason for Caesar's heir to involve himself with Illyricum in 35 may have been other links with the late dictator: it had been part of the provincial command that Julius Caesar had held for ten years from 58 BC, though he had of course spent most of his time conquering Gaul, and is said to have intended at the end of his life to invade the Dacians beyond the Danube, which would have entailed a campaign through northern Illyricum.[34] Perhaps the most obvious reason, however, is that Illyricum was the closest region to Italy in which Caesar could fight a military campaign to show that he was more than equal to Antonius. This he certainly did. In 35 he overcame the northerly tribe of the Iapodes, destroying a stronghold at Metulum after a difficult siege, and then advanced north-west beyond Illyricum into Pannonia, where he captured the town of Siscia (modern Sisak, in central Croatia), perhaps contemplating an advance into Dacia. At the end of the campaigning season he returned to Rome. Dio states that he intended to invade Britain, as Julius Caesar had done, and that he gave to his wife, Livia, and his sister, Octavia, the rights to manage their own affairs without the oversight of a guardian and the sacrosanctity equivalent to that of the tribunes of the plebs.[35] This was an extraordinary move but may have been done in order to present a contrast with Antonius' relationship with Cleopatra in Alexandria. The rights and honours Caesar gave were unprecedented and the fact that the beneficiaries were women so closely related to him suggest the marking out of a Caesarian dynasty; but they were also the wives of the two surviving triumvirs, and these rights gave them responsibilities and protection in a very Roman style which was markedly different from those Antonius had given to Cleopatra and her children in the previous year, to say nothing of those which followed his return from Armenia later in 34.

Whatever Caesar may have been contemplating with regard to Gaul and Britain, in the event he returned to Illyricum. After a visit

---

33. Appian, *Illyr.* 12–13.
34. Vell. Pat. 2.59.4; Suet. *Iul.* 44.3; Appian, *B Civ.* 2.110.
35. Dio Cass. 49.38.1.

to Siscia, where he punished some insurgents, he mounted a campaign against the Dalmatians, further to the south, and after some difficulties succeeded in capturing their stronghold of Promona. At the end of the year he was laying siege to Setovia, whence he departed for Rome to take up the consulship for the second time in January 33. He held office for only a few hours before going back to Dalmatia to complete the siege and the conquest of the region. On his return to Rome, he used cash from the booty he had gained to rebuild a portico near the Circus Flaminius which had been erected by Gnaeus Octavius, who as praetor in charge of the fleet in 168 BC had received the surrender of Perseus, the last king of Macedon, and had celebrated a naval triumph the following year. Here Caesar deposited standards which the Dalmatians had captured from the Roman general Aulus Gabinius in 48 and which had been regained by him after their submission. There could hardly have been a more direct slighting of Antonius, whose disastrous expedition against the Parthians had failed to bring back the standards which Crassus had lost at Carrhae in 53, and the placing of them in the building which Caesar restored but graciously allowed still to be called the Porticus Octavia will simply have underlined the comparison. Nor was this the only change to the physical structure of the city in these years. In 33 BC Agrippa, who had already held the consulship, undertook the more junior magistracy of aedile, a post which involved the care of public constructions in Rome, and as such built a new aqueduct, which in honour of Caesar was named the Aqua Iulia, and also repaired others, as well as refurbishing the sewers and putting on a series of spectacular games.[36] All this substantial and important public work in the heart of the Roman world will again have emphasised the difference between the two triumvirs.

The end of this year in any case was crucial for the relationship between the two men. The second period of the triumvirate, which was to run for five years and the start of which had been backdated to January 37, was due to reach its end on 31 December.[37] The consuls for the following year (32 BC) were Gnaeus Domitius Ahenobarbus and Gaius Sosius, strong supporters of Antonius. He

36. Pliny, *HN* 36.104 and 121; Suet. *Aug.* 42.1; Frontinus, *De aquis urbis Romae* 1.9–10; Dio Cass. 49.43.1–4.
37. See above, p. 56. On the terminal date of the triumvirate, see the discussion by Christopher Pelling in *Cambridge Ancient History* X2, Cambridge: Cambridge University Press, 1996, 67–8.

sent them letters, demanding that the titles and honours that he had
given to Cleopatra and her children and the reallocation of the
provinces he had made should be ratified by the people, offering to
give up his powers as triumvir and requiring Caesar to do the same.
In the event, these proposals were not put to the senate because
(so Dio states) the consuls on entering office were unwilling to do
so, even though Caesar was urging that they should.[38] Nonetheless
Sosius mounted an attack on Caesar, which was only forestalled by
the veto of a tribune. Although no longer properly able to convene a
meeting of the senate now the triumvirate had lapsed, Caesar did so
and, accompanied by a bodyguard and taking his seat between the
two consuls, made an attack on both Antonius and Sosius. When no
response was forthcoming, he called upon the senate to reconvene
on a specified day on which he promised he would produce documents which would show Antonius was in the wrong. Before that
day came, however, the consuls and about one third of the senate
had left to join Antonius.[39]

They found him at Ephesus. Antonius had assembled an army
of some twenty-three legions and a huge fleet of 800 ships, both
merchant ships and warships, of which a quarter were provided by
Cleopatra. From there he moved to Samos (where he is said to have
provided a lavish festival and attracted the support of many eastern
rulers) and thence to Athens.[40] It was probably in Athens that,
enraged by further assaults on him in Rome by Caesar, he divorced
Octavia, who was still living in his house in the capital and bringing
up their children and also his children by Fulvia, with the exception
of the eldest son, Marcus Antonius Antyllus, who was with his
father.[41] Plutarch says that Cleopatra was jealous of the popularity
that Octavia had enjoyed in Athens when she had been there in the
winter of 39/38 with Antonius and, though this may be the result
of Plutarch's own agenda in contrasting the two women, there can
be little doubt that the divorce marked Cleopatra's final triumph
and Antonius' irrevocable commitment to the Egyptian queen rather
than the sister of Caesar. The decision was by this stage inevitable:

38. Dio Cass. 49.41.
39. Dio Cass. 50.2. Augustus, *RG* 25, says that 700 senators fought on his side at
Actium, but the senate at this date comprised about 1,000, and many came over to his
side between early 32 and September 31, when the battle was fought. See A. E. Cooley,
Res Gestae Divi Augusti: Text, Translation, and Commentary, Cambridge: Cambridge
University Press, 2009, 217–18.
40. Plut. *Ant.* 56–7. For the size of Antonius' army, see P. A. Brunt, *Italian Manpower
225 BC–AD 14*, Oxford: Oxford University Press, 1971, 503–7.

Antonius was embarking on a final conflict with Caesar and was reliant on the financial and naval support of Cleopatra; but it also showed that he was prepared to acknowledge publicly that this was the case.

Caesar moved rapidly to make the most of the opportunity this offered. Two of Antonius' long-term supporters, Marcus Titius (who had been responsible for the death of Sextus Pompeius in 35) and Titius' uncle, Lucius Munatius Plancus, the consul of 42, who had been governor of Syria under Antonius also in 35, abandoned him and fled to Rome to join Caesar, apparently because of their dislike of Cleopatra. It was they, according to Plutarch and Dio, who urged Caesar to seize and open Antonius' will, which had been deposited with the Vestal Virgins in Rome and which they had witnessed when Antonius made it. Plutarch also states that the Vestals refused to hand over the will and responded by saying that if he wanted it he should come himself to take it, whereupon Caesar did just that, reading the document by himself and noting passages which were particularly incriminating. He then called a meeting of the senate where he read out some of the material that he claimed to have found, though some senators disapproved of his action in seizing the will and revealing its contents while Antonius was still alive. In the will Caesar claimed to have found instructions that Antonius' body should be buried in Alexandria with Cleopatra, large bequests to Cleopatra's children by him who were named as his heirs, and an assertion that the child that she claimed to have borne to Julius Caesar was indeed the true son of the late dictator.[42] The circumstances of its publication, and especially the suitability of what Caesar read out for his argument that Antonius had severed his links with Rome, have led many scholars to doubt the authenticity of this document. In particular it has been pointed out that its provisions that Cleopatra's children should be Antonius' heirs would have been invalid because they were not Roman citizens and therefore unable to inherit under Roman civil law, and that it would be surprising if Antonius had been unaware of this basic legal requirement.[43] The

41. Plut. *Ant.* 57.
42. Vell. Pat. 2.83.1–2; Plut. *Ant.* 58; Suet. *Aug.* 17.1; Dio Cass. 50.3.1–5.
43. See John Crook, 'A legal point about Mark Antony's will', *Journal of Roman Studies* 47 (1957), 36–8. J. R. Johnson, 'The authenticity and validity of Antony's will', *L'Antiquité Classique* 47 (1978), 494–503, suggests that Antonius made a military will, which among other things allowed soldiers to make non-Romans heirs (Gaius 2.109–10); but Ulpian, *Dig.* 29.1.pr, indicates that this was not available as a general provision until the time of the Flavian emperors.

invalidity of the will does not, however, demonstrate that it was not what Antonius wrote, and indeed the allegation that he was flying in the face of Roman practice was the nub of Caesar's argument. What Caesar claimed to have revealed by reading sections of the will would have hardly been surprising to anyone who had watched Antonius' activities in the east over the past years, and in particular the setting up of Cleopatra's children as rulers over large areas of territory in the famous donations of Alexandria in 34.[44] The exchanges of propaganda between the two triumvirs had been increasingly virulent and highly personal,[45] and in one sense the disclosure of Antonius' will was simply another round in the battle of words. It also marked a change of focus. Antonius' divorce of Octavia was a definitive break, and she is said to have feared that she would be one of the causes of the war that was to follow.[46] Caesar's selective reading of the will was intended to show to the people of Rome and Italy just what that break meant, not least in the assertion that a son of Cleopatra was the true heir of Julius Caesar. When later Nicolaus of Damascus wrote his *Life of Augustus*, he was careful to note that the dictator had specifically stated in his own will that the story that Cleopatra's child was his was a lie.[47]

It was not just through the exposure of Antonius' long-term intentions that Caesar sought to gain the ascendancy in the minds and hearts of those in Rome and Italy over the threat from Egypt and the east. As Antonius moved westwards into Greece, the whole of Italy swore an oath of allegiance to Caesar and demanded that he should lead them in the war in which he emerged as conqueror at Actium; or so he himself tells us in the *Res Gestae*.[48] Just how voluntary the taking of this oath was there is no way of telling, and Suetonius records that Caesar publicly allowed the people of Bononia an exemption from swearing it, on the grounds that they had long been clients of the Antonii.[49] Such an announcement suggests that other communities were not given leave to avoid the oath. It was after all essential to Caesar that this very explicit and public support for his imminent conflict with Antonius should be

44. See above, p. 62.
45. See, for example, Antonius' letter to Caesar in 33 on the latter's sexual appetites, a rejoinder to accusations that he himself was sleeping with Cleopatra (Suet. *Aug.* 69.2).
46. Plut. *Ant.* 57.3.
47. Nic. Dam. *Vit. Aug.* 20.
48. Aug. *RG* 25.2: iuravit in mea verba tota Italia sponte sua et me bel[li], quo vici ad Actium, ducem depoposcit.
49. Suet. *Aug.* 17.2.

Figure 4 Denarius of Marcus Antonius, 31 BC (*RRC* 545.2) (© The Trustees of the British Museum)

seen to be as total as possible, both because it showed him as *dux Italiae*, the chosen leader of the whole of Italy against an enemy who had turned his back on all things Roman, and because, by displaying the people's recognition of the state of emergency that Antonius' threat had brought about, it provided him with legitimacy for raising and leading an army against him.[50] The triumvirate had ended at the close of the previous year and with it Caesar's constitutional power. Whereas Antonius continued to call himself triumvir, not least on the coins which he struck to pay the legions who were to fight for him at Actium,[51] Caesar did not use the title; the oath gave him the constitutional legality he needed and (perhaps more importantly) was a crucial victory in the propaganda war that was the context within which the military struggle would be fought. The point is made in the typically brief but allusive note that follows the mention of the oath in the *Res Gestae*: 'the Gallic and Spanish provinces, Africa, Sicily and Sardinia swore the same oath of allegiance'.[52] The whole of the western half of the Roman world was on his side.

Caesar needed all the support he could muster. In 32 he was not obviously the likely winner in the forthcoming conflict. The large number of senators who had left Roma with the consuls showed the

50. See J. Linderski, 'Rome, Aphrodisias and the *Res Gestae*: the *genera militiae* and the status of Octavian', *Journal of Roman Studies* 74 (1984), 74–80.
51. *RRC* 544; cf. Dio Cass. 50.7.1.
52. *RG* 25.2: iuraverunt in eadem ver[ba provi]nciae Galliae Hispaniae Africa Sicilia Sardinia.

extent of support for Antonius in the capital, and Caesar caused more resentment by imposing heavy taxes on the property of wealthy freedmen in Italy as well as on the income of the free-born. This led to riots and fire-raising.[53] In any case, for all the ingenious and effective political moves that Caesar had undertaken, as the year 32 drew towards its end, Antonius was in a far stronger position militarily and financially than his opponent. He had far larger forces, both on land and sea, than Caesar, and the wealth of the eastern kingdoms, not least Egypt, was at his disposal. It was in this context that Caesar took the formal step of declaring war. Indeed the formalities were strongly emphasised by the use of the allegedly ancient practice of the *ius fetiale* for the declaration of wars, revived or perhaps even invented by Caesar for the occasion, which included the casting of a sacred spear into land in Rome, outside the city walls and close to the temple of the war-goddess, Bellona, which was designated as enemy territory for the purpose. In this case the enemy was not Antonius but Cleopatra. The message was clear. This was a war to be fought against a foreign foe.[54] Antonius was to be regarded as the servant of an Egyptian queen, Caesar as the leader of Italy and the Roman west.

Caesar's victory: Actium and Alexandria, 31–29 BC

At the beginning of the following year, Caesar took up his third consulship. It had been agreed at Tarentum in 37, when their triumvirate had been extended for a further five-year term, that Antonius and he should both be consuls in 31, but on Caesar's urging the senate had stripped Antonius of his forthcoming office some months before, after his will had been read out to the senators.[55] In his place Marcus Valerius Messalla became Caesar's colleague for the first months of the year. By this time Antonius had distributed his troops along the eastern coastline of Greece and much of his fleet anchored at Actium, where an inlet into a large inland lake gave protection, and he himself wintered with Cleopatra at Patrae (modern Patras), in the north-east of the Peloponnese.

53. Plut. *Ant.* 58.1; Dio Cass. 50.10.4–6.
54. Dio Cass. 50.4.4; cf. Plut. *Ant.* 69.1. For the *ius fetiale* and its 'revival', see J. W. Rich, *Declaring War in the Roman Republic in the Age of Transmarine Expansion*, Brussels: Coll. Latomus, 1976, 149; Thomas Wiedemann, 'The *fetiales*: a reconsideration', *Classical Quarterly* 36 (1986), 478–90.
55. Dio Cass. 50.4.3.

He could not risk an attack on Italy, where Caesar held the main harbours at Tarentum and Brundisium, and so had to wait for the arrival of his adversary. Early in the year Agrippa, in command of part of Caesar's fleet, crossed from Italy to interrupt Antonius' supply route and succeeded in taking one of his bases at Methone, in the south-east of the Peloponnese, from where he was able to prevent merchant ships bringing provisions to Antonius' armies. Shortly after, Caesar sailed with his army and 250 ships from Brundisium and was able to cross unopposed to land on the northern side of the inlet at Actium, and set up a camp on a hill overlooking the gulf. Antonius set off rapidly from Patrae and camped initially on the southern side of the inlet, crossing to the northern side once his army had gathered. There he tried to force Caesar to engage in battle, which he refused to do. Agrippa meanwhile captured the island of Leucas just to south, which gave the Caesarian fleet a far safer anchorage, and followed this up with a lightning attack on Patrae, which he took. Antonius was now effectively blockaded and cut off from his supply routes, and was forced to withdraw back across the strait to his previous camp. Already several of his supporters had deserted him and joined Caesar, one of whom, Quintus Dellius, brought the news that Antonius and Cleopatra intended to break out of the gulf in order to sail for Egypt. On 2 September Antonius' ships, which were in many cases larger than those of his opponent, sailed out of the inlet and formed a line across its mouth. Antonius had loaded his treasure chest aboard secretly and had reduced the size of his fleet by burning all but the best, which included a squadron of sixty under Cleopatra's own command, which took up position behind the main line. They were faced by a line of Caesar's ships, mostly more lightly built. For some hours the two lines maintained their positions, each waiting for the other to move, until about midday, when the Antonian left wing began to advance. Caesar made his ships back water to draw those advancing out into more open sea, where the lighter boats had more advantage from their manoeuvrability. As the ships on the two sides engaged, a break began to appear in the middle of the lines, and suddenly Cleopatra's squadron hoisted sail and sped through the midst of the battle out to sea, followed by a galley with Antonius aboard. He was taken onto Cleopatra's ship as it sailed south towards the Mediterranean. The flight of their commander was apparently not seen by those in his fleet, who fought on, to be overwhelmed by the Caesarians, who set fire to many of the ships in

Antonius' fleet while still at sea.[56] Nonetheless, for a battle of such significance surprisingly few casualties were sustained. Plutarch records that only 5,000 were killed, which for an ancient sea-battle is a low number. Perhaps more surprising is the relative ease with which Caesar was able to neutralise the large land forces which Antonius had had at his disposal. The commander in charge of them, Publius Canidius Crassus, who had opposed the notion of risking all on a sea-battle, received an order from Antonius as he fled from Actium to march with his forces through Macedonia to Asia, and the army is said to have held together for seven days after the defeat at sea. Canidius, however, left them so that he could follow Antonius to Egypt, and the army was won over by Caesar as it moved through Macedonia and was added to his own forces.[57] Many of Antonius' army, along with part of his own, he discharged, sending them back to Italy, where Maecenas had been left in charge during Caesar's absence. On their arrival, these soldiers caused problems by demanding the rewards they had been promised, and Caesar sent Agrippa back to Rome to assist Maecenas in dealing with them, and gave them authority to present to the senate the official news of his victory. He meanwhile toured mainland Greece and Asia, settling matters in the regions Antonius had controlled and confirming in place many of the rulers who had been established by his rival. Returning to Italy at the beginning of the year 30, he was met at Brundisium by large numbers of senators and also others from the equestrian order and from the ordinary people, all determined to show enthusiastic loyalty to the victor of Actium. He was also met by the soldiers he had sent back to Italy after the battle, who were demanding the rewards that they had been promised. He used monies that he had gathered in Asia to pay part of the bounties to the veterans, and also gave land to those who had served in his armies throughout the campaign, some confiscated from communities in Italy which had supported Antonius, and some which he took from landowners who were promised payment from the booty he expected to collect from Egypt.[58]

It was in Egypt that the final stage of the war had to be played out. Caesar left Italy and, rather than sailing directly for the east, marched his forces through Macedonia and Asia, receiving as he

56. For an account of the battle, see J. M. Carter, *The Battle of Actium: The Rise and Triumph of Augustus Caesar*, London: Hamilton, 1970.
57. Plut. *Ant.* 67.5; 68.3; Dio Cass. 51.1.4–5.
58. Dio Cass. 51.4.

went embassies from Antonius and Cleopatra. Antonius was in a desperate position: before Actium he had left four legions at Cyrene on the north African coast, probably to keep an eye on Egypt during his and Cleopatra's absence. This was, after the loss of his legions in the aftermath of Actium, his only substantial army, but its commander, Lucius Pinarius Scarpus, had refused to receive him as he fled from the battle and went over to Caesar, the legions being taken over by an equestrian officer, Gaius Cornelius Gallus. Consequently it probably suited Caesar to approach Egypt more slowly, in the hope that he might separate the two, and he is said to have offered Cleopatra better treatment if she killed or banished Antonius.[59] By July Caesar was advancing towards Egypt, with another force under Cornelius Gallus coming from the west with the troops that he had from Scarpus. Antonius, who had unsuccessfully attempted to prevent Gallus by appealing to the soldiers who had served under him, heard that Caesar had seized Pelusium on the eastern edge of the Nile delta, and returned to Alexandria to defend it. He was able to cause Caesar difficulties by a successful cavalry skirmish, but on 1 August in a larger engagement by land and sea, he was deserted by his cavalry and navy. In an infantry battle, Caesar won decisively, and entered Alexandria unopposed. Antonius committed suicide, misled, we are told, by false stories that Cleopatra had already killed herself; and nine days later she too, after and despite a one-to-one interview with Caesar, died from the bite of an asp which she had had smuggled into her room.[60] Caesar, in accordance with a promise he had made to Cleopatra, allowed them to be buried together in a mausoleum the queen had already had built in Alexandria. He also seized the treasure that Cleopatra had gathered together and indeed had threatened to burn in the months before he had arrived in Egypt, and the boy whom she claimed to have borne to Julius Caesar was found and killed, along with Antonius' eldest son, Antyllus. Her other children by Antonius were allowed to live, as were his other children by Fulvia and Octavia, who were with Octavia in Rome.[61]

The deaths of Antonius and Cleopatra after their defeat at Actium marked a watershed at least as significant as that of Philippi. Like Philippi (and perhaps more obviously so) it was a clash between

59. Plut. *Ant.* 72–3; Dio Cass. 51.6–9.
60. Plut. *Ant.* 76–86; Dio Cass. 51.10–14.
61. Dio Cass. 51.15.5–7.

people who intended to be the rulers of the Roman world; but, just as events between the assassination of Julius Caesar and the battles at Philippi had altered and determined the motives and ambitions of Antonius and Caesar, Marcus Brutus and Cassius, so the eleven years from Philippi to Actium changed the context and so the significance of the struggle between Antonius and Caesar. By 31 BC these two, though each aspired to pre-eminence, presented quite different models of what that pre-eminence might mean. The rivalry between them, when it began in 44 and 43, was between two men, each of whom had a claim to be the successor to the dead dictator, either as his senior colleague and champion of his soldiers or as his heir and the bearer of his name. By the late 30s the prize for which they were fighting was no longer expressed in these terms, and (although Antonius continued to promote Caesarion, Cleopatra's son, as Julius Caesar's offspring and young Caesar never gave up his role as his father's avenger) in the virulent propaganda war between the two the name of Julius Caesar is never mentioned. Other things had changed too. After Philippi, Antonius stood unchallenged as the greatest military commander in the Roman world; but the Parthian debacle of Antonius in 36 BC, and young Caesar's success against Sextus Pompeius in the same year and his campaigns in Illyricum from 35 to 33, altered the balance. Nonetheless, on the eve of Actium a shrewd observer might well have assumed that the victor would be Antonius rather than Caesar. Antonius had not only the backing of the queen of the last of the great Hellenistic kingdoms but, by careful and ruthless selection of the rulers of Asia Minor and the kingdoms to the east, he had constructed a solid base of support in the richest and most powerful area of the Graeco-Roman world. It seemed likely that even his failure against Parthia would soon be redeemed: his alliance with the king of Media and the large army that he had amassed on the Parthian frontier suggest that his next invasion would have succeeded, had he not been compelled to move west to face the threat from Caesar. Though Actium turned out to be a surprisingly easy victory (due not least to the intelligence and expertise of Agrippa in cutting Antonius' supply lines), that was not obvious in the weeks before the battle. Antonius' mistakes are clear with hindsight: by allying himself so closely with Cleopatra and adopting the style and methods of the Greek east, he neglected and indeed flouted the expectation and the sensitivities of those (even his own supporters) in Rome and allowed Caesar to present himself as *dux* of Italy and of the western provinces; but it must be remembered that, for all the importance of Rome and Italy as the heartland of the empire, the financial and military strength that Antonius thus accrued was immense. He was in one sense the successor of Pompeius, whose conquests in the east in the 60s BC had brought him vast resources as well as the glory which gave him such pre-eminence in Rome on his return; and the example of Cassius, who for a brief period in 43 BC can be seen attempting the same, shows that others saw this as a way to dominance. Antonius, of course, unlike Pompeius, did not return to Rome and went far further in adopting the trappings of power that marked a Greek ruler in the eastern Mediterranean; but that might be seen as a logical extension of his predecessor's policy, encouraged by the attractions, financial and military as well as personal, of Cleopatra. Had they won the battle of Actium, the Roman empire and its history would undoubtedly have been very different.

It was the capture of Alexandria rather than his success at Actium which marked for Caesar the true victory in his struggle for domination and the beginning of a new world order.[62] Actium of course was significant, and Caesar planned and had constructed a new city, Nicopolis ('City of Victory'), with a monumental sanctuary on the hill on which he had placed his camp, overlooking the site of the battle; games in commemoration of the victory were to be held there every five years.[63] The date of the victory, 2 September, was also marked as a festival day by a decree of the senate, recorded in the calendars of cities throughout Italy.[64] But the day on which Alexandria was taken was marked with even more significance in these same calendars, as the day on which Caesar 'liberated the *res publica* from the most wretched of dangers'.[65] The triple triumph which Caesar celebrated in Rome on 13, 14 and 15 August in 29 BC carried the same message. On the first day it was his victory over the Illyrians and Dalmatians that was celebrated; on the second, the battle of Actium; and on the third, by far the most spectacular of the three, the victory in Egypt.[66] In addition to the huge amounts of

62. On the place of Actium in Augustus' view of history, see R. A. Gurval, *Actium and Augustus: The Politics and Emotions of Civil War*, Ann Arbor: University of Michigan Press, 1995.
63. Strabo, 7.7.6; Dio Cass. 51.1.1–3. It should be noted that another Nicopolis was constructed outside Alexandria (Strabo, 17.1.10; Dio Cass. 51.18.1).
64. *Fast. Arv., Amit.* and *Ant.* See *Inscr. Ital.* 13.2, pp. 32–3, 192–3, 208–9.
65. *Fast. Praenest., Arv., Amit.* and *Ant.* See *Inscr. Ital.* 13.2, pp. 30–1, 134–5, 190–1 and 208.
66. Suet. *Aug.* 22; Dio Cass. 51.5–9.

booty that he had brought back from Alexandria, Caesar had two of
Cleopatra's children, Alexander Helios and Cleopatra Selene, in the
procession, accompanying an effigy of their dead mother, reclining
on a couch. But perhaps the clearest signal that the ending of the war
in Egypt was the crucial change came in the honours that the senate
voted for Caesar when, in his absence, he entered his fifth consulship
in January 29.[67] Included among these was the closing of the gates
of the shrine of Janus, which, as Augustus himself explains in the
Res Gestae, were to be shut when there was peace by land and sea
throughout the whole empire of the Roman people and which had,
'before my birth', been closed only twice since the foundation of the
city. The closing of the gates of Janus signified the coming of peace
to a people who had been wracked by war, and the birth of a new
age.[68]

Nor was it only Caesar who saw it like this. In the year 8 BC, the
senate voted that the month which was called Sextilis should hence-
forward be called 'August', in his honour. Macrobius, writing five
centuries later, reproduces the words of the senate's decree, which
explained that the reason for choosing this month was that it was in
August that the emperor had, in 43 BC, entered his first consulship
and that in the same month he had celebrated his triple triumph; but
also because it was in August that he had brought Egypt into the
power of the Roman people and ended the civil wars; for these
reasons this month was the most propitious for the Roman state.[69]
Velleius Paterculus, writing in the reign of Augustus' successor,
the emperor Tiberius, is (as often) more fulsome. Describing the
effects of Caesar's return to Rome after the capture of Alexandria,
he writes:

> The civil wars were ended after twenty years, foreign wars sup-
> pressed, peace restored, the frenzy of arms everywhere lulled to rest;
> validity was restored to the laws, authority to the courts, and dignity
> to the senate; the power of the magistrates was reduced to its former
> limits, with the sole exception that two were added to the eight exist-
> ing praetors. The ancient and traditional form of the Republic was
> restored, fields were cultivated again, religion respected, people freed
> from fear and everyone sure of their own property; laws were
> usefully amended and new ones passed for the common good, and

67. Dio Cass. 51.20.4–5.
68. Aug. *RG* 13. See Cooley, *Res Gestae*, 157–61.
69. Macrobius, *Sat.* 1.12.35. (Dio Cass. 55.6.6 and Censorinus, *DN* 22.16, place this in
8 BC; Livy, *Per.* 134, says it occurred in 27 BC.)

the roll of the senate was revised without harshness but not without severity. (Vell. Pat. 2.89.3–4)

[Finita vicesimo anno bella civilia, sepulta externa, revocata pax, sopitus ubique armorum furor, restituta vis legibus, iudiciis auctoritas, senatui maiestas, imperium magistratuum ad pristinum redactum modum; tantummodo octo praetoribus adlecti duo. Prisca illa et antiqua rei publicae forma revocata, rediit cultus agris, sacris honos, securitas hominibus, certa cuique rerum suarum possessio; leges emendatae utiliter, latae salubriter, senatus sine asperitate nec sine severitate lectus.]

This is not of course a list of the immediate consequences of Caesar's return in mid-29, and Velleius himself describes it at the end of the passage as an image of his whole reign (*universam imaginem principatus*). It mirrors in many ways the account Augustus himself gave in his *Res Gestae*,[70] but it reflects both the sense of the new beginning that was marked by the end of the war in Egypt and the work of restoration that needed to be done. The twenty years of civil war since the outbreak of hostilities between Julius Caesar and Pompeius in 49 BC had, on this reading, been marked by fighting between Romans, by the collapse of the political and legal structures, by the neglect of the gods and of the cultivation of the fields, and by the loss of security both of persons and of property. The very fact that Augustus, as Caesar was soon to be known, made a reversal of the sufferings of the civil war a centrepiece of his presentation of himself to the Roman world and to posterity inevitably raises suspicions about his motives in so doing. It does not, however, take away the reality of what had happened and the effects of two decades of death, confiscation and insecurity not only on Romans in Italy but on Romans and non-Romans around the entire Mediterranean world.

These are later accounts of the significance of the victory in Egypt and of the civil wars of which it marked the end. They display the importance of the memory of those wars in the work that Augustus was to carry out in the years which followed and its representation in the official propaganda of the regime; they also omit, at first sight surprisingly, some major elements. In particular there is no mention of who it was that was to blame for almost incessant fighting that had characterised the twenty years before the triple triumphs of 29. Antonius is never named in the *Res Gestae*, nor is he mentioned in

70. See Woodman, *Caesarian and Augustan Narrative*, 250–61.

Velleius' eulogy of Augustus' principate. It was not so at the time. After the reports of the deaths of Antonius and Cleopatra had reached Rome, the senate had voted that Antonius' statues should be torn down and that the date of his birth (14 January) should be declared a *dies vitiosus*, on which no public business could be transacted.[71] Such an insult, intended to be set permanently in the annual cycle of the Roman year, was completely unprecedented and as total a rejection of the former triumvir as might be imagined.

Two other pieces of contemporary evidence are more nuanced. Horace produced his book of iambic verse, the *Epodes*, in 30 or thereabouts, and it includes two poems (*Epod.* 7 and 16) from the total of seventeen which lament the horrors of Romans fighting Romans and warn that Rome will be ruined unless civil war is ended. In another poem (*Epod.* 9) he refers directly to the battle of Actium and hopes for an occasion when he and his friend Maecenas, Caesar's ally, can drink together to celebrate Caesar's victory, as they had done when Caesar had defeated Sextus Pompeius in 36. The enemy this time is a Roman soldier, enslaved to a woman and obeying her wrinkled eunuchs; but the enemy is defeated and flees by sea. The poem ends with a call for more wine to suppress the poet's squeamishness and calm his anxiety and fear for the work in which Caesar is engaged. The tone of this poem is not one of unalloyed exultation, and, although the god of the triumph is invoked, this is done to ask why the triumph has not yet taken place when the victor is greater than any other who has defeated African foes. The moment it depicts seems to be between the defeat of Antonius and Cleopatra at Actium and their final overthrow after the capture of Alexandria. Horace's disgust at the un-Roman behaviour of Antonius and his accolade to the success of Caesar are tempered by his anxiety that the job is not yet completed.[72] If this was a feeling held by others in Italy, the enthusiasm which greeted the news that Caesar had finally destroyed the power of Antonius and the Egyptian queen is readily explicable; but it is notable too that at this point Antonius is seen as the leader of the opposing forces, even if himself in thrall to Cleopatra and her minions.

The other contemporary witness is another poet who completed a

---

71. Dio Cass. 51.19.3. It is so recorded in the *Fasti Oppiani* and *Verulani* (*Inscr. Ital.* 13.2, pp. 99 and 158–9).
72. See the exposition of this poem by Gurval, *Actium and Augustus*, 137–59, who also reviews other earlier interpretations. While not completely in agreement with Gurval, I find his close reading of the poem is highly illuminating.

set of poems at just this time. Vergil is said by his biographer, the fourth-century grammarian Aelius Donatus, to have read the whole of the *Georgics* to Caesar on his return to Italy in 29 and to have taken four days to do so, with the assistance of Maecenas.[73] In the proem to the third book Vergil presents himself as constructing a temple near his home town of Mantua, dedicated to Caesar and including images of his achievements. These were to include 'the Nile billowing with war and flowing greatly and columns rising up with the bronze of ships'.[74] The last phrase brings to mind the four bronze columns that Caesar had made from the prows of ships after the victory in Egypt and which were erected in the Forum.[75] The ships were no doubt taken at Actium, and similar prows adorned the sanctuary there at the new city of Nicopolis; but the emphasis in Vergil's temple is to be on Egypt. It is one of a list of places and peoples that Caesar had conquered or would conquer. Here there is no mention of Antonius, or indeed of the civil war. The context, after all, is in a series of poems about farming, the return to the ways of peace.

The absence of Antonius in these places after the capture of Alexandria is almost as remarkable as the fury against him expressed by the senate at the news of his death. It may be that the question of who was to blame for the horrors of civil war simply could not be put. Caesar was at least as responsible for the proscriptions of 43 as his two fellow triumvirs, Antonius and Lepidus, and more so for the confiscations of land in Italy and the Perusine war which followed. No one could deny the terrible things that had happened, though it might be, by stressing, as Velleius was to do, that they had lasted for twenty years that Caesar at least, who was only thirteen when his adoptive father crossed the Rubicon, might be seen as the solution to the problem rather than its cause. In any case, the wars formed the background to the position that Caesar now occupied, since he had emerged as victor. If he was to maintain that position, the problems that they had thrown up were inevitably the agenda for the years that followed.

73. Donatus, *Vit. Verg.* 27.
74. Verg. *G.* 3.28–9.
75. Servius, *Ad G.* 3.29. P. Zanker, *The Power of Images in the Age of Augustus*, Ann Arbor: University of Michigan Press, 1988, 80–1.

CHAPTER 4

Princeps, *29–12* BC

If the closing of the gates of Janus at the beginning of Caesar's fifth consulship in 29 BC was intended to mark the beginning of a new age,[1] this did not mean that Caesar could rest on the laurels he had won at Actium and Alexandria. He was thirty-three years old and, in terms of the age-restrictions of the Republic, nine years below the minimum age at which he was eligible to hold the consulship, an office he was now entering for the fifth time. He had eliminated at Alexandria the only remaining contender for power, a man twenty years his senior, and of his closest associates Agrippa was the same age as he was and Maecenas perhaps a few years older. If Caesar was to retain the total power that he had now achieved, he could not afford to ignore the demands and needs of those who had brought him to where he was, those who had supported him through the years since his arrival on the political scene in 44 and above all the armies, both those that had fought for him and those which had come over to him since Actium, most of whom were now clamouring for discharge and for the rewards they had been promised. There were others too that he had to keep on his side, notably the members of the governing elite, from whom came the people who ran the empire, and the Roman plebs, who through the late Republic and especially in the years of the civil wars had become highly politicised and whose vociferous presence in the capital in large numbers had always to be reckoned with.

Behind all these considerations lay another: who was Caesar? He had emerged in 44 BC as the heir of the assassinated dictator and then as leader of one of the factions which claimed to be his true successors. In taking and using the name of C. Julius Caesar he promised to bring vengeance on the murderers of his adoptive father, and after the battles of Philippi in 42 he vowed to dedicate a temple

1. See above, p. 76.

in Rome to Mars Ultor, Mars the Avenger.[2] In 38, as he began his campaign against Sextus Pompeius (who, to recall his own father, had for some years been styling himself Magnus Pius or Magnus Pompeius Pius[3]), began to call himself on his coinage *Imp. Caesar Divi f.* ('Imperator Caesar, son of the Divine'), which became his new name.[4] Throughout the period of the civil wars he remained Caesar's heir and self-appointed avenger, even though as *dux Italiae*, summoned by the oath of the Italian people and the provinces of the west to be their leader, he claimed to be much more.[5] The aftermath of Actium had seen the deaths of the last two surviving assassins of the dictator, Gaius Cassius Parmensis and Decimus Turullius, and it might seem that, apart from the building of the temple promised at Philippi, which was still not done, the required vengeance had been carried out.[6] More to the point, though his status as Caesar's heir was not forgotten (he still bore the name of the dictator), it was not going to be sufficient to provide an agenda for the next stage.

Reconstituting the *res publica*, 29–27 BC

There was, however, no lack of Caesarism in the days immediately following the triple triumph of 13–15 August 29. On 18 August the temple of Divus Iulius, which had been authorised by all three triumvirs in January 42, but constructed by Caesar, was dedicated in the Forum at the place where the body of his father had been burned, and was now decorated with prows from ships captured at Actium; and on 28 August the senate house, the curia, whose rebuilding had been begun by Julius Caesar just before his assassination, was inaugurated with the dedication of the altar of Victory which stood in its midst; and there too was placed a statue of the goddess, brought from Tarentum, newly adorned with booty from Egypt.[7]

---

2. Ovid, *Fast.* 5.569–78; Suet. *Aug.* 29.1.
3. *RRC* 478, 479 (from 45 BC onwards), 511 (in Sicily, 42–40); *ILS* 8891 (Sicily, 39 or later).
4. *RRC* 534 and 535. See R. Syme, '*Imperator Caesar*: a study in nomenclature', *Historia* 7 (1958), 172–88 (= *Roman Papers*, vol. 1, Oxford: Oxford University Press, 1979, 361–77).
5. See above, pp. 68–9.
6. Cassius: Vell. Pat. 1.87.3; Val. Max. 1.7.7. Turullius: Val. Max. 1.1.19; Dio Cass. 51.8.2–3. Velleius describes Cassius as the last of the conspirators to die, but this seems to have occurred on Caesar's orders shortly after Actium. Turullius was killed as Caesar advanced on Alexandria.
7. Aug. *RG* 19.1; Dio Cass. 51.22. Temple of Divus Iulius: Dio Cass. 47.18.4; *Fast. Ant.*

The result of these buildings was to turn the Forum, the centre of the political life of Rome, into a celebration of the Julian family, with the Curia Iulia at one end, the temple of Divus Iulius at the other, and in the central space the column marking Caesar's victory over Sextus Pompeius at Naulochus in 36 and the four bronze columns, made from metal from still more of the ships from Actium.[8] Just beyond the Curia stretched the Forum Iulium, built by Julius Caesar himself and dedicated on the last day of his triumph in 46 BC, after the crushing of the Pompeian forces in Africa, and containing the temple of Venus Genetrix, the divine founder of the Julian family, the *gens Iulia*. At the beginning of this new age, Rome was marked with the victory of Caesar and of the family.

Other and different changes were also in hand. Late in 29 Caesar and Agrippa, who was designated to be his colleague in the consulship for the following year, were given the power of censors, which enabled them to conduct a census of the citizen population and to review the membership of the senate (*lectio senatus*). The process was completed in the following year with the traditional purification ceremony, the *lustrum*, conducted for the first time in forty-two years.[9] This event showed a combination of respect for the ancient traditions of the Roman *res publica*, and of the intention to reestablish the values which had been so damaged by the period of the civil wars which had now come to an end, with new and unprecedented ways of achieving this. Traditionally the census and the *lustrum* were carried out every five years by the censors, elected for the purpose by the *comitia centuriata*, which also elected the senior magistrates such as the consuls and praetors; but this had not taken place since 70 BC. Dio, indeed, says that in 29 Caesar and Agrippa were censors together but this is certainly wrong. Suetonius states that Augustus, as he was about to become, three times conducted the census but without holding the office of censor,[10] and Caesar and Agrippa are recorded in one of the sets of *Fasti* as having completed the *lustrum* in 28, when both were consuls, by use of *censoria potestas*. This 'power of the censors', which enabled them

(*Inscr. Ital.* 13.2.208). Curia Iulia: Dio Cass. 44.5.1–2; *Fast. Maff.* and *Fast. Val.* (*Inscr. Ital.* 13.2.79, 175 and 503–4).

8. P. Zanker, *The Power of Images in the Age of Augustus*, Ann Arbor: University of Michigan Press, 1988, 79–82.

9 Aug. *RG* 8.2; Dio Cass. 52.42 and 53.1.3.

10. Suet. *Aug.* 27.5: quo iure, quamquam sine censurae honore, censum tamen populi ter egit, primum ac tertium cum collega, medium solus.

to act as censors without actually holding the office, must have been given by a specific legal enactment and some scholars have doubted whether such a grant took place, arguing that technically Caesar would have been able to carry out these functions in virtue of his being consul.[11] Such an action would, however, have been decidedly untraditional, something which Caesar would have been unwilling to undertake at a point when he was emphasising the re-establishment of the norms of the *res publica*; and in any case, if Dio is right in dating the start of the census to 29, it would have applied only to himself, since Agrippa was not consul until the next year.

This division between function and office was to become more and more the way in which the apparent contradiction between a return to the traditions of political life at Rome and the predominance of one individual was handled, and it is worth noting how remarkable this first use of the tactic was. It is true that on at least one occasion in the past consuls had been given the power to undertake tasks normally performed by censors, when in 75 BC the leasing of the contracts for the collection of monies due to the state was assigned by decree of the senate, ratified by the assembly of the people, to Lucius Octavius and Gaius Aurelius Cotta, the consuls of the year.[12] What happened in 29 was far more than this. Not only was the work which the two men granted the *censoria potestas* carried out the most significant and sacred functions of the censors – the census of the Roman people and the purification ceremony of the *lustrum* – but one of them, Agrippa, was at the time no more than a private citizen, even if he was to become consul the following year. Moreover in addition to the numbering of the citizens and the assessment of their place in the property-based class system of the Roman state and to the revision of the role of the senate, a further law, the *lex Saenia*, was passed enabling them to add new members to the list of the old aristocratic families, the patricians, whose numbers had been diminished by the effects of the past two decades of civil war.[13] All this amounted to an extraordinary extension of the

---

11. See the discussion by J.-L. Ferrary, 'The powers of Augustus', in J. Edmondson (ed.), *Augustus*, Edinburgh: Edinburgh University Press, 2009, 90–136, at 104–6. (This is an abbreviated translation of Ferrary's article, 'À propos des pouvoirs d'Auguste', *Cahiers du Centre G. Glotz* 12 (2001), 101–54.) It may be that Agrippa was given the *censoria potestas* by a specific law, as was done for Tiberius in AD 13 (Suet. *Tib.* 21.1; see below, pp. 189–90).
12. Cic. 2 *Verr.* 3.18–19.
13. Tacitus, *Ann.* 11.25; Dio Cass. 42.52.5.

powers of the censors, given to two individuals who were not censors; and the results of their work were no less remarkable. The senate, which had expanded from the 300 that it had been at the time of Sulla's restoration of the membership some half-century earlier to about a thousand, was reduced by the removal, by persuasion and compulsion, of 190 'unsuitable' senators.[14] The number of citizens was given as 4,063,000, over four times the size of the last census of 70 BC, an increase that was perhaps partly the result of under-registration in Republican censuses as well as the grants of citizenship to provincials.[15] Whatever the cause, the huge numbers, the purging of the senate and the potent ceremonies associated with the completion of the *lustrum* were likely to have presented a powerful image of the new Rome, emerging at the end of the horrific period of the civil wars; and this was brought about by the use of the powers of the censors, based on the traditional structures of the old, wielded by two men who, though not censors, stood for the new order. At the end of the process, Caesar, despite his youth, was appointed *princeps senatus*, the leader of the senate, which gave him the first place on the list of senators to be called to express an opinion in a debate.[16] The traditional structure was in place, but in new hands.

As Caesar himself was to record when, as the emperor Augustus and at the end of his reign, he completed the *Res Gestae*, it was in his sixth and seventh consulships (28 and 27 BC), after he had put an end to civil wars and was by the agreement of all holding power over everything, that he transferred the *res publica* (literally 'the business of the people', the government of the state) from his power into the control of the Roman senate and people.[17] The same message can be found on a gold coin issued in 28 BC, showing the head of Caesar on the obverse, with a legend describing him as consul for the sixth time, and on the reverse an image of Caesar seated on the consul's curule chair, holding a scroll and with a document box at his feet, with the legend LEGES ET IURA P R RESTITUIT, 'He restored the

---

14. Dio Cass. 52.42.1–4. On Sulla's senate, see Appian, *B Civ.* 1.100.
15. Aug. *RG* 8.2. See the discussion of the figures in A. E. Cooley, *Res Gestae Divi Augusti*, Cambridge: Cambridge University Press, 2009, 141–2.
16. Aug. *RG* 7.2; Dio Cass. 53.1.3.
17. Aug. *RG* 34.1: In consulatu sexto et septimo, postqua[m b]ella civilia exstinxeram, per consensum universorum [po]tens rerum om[n]ium, rem publicam ex mea potestate in senat[us populi]que Romani [a]rbitrium transtuli. See further below, pp. 204–5.

Figure 5 Aureus of Imp. Caesar, 28 BC (© The Trustees of the British Museum)

laws and rights of the Roman people.'[18] The return to earlier ways was marked by Caesar transferring the *fasces*, the bundles of rods and an axe carried by the lictors which marked the power of the consul, to his colleague, Agrippa, as had been done on a monthly basis under the Republic, to symbolise their sharing of the consular office.[19] Other signs of the return of normality followed. Caesar burned old records of debts to the treasury and annulled decisions made by himself as triumvir, while in the sphere of religion he banned the practice of Egyptian cults within the *pomerium* (the sacred boundary of the city) and restored eighty-two of the city's temples, neglected during the civil war period; and in May, July and August three triumphs were celebrated, from Spain, Gaul and Africa, by individual proconsuls.[20] This was work of restoration, not least of relations with the gods, the disrespect for whose cult was seen by the poet Horace as both the symptom and the cause of the dire state into which Rome had declined;[21] but there was more to the new Rome than simply a return to the old days. The Actian Games were celebrated for the first time in Rome in September, in celebration of the victory of 31 BC, and on 9 October a magnificent new temple was dedicated to Apollo on the Palatine hill, adjoining and attached to

18. J. W. Rich and J. H. C. Williams, '*Leges et iura p.R. restituit*: a new aureus of Octavian and the settlement of 28–27 BC', *Numismatic Chronicle* 159 (1999), 169–213.
19. Dio Cass. 53.1.1.
20. Dio Cass. 53.2.3–5; on the annulment, Tacitus, *Ann.* 3.28; and on the refurbishment of temples, Aug. *RG* 20.4; cf. Suet. *Aug.* 30.2. Triumphs: *Inscr. Ital.* 13.1, 570–1.
21. Thus especially Hor. *Carm.* 3.6.

Caesar's own house. Caesar had vowed to build the temple after the defeat of Sextus Pompeius at Naulochus in 36 BC, but it was the victory at Actium which now predominated.[22] The building was in white marble, decorated with ivory and with precious statues, and the colonnades which surrounded it included two libraries, one for Greek and one for Latin books.[23] This was the home of the god of the new age, alongside that of its founder. Outside the city boundary, on the Campus Martius, another remarkable edifice was being built, circular in design, consisting of two huge cylinders, 87 metres wide and rising nearly 40 metres to the central point. This was to be the Mausoleum of Caesar and his family, and it was sufficiently complete to be put on public display during his sixth consulship in 28, though not finished for some years thereafter.[24] It far outstripped the funerary monuments of the great Republican families that preceded it and, topped with an immense statue of Caesar himself, demonstrated for all to see that not only Caesar but also the family of Caesar was predominant within the newly restored world of Rome after the end of the civil wars.

It was also about this time that Caesar strengthened the already powerful ties between himself and Agrippa, the closest of his associates, by arranging a marriage for him with Claudia Marcella, the daughter of Caesar's sister Octavia, and thus Caesar's niece.[25] Thus it was as part of the family of Caesar that, at the beginning of the following year (27 BC), he and Agrippa again entered the consulship together. On 13 January Caesar read a speech to the assembled senators in which he handed over to the senate and people control of all the mechanisms of the state for them to decide how it should be governed.[26] Dio, who gives the only detailed account of what happened on that day, says that only a few of Caesar's closest supporters knew what he was going to do and that many senators were surprised;[27] but, if this is true, those supporters managed the

22. Vell. Pat. 2.81.3; Dio Cass. 49.15.5, 53.1.3–5. Dedication of temple of Apollo: *Fast. Ant. min.* (in *EJ* 53 and *Inscr. Ital.* 13.2.209, 518–19). For its position and the significance of it, see Zanker, *The Power of Images*, 50–3.
23. Prop. 2.31; Verg. *Aen.* 8.720. Suet. *Aug.* 29.3.
24. Suet. *Aug.* 100.4. For a description, see Zanker, *The Power of Images*, 72–7.
25. Dio Cass. 53.1.2; Suet. *Aug.* 63.1; Plut. *Ant.* 87.2.
26. Dio Cass. 53.3–10 gives his version of this speech, in which Caesar states that he is handing over 'absolutely everything, the army, the laws and the provinces' (53.4.3). In the *Res Gestae*, Augustus says he handed over the *res publica*, that is, all the business of the state (Aug. *RG* 34.1: see above, n. 17).
27. Dio Cass. 53.2.7 and 11.1–4.

outcome skilfully. After pleas from members of the senate that he would not give up power, Caesar agreed to take responsibility for those provinces which were insecure and likely to be troubled either by external enemies or by internal disruptions, while leaving the safer provinces to be allocated, as they had always been, by the senate; and stated that he would limit his tenure of these provinces to ten years.[28] The provinces which were assigned to Caesar were the four provinces of Gaul (Narbonensis, Lugdunensis, Aquitania and Belgica), the two Spanish provinces (Hispania Citerior and Ulterior), Syria (including Cilicia and Cyprus) and Egypt; the other ten were to be 'the people's provinces'.[29]

The result of this was to entrust Caesar with an immense provincial command, which he was to exercise through legates holding the *imperium* of a praetor, and who acted just as provincial governors had done in the past (and as proconsuls sent to the people's provinces continued to do), but were appointed by and directly responsible to Caesar himself. Whatever one thinks of the elaborate preliminaries of his proffered resignation and eventual taking up of a command at the insistence of the senate, the outcome can be seen as in the same style as what Caesar and his associates had been doing over the past few years. No one could doubt that he was the most powerful individual in the Roman world and in effect its sole ruler; but this was expressed in January 27 in terms which were derived from the constitutional structures of the Republican period. The great commands of Pompeius Magnus against the pirates and in the east in the 60s BC and of Julius Caesar in Gaul in the 50s were undertaken using legates, while Pompeius held the two Spanish provinces after 55 BC in the same way. What differentiated this from Caesar's command was, of course, its unprecedented dimensions, in terms both of size and of length of time; but Caesar was without precedent in the extent of his power. This was recognised by individuals and communities across the Roman world from the moment of his victory over Antonius at Actium, and reached a climax at just this point in 27 BC.[30] No one at Rome will have thought any different.

---

28. Dio Cass. 53.12; Suet. *Aug.* 47; Strabo, 17.3.24–5.
29. Dio Cass. 53.12.3–9; Strabo, 17.3. As he explains, Dio has listed the provinces as they existed at the time he wrote. On the nature of the distinction between Caesar's provinces and the people's provinces, see F. G. B. Millar, 'The emperor, the senate and the provinces', *Journal of Roman Studies* 56 (1966), 156–66, and '"Senatorial" provinces: an institutionalized ghost', *Ancient World* 20 (1989), 93–7.
30. See the masterly essay by F. G. B. Millar, 'State and subject: the impact of monarchy',

The supremacy of Caesar was marked by a further measure approved by the senate, perhaps more significant even than the division of the provinces in expressing that supreme position. On 16 January, on the motion of Lucius Munatius Plancus, the senate granted him the name Augustus.[31] This was in many ways extraordinary, and had extraordinary consequences. As Dio notes, the names 'Caesar' and 'Augustus' were used thereafter by the emperors who followed, not because they signified any specific powers that they held but because they showed respectively their pedigree and the splendour of their position (Dio Cass. 53.18.2). Indeed this was true not only of those users of these names who held imperial supreme positions through the whole period of the Roman Empire but of many rulers through the Middle Ages and into the modern period. In 27 BC the new name did not, of course, have this significance, but it was remarkable, not least because of its divine connotations. Dio says that the name implies that Caesar was more than human, and explains that this was why the Greeks used the word *sebastos* to address him, since this meant a person who was revered (Dio Cass. 53.16.8) This was not just the judgement of an historian writing some two centuries later. Livy, who began his history of Rome in these years, uses *augustior*, the comparative form of the adjective *augustus*, to contrast with the adjective *humanus* to mean something 'more than human' on five occasions in the first ten books of his work. Later in Augustus' reign the poet Ovid explains the name in the same way, again contrasting it with *humanus* and writing that the ancestors referred to things holy as *augusta* and that the word *augurium* (augury) had the same root, being brought to fulfilment (he uses the verb *augere*, 'increase') by Jupiter through his own power.[32]

Some of our sources have the story that it was suggested that he should take the name 'Romulus', the first king and founder of the Roman state, but that 'Augustus' was considered more revered and close to the gods.[33] The meaning of the name is nuanced but un-

in F. G. B. Millar and E. Segal (eds), *Caesar Augustus: Seven Aspects*, Oxford: Oxford University Press, 1984.

31. *Fast. Praenest.* (*Inscr. Ital.* 13.2.115 and 400); Aug. *RG* 34.2; Vell. Pat. 2.91.1; Suet. *Aug.* 7.2; Florus, 2.34.66; Dio Cass. 53.16.6. Ovid, *Fast.* 1.589–60, conflates this event with those of 13 January.

32. Livy, *Praef.* 7; 1.7.9; 5.41.8; 8.6.9; 8.9.10; Ovid, *Fasti* 1.605–12 (see L. R. Taylor, 'Livy and the name Augustus', *Classical Review* 32 (1918), 158–61).

33. Suet. *Aug.* 7.2; Florus, 2.34.66. Dio states that the name 'Romulus' was Caesar's

mistakable. Augustus is almost divine, at least superhuman, and is recognised as such by the senate's decree. Alongside this remarkable honour others were decreed: his house on the Palatine hill, a relatively modest dwelling which had once belonged to the orator Hortensius and which adjoined the gleaming new temple of Apollo, was adorned with evergreen laurels on each side of the door, over which was placed a civic crown of oak leaves, a symbol reserved for those who had saved the lives of Roman citizens; and in the senate house a golden shield was placed, recording his valour, clemency, justice and piety towards the gods and the fatherland.[34] The occupant of Augustus' house might still be a human being (though Ovid, writing from exile at the end of Augustus' reign, wondered whether it was in fact the house of Jupiter[35]); but, if so, that human being was truly extraordinary. Even the title by which he referred to himself, *princeps*, which might be translated 'leading citizen' and which could be used of others without offence, expressed (in a more modest way) an undoubted pre-eminence when applied to him.[36]

The events of 28 and of the first month of 27 BC marked a return to normality, but to a normality which included and depended upon an individual placed in a wholly abnormal position. The business of the Roman people (which is one translation of that elusive notion, *res publica*) could continue, freed from the threats and horrors of civil war, under the oversight of its revered protector, the new Augustus. Later in 27, two successful generals celebrated triumphs. In July Marcus Licinius Crassus, grandson of the Crassus who had died at the battle of Carrhae against the Parthians in 53 BC, celebrated victories over the Getae in Thrace; and in September Marcus Valerius Messalla Corvinus was awarded a triumph from Gaul. This was as normal, honouring two successful generals; but even in the midst of such normal honours, the significance of Augustus' position could not be escaped. Dio Cassius states that in 29 BC in the course of his brilliant campaigns Crassus killed with his own hands Deldo, the king of the Bastarnae, against whom he was fighting, and that he would have dedicated the king's armour as

---

preference, but he realised that this would associate him too closely with the notion of kingship (Dio Cass. 53.16.7).

34. Aug. *RG* 34.2; Dio Cass. 53.16.4. On the detailed significance of these honours, see Cooley, *Res Gestae*, 262–71.

35. Ovid, *Tr.* 3.1.31–42.

36. Aug. *RG* 13 (*me principe*) and (used of others) 12.1 (*principibus viris*). Horace (*Carm.* 4.14.6) calls him *maxime principum*, 'greatest of leading citizens'.

spolia opima in the temple of Jupiter Feretrius in Rome, if he had been the general in supreme command.[37] The privilege of making the special dedication of such spoils was very rare, and had, according to our sources, occurred only three times in previous Roman history, the first dedicator being Romulus. It has been widely believed by modern scholars on the basis of Dio's account that Crassus requested permission of the senate to make the dedication and was prevented by Augustus on the grounds that Crassus was not the commander in this war but was fighting under Augustus' command. This notion has been supported by a passage which Livy inserted into his account of an earlier dedicator of the *spolia opima*, Aulus Cornelius Cossus, to the effect that, although earlier writers had believed that Cossus held the rank of military tribune when in the fifth century BC he was allowed to make his dedication, Livy had it from Augustus himself, who had been responsible for the rebuilding of the temple, that an inscription on a linen corselet which was part of the spoils showed he was in fact a consul.[38] This seemed to suggest that Augustus had conveniently found, or perhaps even invented, evidence that would preclude Crassus from dedicating *spolia opima*. This argument collapses, however, because it is clear that Dio is wrong in saying that Crassus did not hold the command in 29, for otherwise he would not have been able to celebrate his triumph in July 27. No doubt it would have been problematic for Augustus if a significant member of a major family from the time of the Republic had been given this very special privilege, associated as it was with Romulus, the founder of the city, but there seems to be no technical reason, in terms of his rank, why Crassus should not have done so. It should be noticed that Dio makes no mention of any request from Crassus being refused, least of all by the senate, and it is perhaps more probable that he never made any formal application, either because he had enough sense to realise that such a move would result in a confrontation with Augustus or because Augustus himself dissuaded him. After the new arrangements for the control of the provinces which had been made in 27 were in place, a similar situation was most unlikely to recur because, unlike Crassus, the legates who commanded most of the legions were now undoubtedly under the command of Augustus himself; and it may be that, if his

---

37. Dio Cass. 51.24.4. On this incident and its significance, see J. W. Rich, 'Augustus and the *spolia opima*', *Chiron* 26 (1966), 85–127.
38. Livy, 4.20.5.

'discovery' of the inscription in the temple of Jupiter Feretrius had a political motive beyond simple antiquarian interest, it was the establishing of the position of these *legati* in respect of their commander rather than a direct rebuff to Crassus.

Augustus had other matters to attend to. In this year he restored the *via Flaminia*, the road which ran from Rome to Ariminium, and encouraged those who had recently celebrated triumphs to use the booty they had brought back with them to refurbish other roads.[39] He left Rome at some point in the year, proceeding to Gaul with the intention (according to Dio) of invading Britain. Whatever the truth of this, he did not go further than Gaul, where he convened an assembly at Narbo, on the Mediterranean coast, and it was probably now that he arranged the structure of the Gallic provinces with Narbonensis in the south and the Three Gauls (Aquitania, Lugdunensis and Belgica) in the territory which Julius Caesar had conquered in the 50s. He also conducted a census of the population, the first of several he was to undertake throughout the empire.[40] By the beginning of January he had crossed the Pyrenees into Spain, and entered his eighth consulship in Tarraco (modern Tarragona).[41] His colleague was Titus Statilius Taurus, who, like his predecessor Agrippa, was a military man who had long been a supporter. As became clear, Augustus' aim was to complete the conquest of the one part of the region which had not been subdued by the Romans after a presence there of nearly two centuries: the mountainous north-west, occupied by the warlike tribes of the Cantabri and the Astures.

Augustus in Spain, 26–24 BC

For the next two campaigning seasons, 26 and 25 BC, Augustus was present in the peninsula. The precise chronology and military detail of the events of these two years have been a matter of considerable debate.[42] The fact that the *princeps* himself was involved, and indeed wrote about these campaigns in his autobiography, gave the war in Spain a particular interest to ancient writers; but inevitably it also meant that they were careful about what they wrote. The picture

---

39. Aug. *RG* 20.5; Suet. *Aug.* 30.1; Dio Cass. 53.22.1–2.
40. Livy, *Per.* 134; Dio Cass. 53.22.5.
41. Suet. *Aug.* 26.3.
42. See particularly R. Syme, 'The conquest of north-west Spain', in *Roman Papers* 2, Oxford: Oxford University Press, 1979, 825–54, and P. Le Roux, *L'armée romaine et l'organisation des provinces ibériques d'Auguste à l'invasion de 409*, Paris: Boccard, 1982, 52–69.

given, even in our fullest source, Dio Cassius, concentrates on the activities of Augustus himself, even though Dio states that the *princeps* fell ill in the process, and seems to have spent the second campaign recovering in Tarraco.[43] Moreover, the extent of the success of these campaigns is undoubtedly exaggerated by all the sources. It is true that for the first time Roman armies confronted the peoples of the mountainous north and north-west, the Cantabri and the Astures, in their own territory, and were successful enough for Augustus to order the closing of the gates of the temple of Janus in Rome, the sign that the world was at peace. Despite this, and the still wilder claim of Velleius Parerculus that even the brigands were cleared from Spain,[44] it is clear that the legions (perhaps as many as seven in the period when Augustus was there) had not succeeded in controlling the area in these two campaigns. One of the commanders who had served under Augustus, Publius Carisius, was again in action against both the Astures and the Cantabri in 22, and in 19 Agrippa himself had a hard struggle to repress the Cantabri. He finally concluded the war which had allegedly been won in 25 by slaughtering the fighting men and forcing the rest to move from their settlements in the mountains down into the more controllable valleys.[45] Agrippa displayed his usual tact in refusing to celebrate a triumph for this victory.

While Augustus was in Spain, his friends were left to control matters in Rome. At the beginning of 26, when Statilius Taurus was the one consul in the city, Messalla Corvinus, who had celebrated his triumph the previous year, was appointed to the office of prefect of the city (*praefectus urbi*), a post whose title went back to the time of Romulus. In the past the prefect had acted in the absence of the consuls (or, initially, the king) from the city, and it might seem reasonable to assume that this was the intention of Messalla's appointment; but later *praefecti* were solely responsible for keeping order in the city itself, and there is no way of telling what Augustus' intentions were for Messalla, since he resigned the post within a few days of accepting it, as though (Tacitus writes) he did not know how to exercise it.[46] As Messalla remained in Augustus' favour, it may

43. Dio Cass. 53.25.5–8.
44. Vell. Pat. 2.90.4.
45. Syme, 'The conquest of north-west Spain', 848–51; Le Roux, *L'armée romaine*, 59–65.
46. Tacitus, *Ann.* 6.11; Seneca, *Apocol.* 10; Jerome, *Chron. sub ann.* 26. See R. Syme, *The Augustan Aristocracy*, Oxford: Oxford University Press, 1986, 211–12.

be that there was a real confusion about the *princeps'* intentions, especially as Statilius Taurus was in Rome as consul during the year.

In any case, in Augustus' absence his interests were maintained by his other allies, notably Maecenas and Agrippa. In these years Agrippa proceeded with the great building programme which had marked the outset of Augustus' period of sole control of the Roman world, and which had been inaugurated even before that by Agrippa during his aedileship in 33.[47] The development of the Campus Martius outside the city walls continued with Agrippa's dedication in 26 of the Saepta Iulia, the great election hall originally mooted by Julius Caesar, and included the construction of a magnificent set of baths in a public park and of a new temple, the Pantheon, dedicated to all the gods.[48] There had been a plan to include a statue of Augustus himself among those of the gods in the interior of the temple, but the *princeps* refused this honour, so that the statue of Julius Caesar was placed there, with those of himself and of Agrippa being set up in the *pronaos*, the porch of the building. Though he was undoubtedly supreme in Rome, Augustus was evidently cautious about claiming divinity there.

However much Rome the city was the capital city of the empire, in another sense the position of Augustus now meant that the centre of power, and hence the centre of attention, was located wherever he was. For much of his time in Spain, this meant the city of Tarraco on the Mediterranean, one of the earliest places to which the Romans had come almost two centuries earlier when they first entered the peninsula with an army, and now carrying the status of a Roman colony. It was here that Augustus came when, owing to persistent ill-health, he had to withdraw from the prosecution of the war in the north-west. In these years, embassies from India, Parthia and the Scythians are said to have arrived to meet Augustus, and inscriptions record the presence of ambassadors from Greek cities, seeking aid over such varied matters as the settlement of a legal case and assistance following an earthquake.[49] Such approaches to major figures were not uncommon in a world which had long been dominated by

47. See above, p. 65.
48. Dio Cass. 53.23.1–2, 27.1–4. Zanker, *The Power of Images*, 139–43.
49. Orosius, 6.21.19–20 (Indians (cf. Aug. *RG* 31.1) and Scythians); Justin, 42.5.6 (Parthians); *EJ* 317 (Chios); Agathias, 2.17, Eusebius, *Chronica* 2.140–1 (Schoene); Strabo, 12.8.18 (Tralles); also possibly from Mytilene, in connection with a treaty (see R. K. Sherk, *Roman Documents from the Greek East*, Baltimore: Johns Hopkins University Press, 1969, 146–57).

Rome, but the number and significance of those who journeyed to Spain in these years were unprecedented.

Although Augustus depended heavily on his friends and allies during his years in Gaul and Spain, one at least, though far from the capital, was deemed to have let him down. Gaius Cornelius Gallus, the officer of equestrian rank who had proved so valuable in the capture of Alexandria after the battle of Actium,[50] had been appointed as prefect of Alexandria and Egypt, to govern the new province directly under the *princeps*. In 27 or 26, he lost the favour of Augustus, for reasons which are not clear. Some sources say that he had made derogatory remarks about Augustus, another that he erected statues of himself in Egypt and placed boastful inscriptions on the pyramids.[51] Augustus forbade him access to any of his own provinces, at which it appears that the senate urged that he should be put on trial.[52] Cornelius Gallus committed suicide, at the news of which, Suetonius tells us, Augustus wept. But though he may well have regretted the inappropriate self-assertion that led to the fall from favour of his former friend, Augustus showed no inclination to reverse either his policy of assigning Egypt to an equestrian prefect or that of vigorous military expansion which Cornelius Gallus had undertaken southwards. A successor, Aelius Gallus, also an equestrian, was sent out with instructions to investigate the geography and the internal situation of Ethiopia and the rich territory of Arabia. This led to a large-scale invasion of the latter by an army, led by Aelius, and consisting of Roman and allied infantry, including Jews and Nabataeans. The intention of this assault was not least the seizure and control of the trade routes which brought spices and other luxury goods from the east. The expedition was a disastrous failure, a fact put down by the geographer Strabo (a friend and confidant of Aelius Gallus) to the treachery of the commander of the

---

50. See above, p. 73.
51. Slanders: Ovid, *Am.* 3.9.63–4, *Tr.* 2.445–6; Suet. *Aug.* 66.2. Boasting: Dio Cass. 53.23.5–7. Though no inscription can be found on the pyramids, a self-congratulatory trilingual example from Philae, dated in its Egyptian form to 15 April 29, may be the basis of Dio's charge (*EJ* 21; *ILS* 8995). See now F. Hoffmann, M. Minas-Nerpel and Stefan Pfeiffer (eds), *Die dreisprachige Stele des C. Cornelius Gallus: Übersetzung und Kommentar. Archiv für Papyrusforschung und verwandte Gebiete* 9, Berlin and New York: Walter de Gruyter, 2009, arguing that the language is conventional for this type of monument and shows no disloyalty to the emperor.
52. Dio Cass. 53.23.7–24.1. On the relationship between the senate's demand and the possible use of the court, see J. S. Richardson, 'The senate, the courts and the *s.c. de Cn. Pisone patre*', *Classical Quarterly* 47 (1997), 510–18, at 514.

Nabataean force, who misinformed the Roman general and sabotaged the invasion. The army which eventually found its way back to Alexandria the following year was severely depleted, though by illness and exhaustion rather than losses in battle. In the *Res Gestae*, Augustus records the incursion but not its result.[53] Failure in Arabia did not discourage him from attempting to achieve success in Ethiopia, and Aelius Gallus' successor, Publius Petronius, responded to an attack on some southern Egyptian cities with a successful invasion, which he reported to Augustus in 24 BC, on Augustus' return from Spain. Petronius also imposed tribute on the Ethiopians. Shortly after this the Ethiopian queen, Candace, attacked garrisons which Petronius had stationed by the Nile, but she was defeated by a rapid response from Petronius, who in 22 BC sent representatives of the queen to the *princeps*, who was temporarily on the island of Samos. There Augustus remitted the tribute which Petronius had required.[54] The southern border of Egypt had been secured and further military operations were not required.

Elsewhere changes were made which show that Augustus, while resident in Spain, was actively concerned with the affairs of the empire as a whole. In 25, in the Alpine region of northern Italy, Augustus' *legatus* Terentius Varro at last subdued the Salassi and sold those of military age into slavery, founding the city of Augusta Praetoria (modern Aosta).[55] In the same year, Juba, son of a former king of Numidia in north Africa, which Julius Caesar had made into a Roman province in 46 BC after the battle of Thapsus, was installed as king of Mauretania, the territory along the coast to the west of the new province; and in central Asia Minor, the area of Galatia, which had been in the hands of Amyntas, who had been placed there by Antonius in 36 but had deserted to Caesar before Actium, became a Roman province following Amyntas' death. At about the same time Polemo, who had been established as king of Pontus in the northeast of Asia Minor by Antonius in 37 and had stayed loyal to him through the Actium campaign, was recognised as a friend of the Roman people.[56]

It was not only foreign affairs which preoccupied Augustus as he rested in Tarraco, beset by illness. He was also clearly thinking about

53. Strabo, 16.4.22–4; Aug. *RG* 26.5.
54. Strabo, 17.1.53–4; Pliny, *HN* 6.181; Dio Cass. 54.5.4–6.
55. Strabo, 4.6.7; Dio Cass. 53.25.2–5.
56. Dio Cass. 53.25.1 and 26.2–3.

a matter which was strictly speaking domestic, the marriage of his only child, Julia, born to Scribonia in 39, shortly before he divorced her to marry Livia.[57] Such marriages were of great importance in major families of the Republican period, often involving political alliances; but in the new world that was the result of Augustus' predominance, there was no other family which stood comparison with that of the *princeps*. This was the message of the Mausoleum in the Campus Martius, a family monument which far outstripped all that had gone before.[58] It is this that led Augustus to choose for Julia's husband not a member of one of the other great families of Rome but a member of his own family, his nephew, Gaius Marcellus, son of his sister Octavia by her first husband, the consul of 50 BC.[59] Marcellus was seventeen years old and Julia thirteen. This was not an exceptionally young age for a woman, but Marcellus' youth suggests that whatever plans Augustus may have had for him were not immediate (despite the precedent of Augustus' own rise to power). This was significant, not least because of Augustus' poor health while in Spain, and it is notable that, when he was unable because of illness to get back from Spain for the wedding, the ceremony was presided over by Agrippa, connected through his marriage to Claudia Marcella to Augustus' family and also his closest political associate.[60]

Augustus returned from Spain at the end of 25, but his illness prevented him from reaching Rome in time to enter his tenth consulship there at the beginning of January 24. His colleague was Gaius Norbanus Flaccus, whose father, consul in 38, had been a successful commander in Spain in the mid-30s. The senate swore an oath to uphold Augustus' acts, as had become usual, and it was announced that a donation would be made to the plebs of 400 sesterces each, as had happened at his triumph in 29. Dio says that at this time a measure was passed by the senate to release him from the constraints of the laws.[61] Dio clearly believed that this was a general measure, placing the *princeps* above the law, which was the case by the time he was writing, but did not apply to Augustus. It seems likely that he has misunderstood a specific grant, enabling Augustus to make such

---

57. Dio says that the divorce took place on the day Julia was born (Dio Cass. 48.34.3).
58. See above, p. 86.
59. See above, p. 7.
60. Dio Cass. 53.27.5
61. Dio Cass. 53.28.1–2.

a donation without falling foul of the law against electoral bribery.[62] Though not free from the law, he was able to determine the holders of magistracies, and appointed his nephew and new son-in-law, Marcellus, as aedile for the following year, and his stepson, Tiberius Claudius Nero (already betrothed to Vipsania, Agrippa's daughter by his first wife), as quaestor, with the additional provision that Marcellus was to be allowed to stand for the consulship ten years earlier than normal, and Tiberius to stand for magistracies five years earlier.[63] The two men were of the same age, and this clearly indicates that Marcellus was his preferred successor, with Tiberius as a second option. These provisions, along with Marcellus' marriage to Julia, show (if there had been any previous doubt) that Augustus was planning a dynastic succession.

Rethinking the model: Augustus' illness and its consequences, 23–19 BC

The following year might have put such plans to the test sooner than Augustus had intended. In January 23 he entered his eleventh consulship along with Gnaeus Calpurnius Piso, a noble who had supported Brutus and Cassius during the civil wars and, though pardoned, had kept away from public life until asked by Augustus to stand.[64] Early in the year Augustus fell seriously ill and feared that he might die. He gathered the magistrates and other leading senators and equestrians, but did not, as had been expected, name a successor (it had been assumed that this would be Marcellus). Instead, after speaking about the affairs of state, he handed over to his fellow consul, Piso, a book containing details of military forces and public revenues, and gave his signet ring to Agrippa. Later, when he had recovered from his illness, after treatment at the hands of his doctor, Antonius Musa, he went to the senate to read out his will, to show that he had not named anyone as his successor.[65] In all this he acted with scrupulous regard for constitutional niceties. Whatever the realities of his control of the state and the expectations of his contemporaries, there was no way in which he could formally

---

62. See P. A. Brunt, 'The *lex Vespasiani de imperio*', *Journal of Roman Studies* 67 (1977), 95–116, at 108–9.
63. Dio Cass. 53.28.3–4. Tiberius' betrothal to Vipsania: Nepos, *Atticus* 19.4.
64. Tacitus, *Ann.* 2.43.2.
65. Dio Cass. 53.30.1–3, 31.1–4. Suetonius, *Aug.* 28.1, attributes Augustus' action to weariness, resulting from his long illness rather than fear of imminent death.

appoint a successor to a post which, in formal constitutional terms, did not exist; and even if the collection of powers he held were to be recognised as a continuing position within the Roman state, it was the senate and people who should appoint its next holder. In reality, the handing over of his ring to Agrippa marked the latter as, at least for the moment, the man to take over from him; but this was not a formal appointment. The question remains why Augustus did not pass his ring to Marcellus; but the answer is probably that given by Dio: that Marcellus was too young for Augustus to have trust in his judgement. The ancient sources, Dio included, also mention another factor: friction between the two men closest to Augustus, the brothers-in-law Marcellus and Agrippa.[66]

Certainly one of the first things that happened once Augustus recovered from his illness was that Agrippa left Rome for the east, charged with governing Syria. He reached the island of Lesbos in the Aegean and settled in the city of Mytilene, controlling Syria by means of *legati*. This is represented in our sources as a withdrawal or even a banishment, brought about by the breakdown of relations with Marcellus;[67] but that does not account for what happened. Agrippa must have held the power of a proconsul (*imperium pro consule*) to act as a governor of Syria, and his base in Mytilene suggests that his remit related to more than just Syria. Moreover, from now to his death in 12 BC he seems to have been given grants of proconsular *imperium* every five years, judging by the somewhat ambiguous remarks by Dio under the years 18 and 13. The Jewish historian Josephus writes of a visit to him by Herod while he was resident in Mytilene, and describes him as 'Caesar's deputy for the lands beyond the Ionian sea'; and a papyrus fragment of the speech which Augustus gave at Agrippa's funeral in 12 BC states that a law (of which the date is not given) was passed that, in whatever territories the Roman state sent him to, no one had power greater than his.[68] All this suggests that Agrippa was given a major role as Augustus' representative in the eastern part of the empire, and that, whatever the problems between him and Marcellus, he was certainly

---

66. On Agrippa's marriage to Claudia Marcella, Marcellus' sister, see above, p. 86.
67. Vell. Pat. 2.93.2; Pliny, *HN* 7.149; Tacitus, *Ann.* 14.53 and 55; Suet. *Aug.* 66.3, *Tib.* 10.1; Dio Cass. 53.32.1. It is probable that the picture given of Agrippa's 'withdrawal' was influenced by that of Tiberius to Rhodes in 6 BC, with which Suetonius, *Tib.* 10.1, explicitly compares it (see below, p. 147).
68. Dio Cass. 54.12.4, 28.1; Josephus, *AJ* 15.350; *EJ* 366, lines 5–10. On the nature of this *imperium* and that given to Augustus late in 23, see below, p. 101.

not banished or withdrawing from public life. Rather this seems to be part of Augustus' devolving of the work of governing the Roman state, which he undertook that year as a consequence of his illness.

In late June or early July, Augustus attended the Latin Games, held on the Alban Mount, just south of Rome. Here he announced that he was giving up his holding of the consulship, and chose as his successor Lucius Sestius, who, like Piso, the other consul of the year, had been a strong supporter of Marcus Brutus and remained devoted to his memory.[69] In place of the consulship, Augustus received a number of additional powers. He was, according to Dio, offered by the senate the tribunate of the plebs for life and in addition given the right to bring a motion on one matter before the senate at each of its meetings, even if he were not consul at the time; he was to be proconsul permanently, so that, unlike all other proconsuls, he did not have to lay down his *imperium* on entering the city; and this *imperium* was to be greater than that of the governors of individual provinces. Dio goes on to say that Augustus and those who succeeded him did not take the title of tribune, but instead were given the right to use the powers of the tribune, the *tribunicia potestas*.[70]

These grants make up what is often called the 'settlement of 23'.[71] It is clear (and Dio says as much) that they were intended to compensate for Augustus' resignation from the consulship, and presuppose that he had indicated that he did not intend to continue to hold the consulship year by year, as he had done since 31. Consequently he is granted the power he needed to be able to act *pro consule*, 'as though a consul', to govern through his legates the huge areas assigned to him in January 27; and, because he also controlled the empire from within Rome itself, he had (unlike all other proconsuls) to be able to retain his *imperium* even within the *pomerium*, the sacred boundary of the city. It was within the city, however, that his resignation from the consulship made the greatest difference. As consul, he had been able to convene the senate, whose formal function was to act as an advisory body to the senior magistrates, and to put motions before them, which, when approved, became *senatus consulta*, decrees of the senate; he had also, as consul, had the right to conduct business with the people in their assemblies.

---

69. Dio Cass. 53.32.3–4. For Augustus on the Alban Mount, see also the *Fasti Feriarum Latinarum* (*Inscr. Ital.* 13.1.151).
70. Dio Cass. 53.32.5–6.
71. For the clearest discussion of the powers of Augustus granted in 23 and their significance, see now Ferrary, 'The powers of Augustus', 99–125.

These were conferred upon Augustus through the *tribunicia potestas*, and indeed so far as meetings of the senate were concerned this was strengthened by the specific grant of the right to present motions. In these ways he was able to act in Rome almost in the way a consul did, with the exception of the election of magistrates, over which the consuls presided. But the major difference from his position in the years since 31 was that, though he might be able to act as a consul did, he was not consul: he was holding and exercising the powers but not holding the office.

This is a pattern that we have seen already in his handling of the delicate matter of managing the constitutional affairs of Rome. In 29 and 28 he and Agrippa had conducted a review of the senate and a census of the people, the task usually undertaken by the censors, using the power of the censors (*censoria potestas*) without being censors.[72] The *tribunicia potestas* was on the same model: Augustus could act as a tribune without holding the office. This too is what lies behind the assemblage of powers which gave him so many of the rights of a consul. Moreover the very fact that he was not holding the office of consul had the advantage that others were able to do so.[73] His continuous tenure of the consulship since 31, combined with the fact that Agrippa had been consul in 28 and 27, and that since 28 the practice, begun by Julius Caesar in 45 and continued through the triumviral period, of consuls abdicating and being replaced by suffect consuls had been abandoned in favour of the Republican pattern of consuls being in office for the whole year, effectively excluded many from the highest constitutional office in the state. In the years to come it was not being consul that marked out the *princeps* from the other leading members of the ruling class but the tenure of the *tribunicia potestas*, which begins to appear on inscriptions from about 18 onwards as marking the years of Augustus' reign, counting from the grant in 23. The result of the changes of that year was not only to free him from the formal duties that the consul had to carry out and from the need to be elected annually but to distinguish him from all others on an enduring basis. Julius Caesar had used the dictatorship for this purpose when in February 44 he had been made *dictator perpetuo*; Augustus chose the apparently more modest means of the *tribunicia potestas*, which, unlike his father's title, was not the distortion of an ancient office of

72. See above, pp. 82–3.
73. So Dio Cass. 53.32.3.

state, but was not an office at all. Moreover, it carried with it the remembrance of the origins of the tribunate of the plebs, created in the earliest days of the Republic to defend the rights of the plebeians. It was this which Tacitus a century later was to call the title that marked supreme eminence.[74] The context in which Augustus acquired it in 23 made it seem a concession to the class from which Julius Caesar's assassins had come and to which the other two consuls of that year, Sestius and Piso, belonged.

Outside the city, in Caesar's provinces and beyond, little was altered by the adjustments of 23. The other grant, that the pro-consular *imperium* of the *princeps* should be greater than that of other proconsuls, has been taken to mean that Augustus held power (called by scholars *imperium maius*) which enabled him to issue orders and decisions which overruled those of the governors of the people's provinces; but recent epigraphic discoveries have shown that *imperium maius* as an overall supremacy over all other holders of *imperium* did not exist. What Augustus obtained in 23 was almost certainly a recognition that his power was to be greater than that of particular proconsuls in whose provinces he found himself from time to time. This would be similar to, though greater than, the power which Agrippa held at some point which was not less than that of proconsuls in such provinces as he was sent to.[75] It is likely that Agrippa's *imperium* was granted by a law later than the grant to Augustus in 23, and the mention of it in the funerary oration of Augustus for Agrippa has no date attached to it. In the case of Augustus, it may have been given in the expectation that the *princeps* would shortly be leaving the capital for the eastern provinces, a visit for which Agrippa's dispatch to the same area may have been a preparation. In any case it is noticeable that, although he undoubtedly held proconsular *imperium* from the time of his resignation of the consulship, Augustus did not call himself 'pro-consul', and the use of the phrase *imperium proconsulare* does not occur until the reign of his successor, Tiberius.[76] Perhaps Augustus

---

74. Tacitus, *Ann.* 3.56: summi fastigii vocabulum. Tacitus also notes the link with Augustus' stance as protector of the people (*Ann.* 1.2.1).
75. See above, p. 98. See the discussion by Ferrary, 'The powers of Augustus', 110–21.
76. Use of *pro consule*: Syme, '*Imperator Caesar*: a study in nomenclature', at 184 (= *Roman Papers* 1, at 374). *proconsulare imperium*: Val. Max. 6.9.7; 8.1(ambust.).2. The one exception to Augustus' non-use of the title occurs in an inscription recently discovered in north-west Spain (*Année Epigraphique* 1999, 915; 2000, 760); but there is doubt about the nature and authenticity of this document (J. S. Richardson, 'The new

did not want to use a title that appeared to put him on a par with senatorial governors of the people's provinces.

The events which surrounded Augustus' illness and resignation of the consulship do not seem to have affected his enthusiasm for Marcellus, even if Augustus did not see him as an appropriate replacement for himself in 23. Marcellus was aedile this year and so responsible for putting on the games which enlivened the city on an annual basis in April (the *ludi Megalenses* and *Florales*) and September (the *ludi Romani*). Augustus lent his help to his son-in-law and the result was a particularly splendid show. The prestige which Marcellus should have gained went for nothing when, either in the midst of the celebrations in April or just after them, he fell ill and died, despite the best efforts of Augustus' doctor, Antonius Musa. Augustus ordered that a golden curule chair, of the type that Marcellus would have used had he lived, adorned with a golden crown be carried in the *ludi Romani*; and his body was buried in the great Mausoleum in the Campus Martius. The theatre, only the second built in stone in the capital, which was being erected just north of the Capitol and much of which can still be seen today, was completed in his memory and named the Theatre of Marcellus.[77]

The death of Marcellus effectively wrecked Augustus' dynastic plans, but that was only one of several problems he had to face at the end of 23 and the beginning of 22. The first were concerned with foreign affairs. In Parthia a civil war had been raging between Phraates IV, the king who had caused Antonius so much trouble in the mid-30s,[78] and a pretender to the throne named Tiridates. By 30 BC Tiridates had suffered reverses but managed to seize a son of Phraates, and approached Caesar as he moved through Syria and Asia after the battle of Actium. No support was given to Tiridates other than being allowed to remain in Syria, but Phraates' son was taken back to Rome. After another failed attempt on the throne, Tiridates fled to Rome and in the latter part of 23 Augustus brought him and ambassadors from Phraates, who had come to complain of Tiridates' behaviour, before the senate. The matter was, not surprisingly, referred to Augustus, and he allowed the pretender to continue to live in style in Syria, but sent Phraates' son back to his father, on condition that he returned the Roman standards and captives

Augustan edicts from northwest Spain', *Journal of Roman Archaeology* 15 (2002), 411–15).
77. Vel. Pat. 2.93.1; Prop. 3.18.13–16. Dio Cass. 53.30–1.
78. See above, pp. 59–61.

which had been taken from Crassus at Carrhae in 53 and later from Antonius. It seems that Augustus wanted to maintain pressure on the Parthian king, without recourse to military action.[79]

The other foreign matter was potentially more embarrassing. Late in 23 or early in the following year (when for the first time since 32 Augustus did not enter the consulship on 1 January) Marcus Primus, who had been proconsul in the public province of Macedonia, was put on trial for having made war on the tribe of the Odrysae, which was friendly to Rome, without authority. The embarrassment occurred when Primus declared at one point in his trial that he had acted with the approval of Augustus, and at another with that of Marcellus. Augustus attended the trial, though he had not been summoned, and in answer to a question from the praetor in charge of the proceedings, denied that he had ordered Primus to wage war against the Odrysae. Primus' advocate, named by Dio as Licinius Murena, demanded to know who had called Augustus to attend, to which the *princeps* replied that it was the public interest. Nonetheless, although Primus was condemned, several jurors voted for acquittal.[80] Shortly afterwards a conspiracy was discovered: its intention was to assassinate Augustus, and those involved in it included Murena and one Fannius Caepio. The plot was revealed by a freedman named Castricius, but the conspirators escaped, Murena having been warned by his sister Terentia, the wife of Maecenas. His close connections to the friends of the *princeps*, both Maecenas and Proculeius, another of Augustus' close associates, who was Murena's half-brother, were of no help to him in the end, since he and Caepio were tried in their absence (Tiberius, Augustus' stepson, acted as prosecutor of Caepio), sentenced to death and killed shortly thereafter. Even so, as in the trial of Primus, the jurors were not unanimous, leading Augustus to introduce a measure that, when defendants were absent, the votes of jurors should not be taken secretly and that condemnation should require unanimity.[81]

Dio dates the trial of Primus and the conspiracy of Caepio and Murena to 22, but many modern scholars have put them in early 23

79. Dio Cass. 51.18.2–3; 53.33.1. Justin, 42.5.6–12, conflates the two episodes. Augustus records Tiridates and Phraates as suppliants who came to him (*RG* 32.1). See A. N. Sherwin-White, *Roman Policy in the East, 168 BC to AD 1*, London: Duckworth, 1984, 322–3.
80. Dio Cass. 54.3.2–3.
81. On the conspiracy, see Strabo, 14.5.4; Vell. Pat. 2.91.2, 93.1; Suet. *Aug.* 19.1, 56.4, 66.3 and *Tib.* 8; Tacitus, *Ann.* 1.10.5. It is also mentioned by Seneca, *Brev. vit.* 4.5 and *Clem.* 1.9.6; Macrobius, *Sat.* 1.11.21.

in the context of Augustus' resignation of the consulship, on the basis of an entry in the *Fasti Capitolini* of consulship held in 23 by Aulus Terentius Murena, who was replaced, for reasons which the inscription recorded but are lost in a lacuna, by Gnaeus Calpurnius Piso. This Murena has been identified with the conspirator and the gap in the *Fasti* filled with a phrase recording his condemnation. It has since been shown that such records in the *Fasti* usually show that the person concerned never entered the consulship and it is probable that Aulus Murena died before he took up office and is not the same man as the conspirator.[82] For this reason there is no reason to doubt Dio's dating, nor to connect the trial of Primus and the conspiracy with Augustus' abdication from the consulship and the measures which followed it. The situation in 22 was nonetheless a difficult one for the *princeps*. The challenge to his position with regard to the provinces which was explicit in the defence Primus had mounted at his trial, followed by a conspiracy involving someone linked by marriage and blood-ties to two of his closest confidants, did not make life easy for Augustus in the aftermath of his own serious illness. The failure to obtain unanimity in the two trials also showed that his pre-eminence was not universally accepted. Perhaps, though, all was not quite as difficult as has sometimes been assumed. It has often been supposed that Augustus lost faith in Maecenas as a result of his indiscretion and it is true that he played a much less significant role in affairs of state in the years that followed; but there is no real evidence of serious rift between them.[83] In the senate at least Augustus had lost none of his influence, and indeed he was, after the trial of Primus, given the additional power to convene the senate whenever he wished, a right that was in principle part of his *tribunicia potestas* but was given explicit expression by this grant.[84]

The other problems Augustus faced in 22 were the result of matters outside the closeted sphere of senatorial politics. The year was a terrible one for the city of Rome. To the plague of the previous year was added the flooding of the river Tiber and a severe grain shortage. At a point when Augustus was away from Rome, the

82. The most cogent argument for the identity of the two men is D. Stockton, 'Primus and Murena', *Historia* 14 (1965), 18–40. On the interpretation of the *Fasti*, see P. M. Swan, 'The consular *fasti* of 23 BC and the conspiracy of Varro Murena', *Harvard Studies in Classical Philology* 71 (1967), 235–47.

83. Tacitus, *Ann.* 3.30 and 14.53, seems to describe a voluntary retirement; and Seneca, *Ben.* 6.32.2, shows Augustus lamenting the loss of Maecenas' advice following the latter's death.

84. Dio Cass. 54.3.3.

people, to whom he had in the year before given grain each month of the year from his own funds,[85] rioted, shutting the senators in the building in which they were meeting and threatening to burn it down over their heads. The people demanded that Augustus be made dictator, which would make him constitutionally superior to all the other magistrates in Rome, and subsequently when he returned to the city urged him to hold not only the dictatorship but also the *cura annonae*, the control of the grain supplies. In a dramatic gesture, in which he tore his toga from his shoulders and went down on his knees, Augustus refused the dictatorship and the alternative of a consulship for life, which had also been offered. He did, however, take the *cura annonae*, and in a few days succeeded in restoring supplies to the city and set up an annually appointed commission of two senators to oversee the distributions of grain for the future.[86]

These events show something even more significant about Augustus' position than his ideas about his constitutional status. To be sure, as Dio notes, he wanted to avoid the dictatorship, an office which, in view of the precedents of Sulla and of Julius Caesar, evoked jealousy and hatred, especially as he already held more real power and prestige than they had had. What the riots and demands of the people in 22 demonstrate is that for many on the streets of Rome, this was not adequate. For a substantial number of citizens below the ranks of the senators and equestrians the careful and elaborate arrangements of 23 were not enough to mark and to guarantee the position of the man they saw as their supporter and saviour. Even if the *tribunicia potestas* had a plebeian flavour, it was insufficient for this purpose, and no tribune (even Publius Clodius, who in 58 BC introduced a free corn dole) had been able to effect what Augustus had done, and what the people wanted him to continue to do. They wanted Augustus to hold an office, whether the dictatorship or the perpetual consulship, which gave him a monarchical position in the state. This was not what Augustus wanted – his policy with regard to power and office in 23 and the years which followed was to secure the former without the latter; but in achieving this he had to take notice not only of those who did not want him holding power but also of those who wanted him to occupy a supreme office.

Another instance in 22 reveals again Augustus' policy in this area.

85. Aug. *RG* 15.1; Vell. Pat. 2.94.3; Suet. *Tib.* 8.
86. Aug. *RG* 5.1–3; Suet. *Aug.* 52; Dio Cass. 54.1.1–5.

He was, according to Dio, offered the censorship for life. In 29 and 28 he and Agrippa had conducted the business of the censors through a grant of *censoria potestas*, but this was only for a limited period.[87] Now he refused the censorship and saw to the appointment of Paulus Aemilius Lepidus and Lucius Munatius Plancus as censors after the traditional model. This return to Republican practice was not a success, and the censors achieved little (they were indeed the last two private citizens to hold the office together); Augustus himself at about this time made changes involving the behaviour of the citizenry. He revived a law passed by Julius Caesar which disbanded the associations (*collegia*), often of artisans, which had been behind some of the street violence of the late Republican period, excepting only the most ancient; and transferred the staging of festivals from the aediles to the praetors, putting limits on the amount of money that could be spent on the festivals. This last may seem surprising, given the lavish games that he had himself helped Marcellus to put on the previous year, but it was no doubt designed to prevent similar displays by others.[88]

On 1 September 22 Augustus dedicated a temple on the Capitoline to Jupiter Tonans ('the Thunderer') in thanksgiving for his escape from being struck by lightning while in Spain.[89] After that, he left Rome, travelling first to Sicily, and then to the eastern provinces. He did not return until 19. His absence again alarmed the populace in Rome, and at the elections in 22 for the consuls of 21 they chose only one consul, Marcus Lollius, keeping the other consulship vacant for Augustus, even though he had not been a candidate. The *princeps* refused either to accept the office or to return to Rome, and when the two men competing for the vacant position presented themselves to him, he ordered that the election should be held in their absence. After a tumultuous further election a second consul, Quintus Aemilius Lepidus, a member of one of the great families of the Republic, was chosen. Augustus sent Agrippa back from Lesbos, where he was based, to ensure that the capital remained under control while he himself was away.[90]

This was not the only reason for Agrippa's return to Rome. Since

87. See above, pp. 82–4.
88. Censorship and Augustus' measures: Vell. Pat. 2.95.3; Dio Cass. 54.2.1–5. *Collegia*: Suet. *Iul.* 42.3; *Aug.* 32.1; *ILS* 4966.
89. Aug. *RG* 19.2; Suet. *Aug.* 29.3; Dio Cass. 54.4.2–4. For the date, see the *Fast. Amit.* and *Fast. Arv.* (*Inscr. Ital.* 13.2.33, 193 and 504).
90. Dio Cass. 54.6.1–4.

the death of Marcellus in 23, Augustus' daughter Julia had been a widow. Agrippa was now to divorce his wife, Marcella, the daughter of Augustus' sister Octavia and the sister of the deceased Marcellus, to marry Julia. Plutarch claims that the idea came from Octavia, even though this involved the divorce of her own daughter; while Dio says that this was in part on the advice of Maecenas, that, since Augustus had made Agrippa so great, he must either have him as a son-in-law or have him killed.[91] Whether Maecenas ever made such a suggestion is unknowable, though the fact that Dio records it indicates that he at least did not think that Augustus had lost trust in Maecenas, despite the problems that the latter's indiscreet revelations to his wife had caused in the aftermath of the conspiracy of Caepio and Murena. In any case the advice both of Maecenas and of Octavia was right. If Augustus were to fall ill again, it would be to Agrippa that he would turn as an immediate successor, and with Agrippa as a close member of his own family he could expect or at least hope for sons who would take his line into a further generation of rulers of Rome. The dynastic policy of the *princeps*, which had received a severe setback with Marcellus' death, was to be firmly re-established. Marcella was divorced and Julia and Agrippa married (as in her marriage to Marcellus, in the absence of the bride's father) in 21.

Meanwhile Augustus was moving slowly eastwards.[92] After leaving Rome he spent a short time in Sicily, where he established colonies of veterans in Syracuse and a number of other cities on the northern and eastern sides of the island, before sailing to Greece. There he rewarded the Spartans, who had provided protection for Livia Drusilla, now the wife of Augustus, when with her first husband and her infant son she fled from Italy in 40 after the Perusine war; and moreover Sparta had, unlike other Greek cities, supported Caesar at Actium, when the present ruler of the city, Gaius Iulius Eurycles, had commanded a warship, as a result of which he was granted Roman citizenship. The island of Cythera, off the southernmost point of Spartan territory, which Augustus gave to the city, was later said by the geographer Strabo to be in Eurycles' private ownership.[93] Athens, by contrast, which had supported

---

91. Plut. *Ant.* 87.4; Dio Cass. 54.6.5.
92. Dio Cass. 54.7.1–3.
93. Plut. *Ant.* 67; Strabo, 8.5.1.

Antonius, was deprived of the nearby islands of Aegina and Eretria, from which they had drawn tax revenue.

From Athens, Augustus sailed to Samos for the winter of 21/20 and in the following year proceeded to the provinces of Asia and Bithyinia, dealing again with the affairs of the cities, rewarding some and punishing others. These were public provinces with senatorial proconsular governors, and it was no doubt in view of his imminent departure for such areas that Augustus had been given *imperium* superior to that of other proconsuls in 23.[94] He was thereby enabled to deprive the city of Cyzicus in Asia of its free-city status, the result of disturbances there which had led to the deaths of some Roman citizens. When he reached Syria (one of Caesar's provinces) he imposed the same penalty on Tyre and Sidon, which had also been the sites of internal political disturbance.[95] The main aim of his presence in Syria, however, was to deal with the potential threat from the Parthians. As we have seen, he had received an embassy from the Parthian king, Phraates, in 23 and heard the case put in person by the pretender to the throne, Tiridates. Then he had pursued a policy of no intervention, but had demanded the return of the standards and prisoners captured from Crassus in 53 and from Antonius' generals during the latter's failed invasion in the 30s. It is clear that many in Rome expected a military invasion of Parthia, and this was trumpeted by poets at the time. It might have happened: not only was Augustus present with his army, but in nearby Armenia his stepson Tiberius was engaged with an army in installing a new king, Tigranes. In the event, Phraates decided that the better course was to carry out the agreement that had been put to him in 23 and handed over the standards.[96]

While Augustus was scoring these diplomatic (or, as he was to describe them, military) successes in the east, the problems that he had left behind in Rome re-emerged. Agrippa had succeeded in controlling the political turmoil that had caused problems that had erupted in 22 and two consuls, Marcus Appuleius and Publius Silius Nerva, were elected in 21 for the following year. In 20, however, Agrippa, now married to Augustus' daughter, was away from the

---

94. See above, p. 101.
95. Dio Cass. 54.7.4–8.
96. See above, pp. 102–3. For the poets, see Prop. 3.4; Hor. *Carm.* 3.5.1–12. Tiberius in Armenia: Vell. Pat. 2.122.1; Tacitus, *Ann.* 2.3.2; Suet. *Tib.* 9.1. Augustus and Phraates: Aug. *RG* 29.2; Strabo, 16.1.28; Vell. Pat. 2.91.1; Suet. *Aug.* 21.3; Livy, *Per.* 141.

city in Gaul. He had been there before, from 40 to 37, which is probably when he had established the basis of an important network of roads, based on Lugdunum (modern Lyons), a city founded in 43 on the instruction of the senate by Lucius Munatius Plancus, in the midst of the military manoeuvrings between Lepidus, Antonius and Caesar.[97] In the following year (19 BC) Agrippa was in Spain, completing at last the conquest of the north-west of the peninsula.[98] The elections in 20 again produced only one consul, Gaius Sentius Saturninus, the other consulship again being kept for Augustus who again refused it. Sentius, admired by Velleius as a consul in the old style, was faced at the subsequent elections with the candidacy of Marcus Egnatius Rufus. This man was a hero of the plebs, because as aedile in 22 he had used his own slaves to put out fires in the city, and on that basis had been elected praetor for the following year. He now was attempting to be elected consul. Sentius, as presiding consul, initially refused to allow him to stand (a two-year gap was required between praetorship and consulship), but then, when this failed, stated that even if Egnatius achieved the necessary votes he would not declare him consul, an essential part of the electoral process. Popular disturbances followed and the senate voted a bodyguard for the consul. Sentius was unwilling to use this, and the senate sent two ambassadors to Augustus, who resolved the matter by appointing one of them, Quintus Lucretius Vespillo, consul. Egnatius and his gang of supporters were rounded up, imprisoned and put to death.[99]

Although later writers put Egnatius into the lists they assembled of those who attempted to assassinate Augustus, and Velleius accuses him specifically of plotting murder, he is in a category quite different from the others who appear in these collections.[100] Unlike the others, Egnatius had a popular following, which Augustus appears to have noticed already in 22, the year of Egnatius' success in his aedileship through the use of his private fire-fighters. In that same year, according to Dio in a passage that has no mention of Egnatius, Augustus ordered that henceforth the curule aediles should

---

97. Lugdunum: Dio Cass. 46.50.4–6. Agrippa's roads: Strabo, 4.6.11.
98. See above, p. 92.
99. Vell. Pat. 2.913–92.5; Dio Cass. 53.24.4–6, 54.10.1–2. Dio puts Egnatius' aedileship in 26 BC (see F. G. B. Millar, *A Study of Cassius Dio*, Oxford: Oxford University Press, 1964, 87–8).
100. Vell. Pat. 2.93.1; Suet. *Aug.* 19.1; Seneca, *Brev. vit.* 4.5; *Clem.* 1.9.6; Tacitus, *Ann.* 1.10.

be responsible for control of fires and gifted 600 slaves for the purpose.[101] This looks very like a response to Egnatius, a trumping of his ace by showing that it was Augustus, not Egnatius, who was the true friend of the people. The honours which accompanied the *princeps'* return to Rome later in 19 seem in part to be designed to promote the same message.

Augustus spent the winter of 20/19 on Samos, where he was visited again by embassies, not least from India. He proceeded from there to Athens, where he was joined by the poet Vergil, who had almost completed his great epic poem, the *Aeneid*, but was now ill. Augustus crossed to Italy, landing at Brundisium, where Vergil died on 21 September. He was 51, seven years older than Augustus. The *princeps* headed to Rome, being met in Campania by a delegation, sent by decree of the senate, of praetors and tribunes of the plebs, accompanied by the consul Lucretius Vespillo. (Dio says that Augustus gave this deputation the slip by entering the city at night.) In honour of his return to the city on 12 October an altar to Fortuna Redux ('Fortune the Home-Bringer') was vowed by the senate to stand at the Porta Capena, where the Appian way entered the city walls. It was dedicated on 15 December. On 12 October an annual sacrifice was to be made there by the consuls and the Vestals; and before the end of the reign the day had gained the name Augustalia.[102]

Although he did not triumph on his return or even, as Dio at one point suggests, celebrate the lesser observance of an *ovatio*, Augustus certainly counted his recovery of the standards from Phraates as a military victory, describing the Parthians as being compelled to hand them over and humbly to request the friendship of the Roman people.[103] The event was acclaimed by the poets, and a scene of a barbarian handing over standards to a Roman officer appears prominently on the breastplate that Augustus wears in the famous Prima Porta statue of the *princeps* as well as on many coins

---

101. Dio Cass. 54.2.4.
102. Aug. *RG* 11–12.1; Dio Cass. 54.9.7–10 and 10.3–4. See J. Scheid, 'To honour the *princeps* and venerate the gods: public cult, neighbourhood cults and imperial cult in Augustan Rome', in Edmondson, *Augustus*, 273–99, at 289–90. On the death of Vergil, Suet. *Vita Vergili* 35.
103. Dio says that he entered Rome on horseback (Dio Cass. 54.8.4), which would imply an *ovatio*, but later says that he entered Rome quietly (54.10.4). Augustus states in the *Res Gestae* that he only celebrated two *ovationes*, which were, as Suetonius notes, those of 40 and 36 (Aug. *RG* 4.1; Suet. *Aug.* 22.1). On the recovery of the standards, see Aug. *RG* 29.2.

of the period.[104] The standards were to be placed in the temple of Mars Ultor which Augustus had vowed after the battles of Philippi in 42, but which was not dedicated until 2 BC, and probably were kept in the temple of Jupiter on the Capitoline hill until that date.[105]

The glory of military victory was central to Augustus' presentation of himself as the leader of the Roman people. This was to result in a major change in the pattern of the celebration of the triumph. Although several proconsuls had triumphed in the years since the victory of Actium, the last non-member of the imperial family to do so, Lucius Cornelius Balbus, was allowed to celebrate his victories in Africa on 27 March 19 BC, while Augustus was on his way back from Samos. The ending of the traditional Republican practice at this moment was not accidental, as can be seen from the fact that the *Fasti Triumphales*, which list all the triumphs from earliest times and were set up in the Augustan period, ends with Balbus' triumph at the very bottom of the last slab of the inscription.[106] No further entries appear, or were intended to appear, not even the *ovatio* which Tiberius celebrated in 9 BC. The triumph, as a sign of the victory of a Roman general, holding the power (*imperium*) of the Roman people and the approval of their gods (*auspicia*), was at an end. Henceforth both *imperium* and *auspicia* were in the hands of the *princeps* and of those members of his family to whom he assigned them.[107] In its place victorious commanders, including those within the imperial family, might be awarded the decorations which had previously been part of the accoutrements of a *triumphator* (called the *ornamenta triumphalia*), but not the great public religious procession that had filled the streets of Republican Rome.

Dio also records other actions of Augustus and powers given to him in connection with his return to the city.[108] His two stepsons,

---

104. Prop. 4.6.79–84; Hor. *Carm.* 4.15.6–8, *Epist.* 1.12.27–8; Ovid, *Fast.* 5.579–96, 6.465–8. For the statue and coins, see Zanker, *The Power of Images*, 186–92.

105. Dio (54.8.3) states that a temple of Mars Ultor on the Capitoline was to be built, but there is no other evidence for this structure, and it is probable that he has confused a decree that the standards should be placed in the temple with its actual construction. See C. J. Simpson, 'The date of dedication of the temple of Mars Ultor', *Journal of Roman Studies* 67 (1977), 91–4. For the vow after Philippi, see above, p. 41.

106. *Inscr. Ital.* 13.1.86–7. M. Beard, *The Roman Triumph*, Cambridge, MA, and London: Harvard University Press, 2007, 61–71.

107. See the comments of Velleius (2.115.3) and Dio (54.24.7–8) on Tiberius and Agrippa.

108. Dio Cass. 54.10.4–7.

Figure 6 The Prima Porta statue of Augustus (© Alinari)

Tiberius and Drusus, the sons of Livia Drusilla by her husband
Tiberius Claudius Nero, were given the rank of praetors within the
hierarchy of the senate and permission to stand for office five years
earlier than the constitutional laws required. Augustus himself was
made supervisor of morality for a period of five years and given the
power of the censors for the same period. He was also given the

Figure 7 Detail of Prima Porta statue of Augustus, showing the breastplate
(© Alinari)

power of the consuls for life, so that he was to be accompanied by
the twelve lectors with their ceremonial *fasces* and to have a seat in
the senate between those of the two consuls of the year; and was to
be able to pass any laws he thought fit, which were to be called
'Augustan laws'. On some of these, Dio is wrong: the supervision of
laws and morals is explicitly denied by Augustus himself in the *Res*

Gestae; and, as he also states there, the legislation which he did indeed propose and carry over the next few years was brought forward through the *tribunicia potestas*, which he had held since 23.[109] It may be that Dio has confused measures urged by the senate but refused by Augustus with those that were accepted. The question of the consular power for life is more difficult, and has been a matter of debate among scholars.[110] Since the arrangements made in January 27, he had held the power of a consul (*imperium consulare*), first as consul and then, after his resignation of the consulship in 23, as proconsul. The difference between a consul and a proconsul under the Republic was twofold: a proconsul had to give up his *imperium* on entering the city of Rome; and a proconsul could not carry out the functions that belonged to the consulship, most notably the convening of the senate and the presidency of elections for the consuls and praetors of the following year. The first of these restrictions no longer applied to Augustus, since the grants which followed his resignation in 23 included an exemption from the need to relinquish his *imperium* on crossing the *pomerium*. The same was true of the convenorship of the senate.[111] It might be thought that the problems that had attended the elections in 23, 22 and 19 were to be dealt with by giving Augustus a position from which he could, as president at the elections, control the chaos that had resulted from his absence; but in fact there is no indication that he acted in this way in the years which followed. Assuming that Dio (our only source on this matter) was right, what was it that Augustus gained in 19? The probable answer is that this was a change not to his powers (a change which he hardly needed) but to the way in which the powers he had were presented while he was in Rome. As Dio says, the result of what happened in 19 was that from then on Augustus, accompanied by the twelve *fasces* or on his seat between the consuls, was seen within the city as a holder of the *imperium consulare*. The people of Rome had, by their demonstrations during the elections of the previous years, demanded that Augustus should at least be one of their consuls, if not sole consul or even dictator. He was not prepared to do any of these things; but his appearance in Rome with the lictors and the *fasces* and his being seated between the consuls would emphasise that he was at least as significant a

109. Aug. *RG* 6.1–2.
110. See now the excellent review and discussion by Ferrary, 'The powers of Augustus', 103–25.
111. See above, pp. 99–101.

person as the consuls, indeed more so because, unlike them, he would be there from year to year, not just for an annual term of office. He did not need more powers – he had all he needed already – but he did need a way of demonstrating his position to the people. That is what he will have achieved by the honours he now had gained.

Establishing the New Age: Augustus and Agrippa, 18–12 BC

If the changes in 19 BC were more to do with the presentation of Augustus' power than with the constitutional arrangements that had underlain it since 27, these arrangements themselves soon required attention. The ten-year long tenure of his massive collection of *provinciae* was due to expire in 17 and was in fact renewed a year early in 18, though only for a period of five years. The areas which were 'Caesar's provinces' were not quite identical to those he had held in 27: Cyprus and Gallia Narbonensis had become 'public provinces' in 20, on the grounds, so Dio tells us, that they no longer needed the military support that Augustus could provide.[112] There was another and more significant difference between what happened in 27 and the extension of Augustus' powers in 18. The earlier arrangements had been made when he was consul and expected to remain so at least for the immediate future. Of the modifications which were made after his resignation of the consulship in 23, some (certainly the grant of *tribunicia potestas* and the rights to present motions to the senate, which extended that grant) were permanent; but others were related directly to his holding of the *imperium consulare* as a proconsul (that is, acting as though a consul) in control of his provinces. These included not having to surrender his *imperium* on entering the city of Rome, the superior nature of his *imperium* over that of proconsuls in public provinces, and the consular honours in the display of his *imperium* when he was in Rome, granted in 19. The renewal of his provinces for a further five years in 18 must have included these elements as well, and as such constituted a combination which, along with the *tribunicia potestas*, represented the constitutional basis of the position of the *princeps*.

The significance of this is underlined by measures taken at the same time with regard to Agrippa. He was not only Augustus' son-in-law as a result of his marriage to Julia but now the father of the

---

112. Dio Cass. 54.12.4. On Cyprus and Gallia Narbonensis, see Dio Cass. 54.4.1.

princeps' grandson Gaius, who had been born in 20. Not only was his *imperium*, assigned to him in 23, renewed (and it is probable that it was at this time that it was made superior to that of proconsuls, on the pattern of Augustus' own, and for five years), but also he was given the *tribunicia potestas*, though (unlike that of Augustus) it was for a period of five years only.[113] The parallels and the differences between Agrippa's position and that of Augustus make it clear that Agrippa was now the second man in the Roman world. His son was Augustus' nearest male blood-relative and, should Augustus die soon (as he nearly did in 23), it would be to Agrippa that his work would be entrusted.

The wish of the senate and people in 19 that Augustus should have supervision of morals and censorial powers, mentioned by both Dio and Augustus himself, indicates a desire for a change. Both the chaos which had attended the elections in the absence of the *princeps* and the repeated demands that he should be present and in control, manifested in popular attempts to make him consul or even dictator, will have shown what might happen to the stability which he had brought to life in Rome and the desire of many, among the people as well as the senatorial class, for firmer foundations in both political and moral spheres. The censors that had been appointed in 22 in the traditional fashion had failed to achieve anything of the sort,[114] and the censorial power, given to Augustus in 19, enabled him to carry out at least one of their functions. In 18 he conducted another review of the membership of the senate, as he and Agrippa had done in 29 and 28.[115] Then the number of senators had been reduced from about one thousand by the removal of 190 senators. Now, according to Dio, Augustus wanted to bring it down to 300, traditionally regarded as the size of the body in the middle period of the Republic, but was persuaded by the outcry from senators to reduce it to 600 instead. If Dio is right, it is probable that the smaller figure was part of Augustus' propaganda rather than a serious intention, since the number of tasks that senators were called upon to fulfil in the structures of government would have made such a drastic reduction inoperable. Even so, the reduction by over 200 was bound to be difficult and contentious and, to reduce the appearance of his creating a senate chosen entirely by himself, he began by setting up

113. *Imperium*: Dio Cass. 54.12.4 (see above, pp. 99 and 101). *Tribunicia potestas*: Aug. *RG* 6.2; Tacitus, *Ann.* 3.56
114. See above, p. 106.
115. See above, p. 84.

a complex process whereby thirty were chosen by him to make a list of five each (not including any of their relatives), one of whom was chosen by lot to be a senator. The resulting thirty men then repeated the process, the intention being to continue by this means until the requisite number was achieved. The process was clearly meant to be scrupulously fair, and even the original thirty did not become members of the senate automatically, but only if they were included in the lists at a subsequent stage and then selected by lot. The very complexity of this scheme produced some interesting results: the eminent legal scholar Marcus Antistius Labeo included in his list of five the name of Marcus Lepidus, the former triumvir and still holder of the office of high priest (*pontifex maximus*), who had been living in exile at Circeii in southern Latium since he had been removed from the triumvirate in 36. Not only did Augustus dislike and despise Lepidus, but his son (also called Marcus Lepidus) had been involved in a plot to kill Augustus shortly after the battle of Actium. In Dio's version of the story, Labeo was challenged by Augustus, on the grounds that the selection for the list was to be of the best men, and indeed both he and subsequent selectors swore an oath that they would only choose such. Labeo is said to have replied that all he had done was to keep in the senate someone whom Augustus was prepared to allow to continue as *pontifex*.[116] In any case Augustus decided after the process had been going for a short time that the lists were being interfered with and made the later selections himself. He did, however, allow those who were not selected to retain some of the privileges allowed to senators, such as the distinctive dress and reserved seats in the theatre.[117]

The object of this reconstruction of the membership of the senate seems to have been the restoring of the senate as an assembly of the 'best' men in the state, something which in the past was believed to have happened through the normal workings of the Republic but which it now needed deliberate and radical intervention to attain. The way in which this was to be achieved was not (as the process devised for the selection of senators in 18 might have led us to expect) by turning the senate into a meritocracy, with members chosen on the basis of their ability, but by an increasingly formal division between senators and their families and other members of

116. Dio Cass. 54.15.4–8. Suetonius, *Aug.* 54, has a slightly different version. On Lepidus, see above, pp. 57–8; and on his son, see Livy, *Per.* 133; Vell. Pat. 2.88; Appian, *B Civ.* 4.50.
117. Dio Cass. 54.13–14.

the propertied classes, who were members of the equestrian order. Already in 22 the children and descendants of senators had been banned from appearing in theatrical performances, and in legislation passed in 18 further restrictions were placed on those whom members of senatorial families could marry.[118] It was also probably at this time that Augustus introduced an increased property requirement for members of the senate of 1,000,000 sesterces, as opposed to the previous figure of 400,000 sesterces, which was the same as that required for membership of the equestrian order.[119] The new figure was not exceptionally high since, although some senators' property fell below this and they appealed to Augustus for grants to bring them up to the level required, the great majority would have been able to meet it easily. The significance of the change was that it separated senators and their families from the rest of the population; and it may be at this point that Augustus began encouraging sons of senators to attend meetings of the senate with their fathers, and permitted them, alone among non-senators, to wear the senatorial tunic with a broad purple stripe once they had assumed the *toga virilis*, which marked their coming of age.[120] The intention was clearly that membership of the senate would pass down the generations of a senatorial family, so that the education of the young within such families should include experience of the senate at the earliest opportunity.

The laws which Augustus proposed and had carried in 18, using his *tribunicia potestas*, often showed a similar preoccupation with the importance and the dignity of the senatorial class, though their primary and announced intention was often different. Perhaps the most controversial related to the encouragement and regulation of marriage. There are indications in the literary sources (and especially in the poets) that there had been attempts to mount a campaign against adultery and extramarital sexual relations, but it seems that this did not result in any legislation.[121] The precise content of

---

118. Dio Cass. 54.2.5 and 16.2. On the legislation of 18, see below, p. 119.
119. Dio Cass. 54.17.3. Dio's dating of this change is not clear at this point, but it was certainly in place five years later (Dio Cass. 54.26.3). Suetonius, *Aug.* 41.1, gives different figures, but is probably confused by a specific case in AD 4 (Dio Cass. 55.13.60). On the senatorial census, see C. Nicolet, 'Le cens sénatorial sous la République et sous Auguste', *Journal of Roman Studies* 66 (1976), 20–38.
120. Suet. *Aug.* 38.2.
121. Hor. *Carm.* 3.6 and 24; Prop. 2.7; Tacitus, *Ann.* 3.28 (dating some unspecified action to Augustus' sixth consulship in 28 BC). See E. Badian, 'A phantom marriage law', *Philologus* 129 (1985), 82–98.

Augustus' laws is complicated by the fact that his legislation in 18 was later modified by a subsequent enactment in AD 9, the *lex Papia Poppaea*, and the two are often discussed in legal sources as though they constituted a single law. The *lex Iulia de maritandis ordinibus* ('about the marriage of different classes', the title given to the law of 18 in both legal and literary sources[122]) is presented by Dio as removing obstacles to marriage between free persons and freed slaves, but also as excluding senators from this option, and Ulpian states that this applied also to their sons.[123] This suggests that marriage was to be promoted, but that the law was careful to require that the bloodline of senatorial families should be kept free from that of former slaves. There were also direct encouragements to those who were married with children. One chapter of the law stated that of the two consuls elected for each year, the senior should be the one with the most children (including in the total any that had been killed in war); and it may be that the precedence accorded to senators who had children or were married in the drawing of lots for the assignment of the public provinces, which Dio mentions when describing the reorganisation of the provinces in 27, was introduced now.[124] On the other hand those who were unmarried were not normally permitted to attend public spectacles, and were penalised by being prohibited from being heirs or receiving bequests, though women were exempted from this prohibition for a year after the death of a husband or six months after a divorce.[125] Legacies that the unmarried were unable to take under the law went to the treasury. Childless husbands and wives who were above the age regarded as appropriate for having children (twenty-five in the case of the man and twenty for the woman) could only inherit one tenth of the other's estate, but if they had a child between them they could take

---

122. Livy, *Per.* 59; Suet. *Aug.* 34.1; Apuleius, *Apol.* 88; Gaius, *Inst.* 1.178; Ulpian, *Dig.* 38.11.1.1; Paul, *Dig.* 37.14.6.4. On the *lex Papia Poppaea*, see below, pp. 181–2.

123. Dio Cass. 54.16.2. See also Ulpian, *Tit.* 13.1, who attributes this specifically to the *lex Iulia*, and applies the exclusion to senators and their sons. It may also have forbidden wills which required the beneficiary not to marry, though this may belong to the *lex Papia* (Terentius Clemens, *Dig.* 35.1.64; Paulus, *Sent.* 3.4b.2).

124. Gellius, *NA* 2.15.3–8; Dio Cass. 53.16.3.

125. Spectacles: *SC de ludis saecularibus* (*EJ* 30A), where special permission was given to allow the unmarried to attend the Saecular Games of 17 BC. Inheritance: Gaius, *Inst.* 2.226; Ulpian, *Tit.* 14. It may be that the unmarried could inherit within the family (see A. Wallace-Hadrill, 'Family and inheritance in the Augustan marriage laws', in Edmondson, *Augustus*, 250–74 (= *Proceedings of the Cambridge Philological Society*, n.s. 27 (1981), 58–80), 256–60 and 271–4), but, even if this is true, it is not clear whether this important exception was part of the *lex Iulia* or of the later *lex Papia Poppaea*.

the whole.[126] Again, the intention is to encourage marriage and child-bearing, though in the matter of rewards and privileges the law seems to be focused particularly on those involved in the political life of the city and whose expectations of benefits from inheritance and legacies were substantial.

At about the same time Augustus carried another *lex Iulia*, in this case on adultery and sex outside marriage. The law forbade sexual relations of a married woman other than with her husband (*adulterium* properly so called); and it also banned those between a man and a girl, an unmarried woman or a widow (this being termed *stuprum*), where the woman concerned was not a slave or engaged in a disreputable trade, such as prostitution or working in a tavern.[127] Adultery was applied as a technical term specifically to the married woman: a husband who discovered his wife's adultery was required to divorce her before making an accusation under the law, and if he failed to do so might be charged himself with acting as a pimp (*lenocinium*) on the grounds of his complaisance. Only after the erring wife had been condemned could he proceed against the lover. A husband who had sexual relations outside marriage could not be accused of adultery on that ground alone, but only if his partner in the offence was herself a married woman.[128]

Augustus' law was clearly focused on adultery as an offence against the family: the father of the offending woman had the right to kill his daughter and her lover if he caught them in the act in his own house or that of his son-in-law, but only if he killed them both.[129] The husband had only the right to kill the lover, and only then if the latter was caught in the act in the husband's own house and was someone who had already been condemned for some other offence or who practised a disreputable trade (such as a pimp or a theatrical performer); he was not permitted to kill his wife, though,

126. Ulpian, *Tit.* 15 and 16.
127. Paulus, *Sent.* 2.26.11; *Dig.* 48.5.14 (13).2 (Ulpian).
128. For the main texts on the *lex Iulia de adulteriis coercendis*, see *Dig.*48.5; Paulus, *Sent.* 2.26; *Collatio* 4.2.2–12. It is probably the background to the debate in the senate related by Dio Cass. 54.16.3–6 under the year 18. For a detailed exposition, see O. F. Robinson, *The Criminal Law of Ancient Rome*, London: Duckworth, 1995, 58–68, which also relates the subsequent development of the law on adultery and sexual misdemeanours. On the context and significance of the law, see also D. Cohen, 'The Augustan law on adultery: the social and cultural context', in D. I. Kertzer and R. R. Saller (eds), *The Family in Italy from Antiquity to the Present*, New Haven and London: Yale University Press, 1991, 109–26.
129. *Collatio* 4.2.6–7 (Paul).

if he had done away with the lover, he had to divorce her; and he was allowed to detain the lover for twenty hours in order to obtain testimony. The father and the husband had sixty days to bring an accusation against the wife, after which it was open to anyone to do so for a further four months. This set of rules, placing primary responsibility for action on the father and on the husband of the wife reflects the traditional Roman view of the nature of the family, with the father, the *paterfamilias*, at its head, and indeed before Augustus' legislation it appears that cases of adultery were dealt with within the family. We know of no laws on the subject from the Republican period, and, although we are told that the *lex Iulia* revoked all previous laws on matters with which it dealt,[130] this probably relates to other sexual offences, covered by the term *stuprum*, on which there was earlier legislation. What Augustus seems to be doing is limiting by legislation the power and activity of the *familia*, and bringing it out of the privacy of the household into the public arena: the new law made adultery a criminal offence, with a new court (the *quaestio de adulteriis*) to try and punish offenders, and, like the *lex de ordinibus maritandis*, it introduced statutory provisions to enforce what were seen as morally desirable aims. The penalties for those condemned were severe but at the time of the law's enactment probably largely financial. A woman convicted of adultery lost half of the dowry she had brought to the marriage and one third of her other property, and was debarred from a further marriage. The man involved, if subsequently convicted, lost half his property.[131]

In addition to these laws, which were novel in that they related to matters which had not previously been the subject of statute law, Augustus also legislated in areas which were already dealt with under laws in the Republican period. Dio, in his account of Augustus' legislation in 18, mentions a law on electoral bribery, which excluded those convicted from holding a magistracy for five years. This was no doubt but one of the provisions of the *lex Iulia de ambitu*, but little else is known about it. Later, when the law was applied to elections to local councils in towns (*municipia*), fines

---

130. *Collatio* 4.2.2 (Paul).
131. Paulus, *Sent.* 2.26.14 states that *relegatio* (deportation) to different islands was also a penalty for both convicted parties. This was certainly the case in the following century (Pliny, *Ep.* 6.31.4–6), and Augustus himself exiled his daughter and grand-daughter to islands on charges of adultery (Vell. Pat. 2.100.5; Seneca, *Ben.* 6.32; Suet. *Aug.* 65.1; see below, pp. 157 and 179). It may be that the *relegatio* provision was added as a result of Augustus' action.

were imposed, and in cases where violence was used the penalty was deportation to an island; but it is quite unclear whether these penalties were specified in the original law.[132] Augustus was following a long tradition of laws against bribery which extended back into the early Republic.[133] Similarly a law limiting expenditure on luxuries (*lex sumptuaria*), which is listed by Suetonius along with the other laws passed at this time, followed a series of laws, beginning with the *lex Fannia* of 161 BC, in limiting the expenditure that was allowed on banquets, with increased disbursements being permitted for festivals, weddings and other special occasions.[134]

It was probably in the following year that Augustus promulgated further legislation on another topic which had been the subject of several laws in the Republican period, namely the organisation of the law courts; two *leges Iuliae iudiciariae*, one on private law procedures and one on the public courts, are referred to in the legal sources. Dio mentions provisions which probably were part of these laws as having been ordered by Augustus in 17; and Modestinus, writing in the third century AD, associates the *lex Iulia iudiciaria* with the *lex Iulia de ambitu*.[135] Both laws seem designed to tidy up and to streamline the judicial processes in the two main areas of the Roman courts: thus in the sphere of private law the old and highly formalised *legis actio* process for actions before the praetor in Rome was ended in almost all cases and it was required that they be conducted under the formulary process.[136] This had been introduced at some point in the late third or second century BC, and consisted of the praetor deciding whether a case brought before him was a cause of action that he was prepared to hear; he promulgated a list of such actions in the edict he issued at the outset of his tenure of the praetorship, and where a particular case was covered by one of the causes in the edict, he prepared a *formula* which made clear the legal basis of the case and appointed a single judge (*iudex*) to decide whether or not the complaint of the plaintiff as defined in the

132. Dio Cass. 54.16.1. On fines in local elections, see *Dig.* 48.14 (Modestinus); and on *deportatio* for the use of violence, Paulus, *Sent.* 5.30a.
133. See A. Lintott, 'Electoral bribery in the Roman Republic', *Journal of Roman Studies* 80 (1990), 1–16.
134. Suet. *Aug.* 34; Gellius, *NA* 2.24.14, who gives a history of *leges sumptuariae*.
135. Dio Cass. 54.18.2–3; *Dig.* 48.14.1.4 (Modestinus).
136. Gaius, *Inst.* 4.30–1. The exceptions Gaius mentions are proceedings in the court of the *centumviri*, which dealt with important cases of inheritance, and cases of *damnum infectum*, involving damage to property caused by the state of a neighbour's adjoining property.

formula was in fact justified, and to condemn or absolve the defendant in terms laid down in the *formula*. Already in the late Republic the praetor's edict had become largely standard, with the contents varying little if at all from year to year. Less is known of the changes to public law, but it appears that here too the emphasis was on adjusting the proceedings of the *quaestiones*, which now included the new *quaestio de adulteriis*, which Augustus had introduced the previous year. The number of advocates that could be used was limited and they were prevented from taking fees; the wording of an accusation was specified; and fines for either the accused or the prosecutors who visited the homes of jurors were laid down.[137]

These technical alterations to the processes of the courts might seem to belong to a quite different area of Augustus' policy from the laws on bribery, marriage and adultery, which modern scholars often describe as 'moral' or 'social' legislation. What links all these together is that they were all enacted by laws proposed by Augustus, using his *tribunicia potestas* (and thus fit in with his remark in the *Res Gestae* that in this way he carried out the reforms to law and customs that the senate wanted, without the need for him to be given a special office for this purpose[138]); and they were all concerned with the application of the law through the courts. Augustus did not of course confine his reforms to juridical matters, and in 18 he also, for instance, made grants to provide food and money to relieve problems caused by shortages of grain and altered the arrangements for grain distribution that he had set up in 22, replacing the two senators responsible with four, chosen by lot from a pool nominated by serving magistrates.[139] The laws that he brought forward in 18 and 17, however, had a special place in his avowed intention of restoring and renewing the life and institutions of the Roman people. In his account of his achievements at the end of his life, he records the growth in the numbers of citizens recorded in the censuses conducted during his reign, and concludes with the statement that 'by means of new laws brought in under my sponsorship, I revived many exemplary ancestral practices which were by then dying out in our generation, and I myself handed down to later generations

137. Advocates: Asconius, *In Scaur.* 20 (C); Dio Cass. 54.18.2. Accusation: *Dig.* 48.2.3.pr (Paul). Visiting jurors: *Dig.* 48.14.1.4 (Modestinus); this is probably the explanation of Dio's surprising remark that jurors were not allowed to visit anyone's house during their year of service (Dio Cass. 54.18.3).
138. Aug. *RG* 6.1–2. See above, pp. 113–14.
139. Aug. *RG* 18; Dio Cass. 54.17.1. See above, pp. 104–5.

exemplary practices for them to imitate'.[140] Suetonius records an edict of Augustus which may well come from these years, in which he expresses the hope that he may be able firmly to establish the state (*res publica*) and may be known to posterity as the originator of the best possible form of government (*optimi status auctor*).[141] Whatever particular changes he was trying to achieve in the structures of Roman society and morality, the overt and public aim was to re-create Rome after the breakdown of its life in the years that had followed the death of his adoptive father in 44, and this renewal was to be achieved as much by the new laws that he put in place in 18 and 17 as by the re-establishment of Roman power from Spain to Parthia in the years immediately preceding. The social and juridical reforms, along with the military and diplomatic successes, were to mark the beginning of a new age for a Rome, re-established and revived by the new regime.

So it was that from 31 May to 3 June of the year 17 BC the Saecular Games were celebrated, including a variety of dramatic performances and followed by more theatrical shows, chariot races and a display of hunting extending over a further seven days. This extensive and spectacular celebration was based on festivities which had been held every hundred years to mark the end of each century from the founding of the city, with sacrifices to the gods of the underworld, Dis Pater and Proserpina.[142] Augustus' version seems to have been different from these in a number of significant ways, and was based on a Sibylline oracle, probably 'discovered' when in 18 BC, at the *princeps'* command, the books containing these oracles were copied afresh and kept by the college of fifteen priests responsible for them (the *quindecemviri sacris faciundis*), of which he himself was a senior member.[143] This laid down that the *saeculum* which was being celebrated was not, as had previously been held, 100 years but 110,

---

140. Legibus no[vi]s m[e auctore l]atis m[ulta e]xempla maiorum exolescentia iam ex nostro [saecul]o red[uxi et ipse] multarum rer[um exe]mpla imitanda pos[teris tradidi] (Aug. *RG* 8.5).

141. Suet. *Aug.* 28.2.

142. Censorinus, writing in the third century AD, cites Varro and Livy (Censorinus, *DN* 17.8). See M. Beard, J. North and S. Price, *Religions of Rome*, Cambridge: Cambridge University Press, 1998, 1.201–6.

143. Dio Cass. 54.17.2. For the text of the oracle, see Phlegon, *De macrobiis* 5.2, and Zosimus, 2.6. It is translated in D. Braund, *Augustus to Nero: A Sourcebook on Roman History, 31 BC–AD 68*, Totowa, NJ: Barnes and Noble, 1985, 296–7. Although the text may contain some archaic elements, much of it seems to be of later, and probably Augustan, date (H. Diels, *Sibyllinische Blätter*, Berlin: Georg Reimer, 1890, 13–15).

which led, most conveniently, to the date of the fifth celebration being in or about 17 BC. The details of the event were recorded on an inscription, set up by the river Tiber, where on each of the three nights of the festival the sacrifices were made, which has survived largely intact.[144] The proceedings were as prescribed by the oracle, with sacrifices not to the gods of the underworld but, by night, to the Fates (Moirae), the goddess of childbirth (Ilythia) and Mother Earth (Terra Mater), and by day to Jupiter, Juno, Apollo and Diana, ending with a hymn, sung by a choir of twenty-seven boys and twenty-seven girls, first on the Palatine at the temple of Apollo, which adjoined the house of Augustus, and then on the Capitoline. The hymn, as the inscription records, was written for the occasion by the poet Horace. This poem, the *Carmen Saeculare*, brings together themes which stand out in the whole celebration. The choir prays to Ilythia for protection for Roman mothers in childbirth, and that she should bless the decrees of the senate and the law on marriage; and that Apollo and Diana should aid Augustus, described as the descendant of Anchises and the goddess Venus (the parents of Aeneas whose son, Iulus, was claimed as the ancestor of the Julian family[145]), who, fierce in war but mild to the defeated, has made the Parthian fear Rome's might by land and sea, and brought respectful embassies from the proud Scythians and now even from India. Already, they sing, Good Faith, Peace, Honour, ancient Modesty and neglected Virtue dare to return, along with blessed Abundance; and they pray that Apollo, accepting the offerings made at the altars at his temple on the Palatine, may bring in another and better age; and that Diana, who inhabits her temple on the Aventine, may listen to the prayers of the college of the *quindecemviri* and hear the vows made by the singing children.

The emphasis in Augustus' secular celebration is on the dawn of a new age, brought in by the victories of Roman arms and the restoration of the ancient Roman virtues. On each of the three nights of the festival itself, after the sacrifices by the Tiber, 110 married women (one for each year of the *saeculum*), specially selected by the *quindecemviri*, conducted banquets in the presence of the goddesses Juno and Diana; and on the second day, when sacrifice was made to Queen Juno on the Capitoline, they made a special prayer to the

---

144. *ILS* 5050. Translations in Braund, *Augustus to Nero*, 293–6, and Beard et al., *Religions of Rome*, 2.139–44.
145. Verg. *Aen.* 1.287–8.

goddess on behalf of the Roman people, as had been laid down in the oracle. This reflected in a religious context the emphasis placed on marriage and on the importance of married women in the legislation of the previous year.

There was another, parallel emphasis on a particular family. The night-time sacrifices were all conducted by Augustus himself, but for those in the daytime he was joined by Marcus Agrippa, not only a great general but also his son-in-law. Agrippa was also a member of the *quindecemviri*, though not a senior member, and his prominent role in the ceremonies was due to his relationship to the *princeps*. He and Julia had another son, Lucius, early in the year, and Augustus adopted his two grandsons as his own children.[146] Augustus' dynastic intentions for his family were clear, and in this context his use of the traditional prayer at the sacrifices not only for the Roman people and for the college of the *quindecemviri* but also for 'myself, my house, my family' will have had a special significance.

The coming of the new era was, of course, stage-managed by Augustus, but must have impressed many of the inhabitants of Rome, perhaps especially those who, during Augustus' absence from the city after his abdication from the consulship in 23, had been vocal in demanding his presence, even to the point of disrupting the election of magistrates who might appear to be taking responsibility into their own hands. Doubtless not everybody was impressed, and Dio records that there were conspiracies in 18 against Augustus and Agrippa. The legislation on marriage may well have made some unhappy, especially those in the richer classes most likely to be affected by the penalties imposed, and the displeasure of members of the senate is perhaps reflected in the sharpness of the debate which accompanied it.[147] Moreover, it remained to be seen what the new *saeculum* was actually like, and how many of the prayers uttered during the *ludi saeculares* would be answered by the gods to whom they were addressed.

In the year 16 BC, both Augustus and Agrippa left Rome, Augustus for Gaul and Agrippa for the east, and they did not return for three years. Agrippa again seems to have been acting, as on his previous period there in 23 to 21, as the responsible agent of the Roman power in the region, as might be expected from the position that the

---

146. Vell. Pat. 2.96.1; Tacitus, *Ann.* 1.3; Suet. *Aug.* 96.1; Dio Cass. 54.18.2.
147. Conspiracies: Dio Cass. 54.15.1. Debate on marriage legislation: Dio Cass. 54.16.3–6.

grants of *imperium* and *tribunicia potestas* in 18 had given him.[148]
This included helping to install Polemo, the ruler of Pontus on the
south side of the Black Sea, as king of the Cimmerian Bosporus, on
the north-east of the sea, in 14 BC,[149] and issuing a letter supporting
the rights and privileges of the ancient *gerousia* of the city of
Argos (at this date probably a college of aristocrats with religious
functions), and others (recorded by the historian Josephus) requiring
the cities of Ephesus in the province of Asia and Cyrene in north
Africa to respect the permission granted to the Jews to send sacred
tribute money to the temple of Jerusalem; Agrippa also visited Syria
and Judaea, where he was shown round Jerusalem by his friend king
Herod, and was subsequently visited by him.[150] These random
instances clearly did not take up all Agrippa's time during his three
years in the east, but may give a flavour of some of the work he
undertook there.

Augustus was more heavily engaged in military activity. He did
not leave Rome until after the dedication of the restored temple of
Quirinus, the god identified with Romulus, the founder-king of the
city, on 29 June.[151] He proceeded to Gaul, where raids by German
tribes from across the Rhine had been causing problems, though the
immediate reason for his departure may have been (as Dio relates) a
defeat suffered by the *legatus* in charge of the area, Marcus Lollius,
which had resulted in the loss of a legionary standard. The problem
was less severe than later writers suggested and the Germans withdrew and made peace shortly after Augustus arrived (no doubt
also returning the standard), without the need for further military
engagement.[152] Lollius' defeat was no doubt a potential setback to
the prestige of the Romans that needed to be reversed rapidly, but it
was not the reason for Augustus' presence in Gaul, or for the extension of Roman control of the areas to the north of Italy and on the
eastern boundaries of Gallia Lugdunensis which followed. In 17 and
16 Publius Silius, proconsul in Illyricum, left his province to fight
successfully against two tribes in the region north of modern Brescia

148. See above, pp. 98 and 116.
149. Dio Cass. 54.24.4–6. On Polemo, see above, p. 95.
150. Rights of Argive *gerousia*: EJ 308; Jews in Ephesus and Cyrene: Josephus, *AJ*
16.167–70 (= EJ 309–10); visits Syria and Judaea, and is visited by Herod: Josephus, *AJ*
16.12–15.
151. Dio Cass. 54.19.4. For the date, Ovid, *Fast.* 6.795–6; *Fast. Ven.* (*Inscr. Ital.*
13.2.59 and 475).
152. Dio Cass. 54.20.4–21.1; Vell. Pat. 2.97.1; Tacitus, *Ann.* 1.10; Suet. *Aug.* 23.1.
Horace, *Carm.* 4.14.51–2, celebrates Augustus' success.

on the Italian side of the Alps before having to return to deal with insurrections from the Pannonians and Norici in his own area.[153] The fact that Silius had to come from Illyricum suggests that that this was a response to an unexpected attack rather than a planned Roman initiative, but it will have drawn attention to the vulnerability of Italy's northern area to incursions from the Alpine region. In 15 Augustus not only sent in Roman forces to subdue the region but chose as the legates for the task his two stepsons, Tiberius and Drusus, the children of his wife Livia by her former husband, Tiberius Claudius Nero. This was not only to be a move to ensure the strategic safety of Italy but also an opportunity to display the military prowess of the imperial family. The two men coordinated attacks on the area, with Tiberius advancing from the west to meet Drusus advancing from the south, and they overwhelmed the Raeti and Vindelici in eastern Switzerland and the Tyrol in a single campaign.[154] In the following year, the region north of Nice was subdued and became an area, called the Maritime Alps, under the control not of a *legatus Augusti pro praetore* but of an equestrian *praefectus*; the region further north, called the Cottian Alps, came under a similar regime in 9–8 BC, but was governed by one Marcus Iulius Cottus, son of king Donnus (who had ruled the area previously), who was now also ranked as an equestrian *praefectus* and who erected an arch, dedicated to Augustus, to mark the event. Augustus placed a monumental trophy at La Turbie, just north of Monaco, in 7–6 BC, recording victory over all the peoples of the Alps under his leadership and auspices.[155] In the *Res Gestae* he added that he had not unjustly attacked any of the peoples he had conquered, a sentiment supported by horrendous stories of atrocities committed by the Raeti to be found in Strabo and Dio; and Horace celebrated the victories that Drusus and Tiberius achieved against the Raeti and the Vindelici.[156] The campaigns in the Alps were to be seen not just as a military and strategic necessity but as an exemplification of the

153. Dio Cass. 54.20.1.
154. Dio Cass. 54.22.3–4; Vell. Pat. 2.95.1–2; Strabo, 4.6.8–9; Suet. *Aug.* 21, *Tib.* 9; Florus, 2.22.
155. Dio Cass. 54.24.1. Cottus' arch: *EJ* 166. *Praefectus* of the Maritime Alps: *EJ* 243. Augustus' trophy monument: *EJ* 40; Pliny, *HN* 3.136–8. On the occupation of the Alpine region, see C. M. Wells, *The German Policy of Augustus*, Oxford: Oxford University Press, 1972, 59–89.
156. Aug. *RG* 26.3 (cf. Strabo, 4.6.9, and Dio Cass. 54.22.1–3); Hor. *Carm.* 4.4.17–18 and 14.7–19.

values of the new age which the *ludi saeculares* had ushered in, brought about by the members of the imperial house.

Not all Augustus' activities in Gaul at this time were so significant, or so readily appropriated into the propaganda of the 'new age'. A recently discovered inscription from El Bierzo in north-west Spain contains what appears to be two edicts from the emperor, issued from Narbo Martius in February of the year 15, dealing with the lands and immunity from tribute of a small community. If this is genuine (and there are strong reasons for believing that it is not), it shows Augustus involved with the minutiae of provincial administration in one of his Spanish provinces.[157] He was, however, certainly concerned about the activities of one of his freedmen, a certain Licinus, a Gaul who had been a slave of Julius Caesar's and was now in charge of financial matters in Gallia Lugdunensis. He had made himself immensely rich at the expense of the provincials by various unscrupulous means, and was to become proverbial for his wealth in the literary tradition.[158] When the Gauls complained to Augustus about his about his behaviour, Licinus is said to have to have taken the *princeps* to his house, displayed his riches and explained that he had taken the money in order to keep the Gauls from becoming too powerful and was, of course, keeping it to give to Augustus; and in this way he escaped punishment. As Augustus' *procurator* in Lugdunensis (and the only freedman known to have held such a post in one of Caesar's provinces), Licinus was properly speaking the emperor's agent and, if the story is true, successfully deployed his position to avoid his patron's wrath.

It was not the details of provincial administration that were to the forefront when in 13 Augustus returned to Rome. Tiberius was one of the consuls for the year, along with Publius Quinctilius Varus, who, like Tiberius, was married to a daughter of Agrippa. As

157. For the text and a sceptical view of its genuineness, see Richardson, 'The new Augustan edicts', 411–15.

158. Dio Cass. 54.21.2–8. He is listed with Crassus, Pallas, Maecenas and others as a man of extraordinary wealth by Persius (2.36), Seneca (*Ep.* 119.9, 120.19) and Juvenal (1.109), and both Martial (8.3.6) and Juvenal (14.306) use him as a type of the rich man. Seneca (*Apocol.* 6.1) writes of him as 'reigning for many years' in Lugdunum, with reference to the emperor Claudius' birth in the city. An early scholion on Juvenal, 1.109, says that he died in the reign of Tiberius (P. Wessner, *Scholia in Iuvenalem Vestustiora*, Stuttgart: Teubner, 1967, 11–12). The mock epitaph by Terentius Varro Atacinus (J. Blänsdorf, *Fragmenta Poetarum Latinarum*, 3rd edn. Stuttgart and Leipzig: Teubner, 1995, 240) probably refers to a different Licinus (T. P Wiseman, 'Some Republican senators and their tribes', *Classical Quarterly* 14 (1964), 122–33, at 132–3).

Augustus approached the city, the senate, under Tiberius' presidency, voted that among other honours, an altar should be erected in the senate house to mark his return. This was declined, as were the other honours, but on 4 July (probably the day on which the *princeps* entered Rome) an altar was decreed, dedicated to Augustan Peace (*Pax Augusta*), to be situated in the Campus Martius. This Ara Pacis was consecrated some four years later, on 30 January in 9 BC, and showed, in addition to images of the victory of a personified Rome, a scene of a religious procession and a sacrifice, presided over by Augustus and Agrippa, in the presence of other members of the imperial family, including young Gaius and Lucius Caesar, Agrippa's young sons and, since 17 BC, the adopted children of Augustus.[159] The overall message is clear, even if the identification of some of the figures is still debated: the peace which Rome enjoyed, at the expense of warfare in the rest of the empire, was attributable directly to the gods of Rome and to the family of Augustus. As in 19, Augustus did not celebrate a triumph for the victories won by his *legati* (who in this case were also his stepsons), but instead erected a lasting monument in the form of an altar to the gods on whom Rome's safety depended;[160] and it can hardly have been a coincidence that the consecration of the altar in 9 BC took place on the birthday of Livia, his wife.

Over the next years the Campus Martius was to become increasingly a showplace for the glories of Augustus and the imperial family. As well as the Mausoleum, which had been built there in the early 20s, in either 13 or 11 the great theatre named for Marcellus, who had died in 23, was dedicated at the southern end of the area; and in 10 BC one of two massive obelisks brought from Egypt was set up to mark by the changing length of is shadow the alteration in the lengths of the days throughout the year.[161] The Greek geographer Strabo wrote admiringly of the beauties of the Campus Martius,

159. Aug. *RG* 12.2; Dio Cass. 54.25.2. Quinctilius Varus was Agrippa's son-in-law: *EJ* 366. Dates of decree and consecration of the Ara Pacis: *EJ* 49 and 46 (= *Inscr. Ital.* 13.2.189, 208 and 476; 117, 161 and 404–5). Images of the Ara Pacis: Zanker, *The Power of Images*, 120–3, 172–5, 203–4.

160. See above, p. 110.

161. Mausoleum: see above, p. 86. Theatre of Marcellus: Dio Cass. 54.26.1 (13 BC); Pliny, *HN* 8.65 (11 BC); see above, p. 102. Obelisk: Pliny, *HN* 36.72–3 (see T. Barton, 'Augustus and Capricorn: astrological polyvalency and imperial rhetoric', *Journal of Roman Studies* 85 (1995), 33–51, at 44–6). The other obelisk was placed in the Circus Maximus, and both record the bringing of Egypt under the power of the Roman people after Actium (*CIL* 6.701 and 702).

Figure 8 Section of the frieze from the Ara Pacis, showing Augustus and his family (© Iberphoto/Alinari)

mentioning particularly the Mausoleum, and noting that the Campus also had large grassy spaces where young men could exercise both on foot and on horseback.[162] This too was part of Augustus' policy, in pursuance of which he encouraged the practice of the 'Troy game' (*lusus Troiae*), involving upper-class youngsters in complex equestrian exercises; and in 13 his adopted son Gaius took part.[163]

These celebrations and displays were a central part of Augustus' return to Rome, but there was also other business to be attended to. The first matter that he brought to the senate, according to Dio, related to the conditions of service of his soldiers. A major problem through the late Republican and triumviral periods had been the demands of soldiers at the ends of their campaigns for land on which to settle. Augustus had dealt with this by establishing settlements, both in Italy and in the provinces, but especially in Italy this had caused grief among those who found themselves dispossessed in order to make way for disbanded veterans. In 13, perhaps under the pressure created by the large-scale discharges which took place in 14

162. Strabo, 5.3.8.
163. Dio Cass. 54.26.1. On Augustus and the *lusus Troiae*, see Suet. *Aug.* 43.2.

of soldiers who had been serving since the Actium campaign, he proposed a new way forward: he specified periods of service (twelve years for members of the praetorian guard and sixteen for others) and the amounts of money they were to be granted on discharge.[164] This was a major change. Until this time there had been no fixed periods of service, since in principle armies had been recruited to fight individual campaigns, even though in practice the same soldiers served in successive wars for years on end as the demands of Roman conquest and then civil conflicts increased. After 13 the army became recognised as a professional body (which in effect it had become already), and the establishment of colonies of veterans ceased, at least for the rest of Augustus' reign.

Dio also records a revision of the membership of the senate in 13, connecting it with difficulties in persuading people to become senators. There is a problem here, since Augustus himself states that he undertook such a review three times, whereas Dio mentions five.[165] The account of the review of 13 is strangely confused, and includes Augustus compelling all holders of the senatorial census who were younger than thirty-five to become senators. There may have been some changes introduced in this year, and it may also be that Dio is conflating with such changes the reforms that Augustus undertook four years later, or that he has mistaken an examination of those members of the equestrian order who held the privilege of a 'public horse' in addition to being within the census class, an honour which went back to the early days of the Republic, for a review of the senate;[166] but what precisely was done in 13 is impossible to determine.

This year did certainly see the renewal of the constitutional powers of the two rulers of the Roman world. Augustus' *imperium* was extended for a further five years as was that of Agrippa, whose *tribunicia potestas* was also granted for a further five years.[167] By this time, if not before, Agrippa's *imperium* was made greater than that

164. Aug. *RG* 6.3 and 16.1; Dio Cass. 54.25.5–6. L. Keppie, *Colonisation and Veteran Settlement in Italy, 47–14 BC*, London: British School at Rome, 1983, 82–6, 208–9.
165. Dio Cass. 54.26.3–9; cf. Aug. *RG* 8.2; Dio Cass. 52.42.1 (29 BC); 54.13.1 (18 BC); 54.26.3 (13 BC); 54.35.1 (11 BC); 55.13.3 (8 BC). A. H. M. Jones, 'The censorial powers of Augustus', in *Studies in Roman Government and Law*, Oxford: Blackwell, 1968, 21–6, at 22–3. On the reforms of 9 BC and Dio's probable confusions, see below, p. 140 and n. 16.
166. Dio Cass. 54.35.1. On the possible confusion with the review of *equites*, see Jones, 'The censorial powers', 22–3.
167. Dio Cass. 54.28.1 on Agrippa; cf. Dio Cass. 54.12.5 on Augustus.

of any other Roman official he might meet in his travels across the empire, and there can have been no doubt that in terms of the structures of the Roman constitution as well as in the propaganda messages that are represented in the sculptures of the Ara Pacis, he was second only to Augustus himself, and the two men were shown as colleagues on coins issued in 13.[168] Before the end of the year he had left Rome for Pannonia, where the troubles which had broken out in 18 had recurred.[169]

One other event, either in this year or perhaps early in the next, made possible yet a further marking of Augustus as the leader of the Roman state. Lepidus, who in the years after 43 was the colleague of Antonius and Caesar (as Augustus was then called) as *triumvir reipublicae constituendae*, died. He had been chosen, in the midst of the turmoil of 44, as successor to the murdered dictator as *ponitfex maximus*, the leader of the priestly college of the city. Augustus had ostentatiously refused to take the office while Lepidus was alive, but on 6 March 12 he was elected by a great crowd of people from all over Italy who flocked into the city for the purpose.[170] He was now beyond doubt not only the head of the civil and military establishment but also the leading religious figure in Rome.

This high point in the development of the new age, which had been announced in 17, was followed by a setback which Augustus could not have foreseen. As he presided over the games that were part of the celebration of the festival of Minerva, held 19–23 March, news was brought to him of the death of Agrippa, who, after a brief and successful campaign in Pannonia, had returned to Italy only to fall ill and die in Campania. The games continued but Augustus had Agrippa's body brought back to Rome, where he himself pronounced the funeral oration over the body, which was shielded from his view, probably because as *pontifex maximus* he was debarred from seeing a corpse. Agrippa's ashes were buried in due course in Augustus' Mausoleum, though he himself had previously chosen another site for his tomb on the Campus Martius.[171]

---

168. *EJ* 366; *RIC* I².73, nos 406–7. See above, pp. 98 and 101.
169. Dio Cass. 54.28.1. See above, pp. 127–8.
170. Aug. *RG* 10.2; *Fast. Maff. Praenest.* and *Fer. Cum.* (*EJ* 47 = *Inscr. Ital.* 13.2.74, 121, 279, 420); Ovid, *Fast.* 3.415–28. Dio (Dio Cass. 54.27.2) places the death of Lepidus and the election of Augustus in 13.
171. Dio Cass. 54.28.2–5, 29.6. A fragment of Augustus' oration has survived in a Greek papyrus (*EJ* 366). Dio doubts that the reason Augustus could not look at the corpse was because he was *pontifex maximus*, but compare Servius on Verg. *Aen.* 3.64

The death of Agrippa was a personal loss for Augustus, but it was also much more than that. The two men, who were almost the same age, had been close friends since before the assassination of Julius Caesar,[172] and Agrippa had been the leading Caesarian general throughout the years of the triumvirate. It was he who had been consul with the *princeps* in the crucial years 28 and 27 when the Roman state took shape in the aftermath of Actium, and by his contributions to the buildings and the aqueducts of Rome and across the empire he had presented the new regime with a new face, both splendid and practical. He was also a very rich man, leaving most of his wealth to Augustus, including large estates in the Thracian Chersonnese (modern Gallipoli), and bequeathed gardens and a set of baths in Rome to the people of the city. After the illness of Augustus and the death of Marcellus in 23, he became not only Augustus' intended successor, should the *princeps* die, but, through his marriage to Julia, Augustus' son-in-law and the father of his heirs. He was also the father-in-law of Augustus' stepson Tiberius. The new age, heralded by the reforms of 18 and the *ludi saeculares* in 17, showed Agrippa as second only to Augustus himself. The nature of his *imperium* and his holding of the *tribunicia potestas* marked him as a virtual co-emperor, and the two men were, in all but name, a pair of permanent consuls. Between them they were to embody the shape of the world to come. Now Agrippa was dead, and the question arose again, as it had after Actium and in 23: what was the Roman world to be like?

and 6.176. The funeral games for Agrippa did not take place until 7 BC (see below, p. 144).
172. See above, pp. 15 and 24.

CHAPTER 5

Emperor and empire, 12 BC–AD 14

The death of Agrippa cast a shadow over what had been for Augustus a decade which had seen not only a recovery from the dangers of the year 23, when he himself had been desperately ill and his chosen heir, Marcellus, had died, but also of achievement in social reform in Rome and military and diplomatic success across the Roman world. Agrippa's campaigns in Spain, the recovery of the standards from Parthia and the victories of Tiberius and Drusus against the Raeti and Vindelici displayed the 'new age' of Augustan Rome as much as did the *ludi saeculares* in 17 or the dedication of the Ara Pacis in 13; and at the centre of all this was the imperial family, as predominant in the field of war as they were exemplary of the society that the reforms of 18 were intended to re-create, especially among the upper classes. Moreover, that imperial family offered hope for the future, notably in the persons of Gaius and Lucius Caesar, born to Agrippa and Julia, adopted by their grandfather Augustus, and who now had another brother, born to Julia after Agrippa's death and called therefore Agrippa Postumus.

The centrality of the family of the *princeps* in the propaganda of the new age resulted in two weaknesses, one inevitable and the other contingent. The first was that, within the structures of the *res publica*, the business and activity of the Roman people, there was no place for a dynastic dominance by one family. This could be managed by an imaginative and careful use of the structures that had been shaped by the history of the Roman Republic, and in particular by the separation of the various powers that had been held by magistrates from the magistracies themselves. This provided, as has been seen, a constitutional basis for the positions that Augustus and Agrippa had held, notably through the use of *imperium* and the *tribunicia potestas*, and was to be continued through the remainder of Augustus' reign. The second problem lay in the shape of the family: the emphasis of the past decade with regard to the future had been on Agrippa's and Julia's children, but in 12 BC they were far too young to take on the continuation of Augustus' regime, should the *princeps* die, and the obvious candidate, at least until they reached maturity, was Agrippa himself, who was now dead. That left Augustus' stepsons, Tiberius and Drusus, Livia's children by her former husband, Tiberius Claudius Nero, who had led the assaults on Raetia and Vindelicia under Augustus' overall command. Tiberius and Drusus belonged to the generation between that of Augustus and Agrippa and that of Agrippa's and Julia's children (at the time of Agrippa's death, they were respectively 29 and 25 years old), but despite their comparative youth it was they who would have to take on at least some part of the role that had previously been Agrippa's. It was too soon for them to be, as Agrippa had been, a virtual co-ruler with Augustus, but within the family and to an extent in the military field they had to fill the gap Agrippa had left.

After Agrippa: the campaigns and the roles of Tiberius and Drusus, 12–6 BC

So it was that Tiberius was dispatched to fight against the Pannonians, who had been frightened into peace by the presence of Agrippa but resumed hostilities on hearing of his death. Tiberius was successful in holding them down, aided by the neighbouring Scordisci, but this was not the only way in which he was required to substitute for Agrippa. Before he left Rome he was required to divorce his wife, Vipsania Agrippina, Agrippa's daughter, and was betrothed to Agrippa's widow, Julia, Augustus' daughter, though the marriage did not take place until late in the following year.[1] By that time, Tiberius had spent a second campaigning season subduing the Pannonians, who had combined with the Dalmatians in the same region of northern Illyricum in resisting the Romans. Drusus in these two years had been undertaking more spectacular campaigns in Germany: in 12 he ravaged the territory of the Sugambri on the eastern bank of the Rhine and, sailing down the river and using a canal which he had constructed to link the Rhine to the Ijselmeer, won over the Frisii on the coast of the North Sea and invaded the lands of the Chauci on the banks of the river Weser. He returned briefly to Rome, where he was *praetor urbanus* in 11, but returned to Germany in the spring. He invaded the Sugambri, who had

---

1. Dio Cass. 54.31.2–4. See above, p. 133. On Tiberius' betrothal to Julia, see also Suet. *Aug*. 63.2, *Tib*. 7.2. On their marriage, Dio Cass. 54.35.4.

attacked their neighbours, the Chatti, and reached the territory of the Cherusci on the river Weser. He was, however, prevented from crossing by a shortage of supplies and unfavourable weather and so returned to the Rhine, where he set up fortifications, probably to protect the Chatti from the Sugambri.[2] Both he and Tiberius were rewarded by the grant of independent *imperium pro consule*, which meant that they were no longer acting as Augustus' *legati* thereafter. Tiberius and Drusus were also awarded the *ornamenta triumphalia* in place of a full triumph for their successes in these campaigns, as was Lucius Piso, who put down a revolt in Thrace during the same period.[3]

It was probably in the winter that followed that two significant events took place that marked the change in the imperial family from the previous decade. As noted, it was now that the marriage between Julia, Agrippa's widow and Augustus' daughter, took place; and about the same time, Augustus' older sister Octavia died, and was buried in the Mausoleum, after a funeral in which orations were pronounced by both Augustus himself and Drusus, whose wife, Antonia, was the daughter of Octavia and Marcus Antonius.[4] She had been a woman of major importance to Augustus, not only as Antonius' wife and a link between the two triumvirs through the turbulent 30s, but also, along with Livia, as an honoured member of Augustus' family. As early as 35 the two women were together granted tribunician sacrosanctity and the right to manage their own affairs, and they are mentioned together by Strabo as builders of monuments in Augustus' spectacular beautification of Rome.[5] Horace also links them, placing them at the head of a list of those rejoicing in the safe return of Augustus in 24 from his campaigns in Spain.[6] In some ways Octavia's death must have been, like that of Agrippa, a reminder of the ageing of Augustus' contemporaries and the passing of many of those who had been responsible for and symbolic of the making of his 'new age'.

2. Dio Cass. 54.32–4; Suet. *Claud.*1.2; Tacitus, *Ann.* 2.8.1.
3. Dio Cass. 54.33.5 and 34.3. *Ornamenta triumphalia*: Tiberius (Dio Cass. 54.31.4; Suet. *Tib.* 9.2); Drusus (Dio Cass. 54.33.5); Piso (Dio Cass. 54.37.4); see above, p. 111. Suetonius notes that Tiberius was the first to be granted the *ornamenta*.
4. Dio Cass. 54.35.4. There are problems with Dio's chronology at this point in his history since he has run together the years 11 and 10, and it is possible that the death of Octavia and the marriage of Tiberius and Julia took place in late 10 (see J. W. Rich, *Cassius Dio: The Augustan Settlement (Roman History 53–55.9)*, Warminster: Aris and Phillips, 1990, 214–15).
5. See above, pp. 64 and 130–1.
6. Hor. *Carm.* 3.14.5–12

In the following year Augustus accompanied the brothers Tiberius and Drusus to Gaul, basing himself again at Lugdunum, where an altar was dedicated to Augustus and Rome on 1 August, the same day that a second son, the future emperor Claudius, was born to Drusus and his wife Antonia, the daughter of Marcus Antonius and Octavia.[7] By that time Tiberius had been sent back to Pannonia to deal with further trouble, caused by a crossing of the frozen Danube by Dacians, living in what is now Transylvania in modern Romania, and by another revolt by the Dalmatians. This time, he seems to have been successful in restoring peace. Drusus was engaged in further fighting across the Rhine, largely against the Chatti, who, despite his campaigns of the previous year, had joined forces with the Sugambri. At the end of the year, the two brothers accompanied Augustus on his return to Rome.[8]

In 9 BC Drusus, who was consul in that year, undertook a further advance into Germany, first against the Chatti, then against the Suebic tribes, who lived in the upper reaches of the river Main, where with some difficulty he defeated the Marcomanni. He then moved north into the territory of the Cherusci and this time succeeded in crossing the Weser, which he had failed to do in 11, and advanced as far as the river Elbe. This was the furthest extent of his expedition and, having erected a trophy on the banks of the Elbe, he headed back towards the Rhine. As he returned, his triumphant progress through Germany, which was surely intended to be resumed the following year, came to an abrupt end: he was thrown by his horse, which rolled over on him, breaking his thigh, as a result of which he sickened and died within thirty days.[9]

Tiberius had been engaged in repressing once again the Dacians and Pannonians, but had joined Augustus at Ticinum (modern Pavia) in northern Italy at the end of the campaigning season when the news came of Drusus' accident and his precarious state of health. He was immediately dispatched by Augustus and, making remarkable speed (he is said to have covered 200 miles in a night and a day), arrived just before his brother died. Restraining the mourning of Drusus' grief-stricken soldiers, he accompanied the body back to Ticinum and thence to Rome, where the swelling crowd of people

---

7. Dio Cass. 54.32.1 seems to date this to the year 12 (as also Livy, *Per.* 139); but Suetonius (*Claud.* 2.1) dates it precisely to 1 August 10, the day on which Claudius was born at Lugdunum.

8. Dio Cass. 54.36.3–4.

9. Dio Cass. 55.1.2–5; Florus, 2.30.23–7; Strabo, 7.1.3; Livy. *Per.* 142; Suet. *Claud.* 1.2.

from Italy and beyond who followed made the eventual entry into the city (so we are told by Seneca) seem more like a triumph than a funeral. The solemnities that followed were on the pattern of those for other members of the imperial family: Augustus gave a funeral laudation in the Circus Flaminius, outside the city walls, and Tiberius a second in the Forum, and Drusus' ashes were interred in the Mausoleum in the Campus Martius. The senate also played its part, voting the posthumous grant of the name Germanicus to Drusus and to his descendants, in recognition of his great victories. Statues were decreed, with an arch on the Appian Way, leading south out of Rome, and a cenotaph, erected beside the Rhine.[10]

This was the third death in the imperial family in four years and perhaps the most difficult for Augustus. Drusus had been his favourite of the two brothers, being named in his will along with his adoptive sons, as well as being popular with the people,[11] even though the distribution of commands and of honours suggests that for the time being at least the two were seen jointly as filling the role left vacant by Agrippa; and indeed it was Tiberius, not Drusus, who had married Julia. The *princeps'* intentions, in terms of a succession, seem to have been focused on Gaius and Lucius, but the immediate problem was the working of his government of the state until such time as they were of age to hold the reins of power. Agrippa, his coeval, had gone, and now one of the two who might fill that gap from the following generation was also dead. The inevitable flimsiness of a family-based regime, set within the structures determined by the constitution of Republican Rome, become increasingly clear.

Immediately after the funeral of Drusus, Tiberius celebrated an *ovatio* for his successes in Illyricum, an honour that it had been intended to give also to Drusus, who was to have had the additional celebration of a triumph outside Rome on the Alban Mount, during the festival of the *Feriae Latinae*. This was a form of the triumph used in the middle years of the Republic by generals who had been unable to hold a full triumph, and on one occasion had been

10. Dio Cass. 55.2.1–3; Suet. *Tib.* 7.3, *Claud.* 1.3; Tacitus, *Ann.* 3.5.2; Livy, *Per.* 142; Val. Max. 5.5.3; Seneca, *Ad Marc.* 6.3.1–2, *Ad Polyb.* 11.5.5; [Ovid], *Consolatio ad Liviam* 167–270; Pliny, *HN* 7.84.
11. Suet. *Claud.* 1.5; Tacitus, *Ann.* 1.33.2, 2.41.3, 6.51.1. Suetonius reports Republicanist tendencies (see also *Tib.* 50.1), but this is probably a deduction from Drusus' popularity. See J. W. Rich, 'Drusus and the *spolia opima*', *Classical Review* 49 (1999), 544–55.

followed by an unusually splendid *ovatio*.[12] Tiberius had now to fulfil the role which had been assigned to himself and his brother, and the death of Drusus would shape his future in a variety of ways over the rest of his life. It was equally crucial to other members of the imperial family. Despite pressure from Augustus, Drusus' widow Antonia never remarried, though she was only twenty-seven at Drusus' death, and she brought up her three surviving children, Germanicus, Livia Julia (often called Livilla) and Claudius, establishing a household from which she was to exercise great influence and patronage.[13] Livia, Drusus' mother and the *princeps'* wife, whose prime significance in the family had been emphasised by the dedication of the Ara Pacis in the Campus Martius on her birthday on 30 January earlier in the year,[14] was honoured with statues and enrolled among those women who had special privileges for being mothers of three children, a right probably instituted under the *lex Iulia de maritandis* of 18, even though she had only two surviving sons.[15] For her too, the loss was not only that of a son but of one who was intended to play a major role in the development of the continuing supremacy of the imperial house.

The year 9 BC was not entirely taken up with the successes and tragedies of the imperial family. At some point, perhaps early in the year, Augustus introduced a number of reforms to the senate and its procedures, which may have been part of a law on senatorial procedure referred to by later writers.[16] These included specifying that the senate should meet twice monthly and that attendance should be compulsory, except in the months of September and October, when a number sufficient to ensure a quorum were drawn by lot from the total; the posting of the names of senators on a white board; and the increasing of the fines for unjustified absence. Augustus also posted details of any legislation he was intending to introduce and invited

12. Dio Cass. 55.2.4–5. Tiberius: Vell. Pat. 2.96.3, 97.4, 122.1; Suet. *Tib.* 9.2. Drusus' intended triumph is mentioned in the anonymous *Consolatio ad Liviam* 21–8, 205–6, 329–38, 459–62, though without reference to the Alban Mount. On the latter, cf. Marcus Marcellus in 211 BC (Livy, 26.21.1–10).
13. Antonia's widowhood: Val. Max. 4.3.3; Josephus, *AJ* 18.180. Children: Suet. *Claud.* 1.6; *EJ* 93.
14. See above, p. 130.
15. Dio Cass. 55.2.5–6. On the *lex Iulia*, see above, pp. 119–20.
16. Dio Cass. 55.3.1–4.1; Suet. *Aug.* 35.3. On the law, Pliny, *Ep.* 5.13.5–7, 8.14.19; Gellius, *NA* 4.10.1. On Augustus' reforms at this point, see R. J. A. Talbert, *The Senate of Imperial Rome*, Princeton: Princeton University Press, 1984, 222–4. It is probable that Dio's confused notice of a review of senate membership and quorum in 11 BC (54.35.1) is a misplaced anticipation of these reforms (Rich, *Cassius Dio*, 215).

senators to make comments which might lead to improvements. All this was in line with his previous legislation, such as that carried in 18 and 17, to support by law what he regarded as good practice from the Republic. The very fact that that legislation was now required shows, of course, that the social and political context of the Republican period had been changed totally, and that the institutions of an earlier time were being used for quite different purposes.

The following year, 8 BC, marked the twentieth from Augustus' beginning of the process of handing back the business of the state, the *res publica*, to the senate and people.[17] Augustus had remained outside the city since his return from northern Italy after Drusus' death, but now re-entered, depositing the laurels which marked the successes in Germany and Illyricum in the temple of Jupiter Feretrius on the Capitoline rather than that of Jupiter Capitolinus, which would have seemed too like a triumph, and avoided any further celebration in view of the loss Drusus. The consuls, however, held games to give thanks to Jupiter for the *princeps*' safe return.[18]

In 13 BC, Augustus and Agrippa had had their *imperium* extended for five years, and so Augustus' again required renewing. On this occasion he was granted a period of ten years rather than five, but, perhaps surprisingly, Tiberius was not given any similar grant. It may be, however, that it was this *imperium* to which Augustus refers when he states in the *Res Gestae* that it was while holding consular *imperium* that he completed a second census of Roman citizens in this year. The first had been completed twenty years before, with Agrippa as his colleague.[19]

There were other reminders that time had passed since those days. Maecenas died towards the end of this year, as did the poet Horace, who had played a significant part in the propagation of the message of the 'new age'.[20] The loss of Maecenas, like that of Agrippa four years earlier, was felt by Augustus, not least because these two had been his companions since the earliest days and could be relied upon to give advice on problematic issues, including those involving the

17. See above, pp. 84–6.
18. Dio Cass. 55.5.1–2; *EJ* 38.
19. Dio Cass. 55.6.1, 12.3 (on the grants of 13 BC, see above, p. 132). On the censuses, Aug. *RG* 8.2–3; see above, pp. 82–4; J.-L. Ferrary, 'The powers of Augustus', in J. Edmondson (ed.), *Augustus*, Edinburgh: Edinburgh University Press, 2009, 90–136, at 104–6. The number of citizens registered was given as 4,233,000, a rise of 4 per cent since 18 BC.
20. Dio Cass. 55.7; Suet. *Vita Hor.* (as supplemented by I. Vahlen, 'Varia', *Hermes* 33 (1898), 245–61, at 245–6).

imperial family. Though Maecenas had not played the role which Agrippa had occupied and had largely been out of the public arena for the past decade, that advice was sorely missed.[21] Maecenas made Augustus his chief heir, with instructions to make such gifts as seemed appropriate to him to some of his friends (including Horace), and Maecenas' splendid house and gardens on the Esquiline hill in Rome became and remained imperial property.

In other ways the activity of the *princeps* and the political classes in Rome showed a familiar mixture of Republican structure and monarchical ceremonial. On the one hand the elections for the magistracies went ahead, though it is interesting to note that these were evidently more genuinely competitive than might have been expected after twenty years of the principate. Ironically this was revealed by allegations being made that all the magistrates elected the previous year for service in 8 BC had been involved in bribery. Augustus declined to conduct an investigation of these charges, but did introduce a system whereby candidates had to pay a deposit before the elections which they forfeited if they were found to have bribed the electorate. This scheme was an attempt to repress bribery without the use of the law court which Augustus had himself set up in 18.[22] The need for its introduction presupposes that there were more candidates than available magistracies and that the elections were not simply predetermined by the *princeps*. On the other hand Augustus was once again given exceptional and extraordinary honours. In place of a triumph for the successes in Germany, which he refused, the senate decreed that his birthday should be celebrated annually with horse races; and the eighth month of the year (previously named Sextilis) was renamed 'Augustus', to mark the month in which he had first been made consul and in which he had captured Alexandria in 30 and had celebrated his triple triumph in 29.[23] Such a renaming had last been done for the dictator Julius Caesar after his return from Spain in 45, when the month Quinctilis was renamed 'Iulius'; the flavour of autocracy is unmistakable.[24]

For the latter part of the year Augustus was once again involved

21. Seneca, *Ben.* 6.32.2. See above, p. 104.
22. Dio Cass. 55.5.3. See above, pp. 121–2.
23. Dio Cass. 55.6.6. August: Suet. *Aug.* 31.2; Macrobius, *Sat.* 1.12.35; 1.14.13–15. Dio also mentions that he extended the sacred boundary of the city, the *pomerium*, but this is probably a mistake, as it is not mentioned in either the *Res Gestae* or the section of the *lex imperii Vespasiani* which relates to the *pomerium* (*EJ* 364, lines 14–16). See M. T. Boatwright, 'The pomerial extension of Augustus', *Historia* 35 (1986), 13–27.
24. Appian, *B Civ.* 2.106. On Marcus Brutus' view of this, see above, p. 19.

in the German wars, remaining on the western side of the Rhine while Tiberius crossed the river to complete the work which Drusus had been undertaking when he died. Tiberius seems to have been successful in establishing Roman control of the huge area between the Rhine and the Elbe, though the claim of Velleius Paterculus that he made Germany virtually a tax-paying province is clearly excessive.[25] The main opposing group, the Sugambri, were moved from their territory to the Gallic side of the Rhine (Suetonius states that this involved 40,000 of them), and some tribes migrated eastwards, the Marcomanni into Bohemia and other Suebi to the eastern side of the Elbe;[26] but the result from a Roman point of view was the establishment of a peaceful conclusion to the wars, and this allowed Augustus in the *Res Gestae* to claim that he had brought under control 'the Gallic and Spanish provinces and also Germany, where the Ocean forms a boundary from Cadiz to the mouth of the Elbe' (*RG* 26.2). For Tiberius' success, Augustus received his fourteenth acclamation as *imperator* (marked in a bilingual Latin and Neo-Punic inscription from north Africa) in the summer of 8 BC and Tiberius his second.[27] Though Germany was by no means wholly conquered, the effect of these campaigns was to provide comparative peace on the far side of the Rhine for the next decade and a half, and, more immediately, evidence of the imperial house expanding the extent of Rome's power into regions beyond those previously touched by the power of the Roman people (*imperium populi Romani*).

So it was that at the beginning of the following year (7 BC) Tiberius, as consul for the second time, summoned the senate to a meeting in the Porticus Octavia, in the south of the Campus Martius and outside the boundary of the city, for he was about to make a full triumphal entry into Rome. This was the first full triumph since that of Lucius Cornelius Balbus in 19 and so marked both the grandeur of Tiberius' achievement and the significance and importance of the individual who celebrated it.[28] When Augustus re-entered the city later, games were held once again in the names of the two consuls, Tiberius and Gnaeus Calpurnius Piso, but Tiberius was by then away in Germany, suppressing an uprising, and his place was taken (so Dio states) by the *princeps'* adoptive son, Gaius Caesar, the elder son

25. Dio Cass. 55.6.1–3; Vell. Pat. 2.97.4; Tacitus, *Ann.* 2.26.
26. Vell. Pat. 2.108.2; Strabo, 7.2–3.
27. *EJ* 39 and 105b.
28. Dio Cass. 55.8.2. On Balbus' triumph and the change in practice, see above, p. 111.

of Agrippa, then only thirteen years old. If this is right, it shows clearly the predominant place of the imperial family and of the young man whom Augustus intended as his successor.[29] The memory of Agrippa was present too, since funeral games in his honour were conducted at this time in the great piazza of the Saepta, the building erected by Agrippa in 26 BC in the Campus Martius for the holding of elections.[30]

The reason for this use of the Saepta was not only out of respect for Agrippa but because a serious fire had damaged the centre of the city, including the Forum, where such games were often held. Augustus had previously attempted to improve fire control in Rome in 22 BC by making the aediles responsible for putting out fires and giving them 600 slaves of his own, whom he had used for this purpose. Now he instituted a new organisation of the city into fourteen regions, each the responsibility of one of the praetors, tribunes or aediles (selected by lot from these colleges of magistrates), the regions being subdivided into 265 *vici* (blocks of streets), each of which was under four *vicomagistri*, elected by the inhabitants of the *vicus*.[31] This looks like an attempt to ground the security of the city from fire in the local areas, but the change also included a religious element. *Vici* had existed in the Republican period, when the city was divided into four regions, when the *magistri* were responsible, along with associations (*collegia*) of local residents, for the cult of the *lares Compitales* (the guardian deities of the crossroads) and the festival of the *Compitalia* held at the New Year, but these had been suppressed because they were associated with demonstrations and other street violence. Augustus revived the cult, renaming the *lares* as *lares augusti*, and attached to it two additional feast days, on 1 May and 27 June each year.[32] The reorganisation of local government thus became an opportunity for the incorporation of Rome

29. Dio Cass. 55.8.33. An inscription records the games as given by Tiberius, with Piso as his colleague. The latter's name was subsequently erased after his condemnation for the death of Germanicus in AD 20 (*EJ* 39).
30. Dio Cass. 55.8.5. On the Saepta, see above, p. 93.
31. Dio Cass. 55.8.6–7; Suet. *Aug.* 30.1; Pliny, *HN* 3.66. For Augustus' arrangements in 22 BC, see above, pp. 109–10.
32. On the *vici*, see J. Bert Lott, *The Neigborhoods of Augustan Rome*, Cambridge: Cambridge University Press, 2004. On the religion of the *vici* and the *lares*, see also John Scheid, 'To honour the *princeps* and venerate the gods: public cult, neighbourhood cults, and imperial cult in Augustan Rome', in Edmondson, *Augustus*, 275–309, at 296–8; and Mary Beard, John North and Simon Price, *Religions of Rome*, Cambridge: Cambridge University Press, 1998, 1.184–6. On the earlier suppression of the *collegia*, see above, p. 106.

into the religious activity of the whole state, linked by the name of Augustus with the imperial house.

This year also saw a further public linking of religion with the imperial family. When Tiberius as consul summoned the senate to its meeting at the Porticus Octavia, he announced that he would undertake the rebuilding of the temple of Concordia, which stood at the northern end of the Forum, under the Capitol. The construction of temples was a traditional way for those celebrating triumphs to mark their thanks to the gods, but this particular rebuilding carried other messages as well. The temple was associated with concord between the citizens of Rome and had last been rebuilt by Lucius Opimius, who during his consulship in 121 BC had repressed the rioting which marked the end of Gaius Gracchus' attempts at reform in the two previous years. It was surely not this event to which Tiberius was relating when he proposed to reconstruct the temple but rather the general idea of harmony among the citizen body, and in any case he had another instance of concord that he wished to mark. He told the senators that he would make the dedication both in his own name and in that of his dead brother, Drusus, thereby honouring their joint victory over the Germans and also the unity of the imperial house, which had brought harmony to the Roman people. When he eventually dedicated it in AD 10, at a time when affairs in Germany were far less happy for Rome, it was named the temple of Concordia Augusta.[33]

Though there was for the moment peace in Germany, problems loomed in the east in the kingdom of Armenia. Tigranes, the king that Tiberius had installed in 20 BC, had died and been succeeded by his son, also called Tigranes, and his daughter, Erato, who were apparently hostile to Rome. Tiberius was to be sent to deal with this problem, and was given not only a renewed *imperium* but also a grant of *tribunicia potestas* for five years, showing clearly that he was to hold the position that had been Agrippa's in the years after 18.[34] As Velleius Paterculus, as always adulatory of Tiberius, puts it, he was 'made the equal of Augustus in the sharing of *tribunicia postestas*, the most eminent of all Roman citizens save one, ... indeed the second eye and head of the *res publica*'.[35] The scene

---

33. Dio Cass. 55.8.2; Ovid, *Fast.* 1.637–50; Suet. *Tib.* 20.1. The date and title of the temple are also recorded in the *Fast. Praenest.* (*Inscr. Ital.* 13.2.114–15).
34. On Tigranes' accession, see above, p. 108; on the situation in Armenia, Tacitus, *Ann.* 2.3.2–4.1. On Agrippa's position, see above, pp. 115–16.
35. Vell. Pat. 2.99.1: tribuniciae potestatis consortione aequatus Augusto, civium

appeared to be set for a re-run of the pattern which had been in place before Agrippa's death, with Tiberius, the husband of Agrippa's widow, playing the role Agrippa had played as the co-ruler of Rome until such time as Gaius and Lucius Caesar, Agrippa's and Julia's offspring and Augustus' grandchildren and adopted sons, might be old enough to succeed. The only difficulty was that Tiberius was unwilling to play his part. He informed Augustus, his stepfather and father-in-law, that he wanted a respite from his labours, and, despite the pleas of his mother, Augustus' wife Livia, and a brief pause when Augustus appeared to be ill once again, set sail for the island of Rhodes, which was to be his home for the next eight years.[36]

The question that this about-face immediately raises is why it happened. The ancient sources provide a variety of reasons, some being explanations which Tiberius is said to have given at the time and later on, some being what the writers believed to be the real cause. The reason given in 6 BC by Tiberius was, it seems, that he needed a rest after all he had done in Germany and as consul and that he wanted to further his education, especially in philosophy. Though Dio (or to be more precise, an abbreviator of Dio's history, for the manuscript of his history has a gap at this point[37]) regards this as a pretext, it is clear that during his time on Rhodes Tiberius did take part in philosophical discussions, was involved in the life of the city and even entered a four-horse chariot in the Olympic Games, which won a victory.[38] This, however, hardly seems an adequate reason for turning down Augustus' assignment to him of an important task in Armenia. Another reason, which Tacitus believed was the underlying cause, was said to be the desire to get away from his wife, Julia, either because of her disdain for him as an inferior or because of her notorious promiscuity.[39] This too seems an odd explanation since it was not for another four years that Augustus (and as a result Tiberius) took action against Julia for her immorality, and, if Tiberius wanted to get away from his wife, the work that he had been asked to do in the east would have achieved this without the need for him to refuse Augustus' commission to Armenia. Tiberius had, after all, hardly been in Rome during the years of the German campaigns. A third explanation, and one which is said to have been given by Tiberius himself at a later date, relates to the increasingly

post unum (et hoc quia volebat) eminentissimus, ducum maximus, fama fortunaque celeberrimus et vere alterum rei publicae lumen et caput.
36. Dio Cass. 55.9.5–8; Vell. Pat. 2.99.1–100.1; Suet. *Tib.* 10.1–11.1.
37. See further below, p. 152.

important place of Gaius and Lucius Caesar, Augustus' adopted
sons, in the *princeps'* plans for the succession to his power. Dio says
that at the consular elections in 6 BC for the following year Gaius
was elected, which, had he taken up the office, would have meant his
becoming consul at the age of fifteen.[40] This would have been extraordinary, and, according to Dio, Augustus refused to countenance it,
appointing the boy instead to a priesthood with the additional right
to attend meetings of the senate (which took effect the following
year[41]), and giving the *tribunicia potestas* to Tiberius. The attempt
to get Gaius elected has been interpreted as a move by a group of
supporters of Julia to advance the claims of her sons, which led
Tiberius to decide that the people had no confidence in him and
that he should withdraw from any contest between himself and the
two young Caesars for the succession.[42] Tiberius himself said later
(according to Suetonius[43]) that he did not want his presence in Rome
to get in the way of their careers in public life. Suetonius explicitly
makes the comparison with Agrippa's departure to Mytilene in
23, which he believes was the result of Augustus' decision that
Marcellus should be his successor. The similarities and differences of
the positions of the two men are instructive. When Agrippa left for
the east it was (as we have seen) to act as Augustus' representative
in the eastern part of the empire, and the years that followed showed
him as in effect the *princeps'* co-ruler, second only to Augustus'
himself.[44] That was the position that was on offer to Tiberius in 6,
and the renewal of his *imperium* and the grant of *tribunicia potestas*
underline the similarity of their positions; but while Agrippa's move
to Mytilene was a result of Augustus' intentions, Tiberius' departure
for Rhodes was clearly his rejection of them. Had he gone to sort
out the problems that had arisen in Armenia, he would have been
following the path that Agrippa had taken; instead he retired as a
private citizen (albeit one holding the *tribunicia potestas*), dis-
sociating himself from the work which Augustus had intended for

---

38. Dio Cass. 55.9.5; Suet. *Tib.* 11.1–3; *EJ* 77b and 78.

39. Tacitus, *Ann.* 1.53: fuerat in matrimonio Tiberii florentibus Gaio et Lucio
Caesaribus spreveratque ut inparem; nec alia tam intima Tiberio causa cur Rhodum
abscederet. See also Suet. *Tib.* 10.1; Dio Cass. 55.9.7.

40. Dio Cass. 55.9.2.

41. See below, p. 150.

42. See, for instance, Barbara Levick, *Tiberius the Politician*, 2nd edn., London: Routledge, 1999, 35–40.

43. Suet. *Tib.* 10.1–2.

44. See above, pp. 98 and 115–16.

him. He seems to have decided that he had no wish to be a second
Agrippa; and he had friends and supporters in the Greek world who
might prove useful to him, especially should Augustus' plans for
Gaius go awry. Moreover he was, at least in the earlier years, visited
by Roman officials and governors on their way to their provinces,
which suggests that they at least recognised his significance.[45]

There is one obvious difference between Agrippa and Tiberius:
they belonged to different generations. Agrippa was Augustus'
coeval and could only expect to hold supreme power in the event of
the latter dying before him (something which from time to time
seemed only too likely). Tiberius was the son of Augustus' wife
and the husband of the mother of the young Gaius and Lucius.
Augustus' intention that these two should be his descendants and
successors had been clear ever since their adoption in 17, thereby
skipping the generation to which Tiberius belonged, but it did not
follow that everybody, and in particular Tiberius, was content with
this. It seems that at some point in 6 BC Tiberius decided that he had
had enough of being the second string to the emperor, perhaps
particularly when this meant acting as a preparer of the way for the
children of his wife, with whom his relations had been deteriorating.
The extent to which this was the result of rival factions, supporting
or working against the emperor's dynastic policy, is hard to determine; but there is no doubt that Augustus was enraged by what he
described to the senate, so Suetonius states, as his desertion by his
stepson. This at least gave the lie to the official position over the past
years that the imperial family was united in its mutual support.
For Tiberius, the Concord to which he had vowed a temple at the
beginning of the previous year seemed most notably to be between
himself and his deceased brother, Drusus, rather than binding him
to his stepfather and his adoptive children. Dio records that on
Tiberius' way to Rhodes he stopped at the island of Paros, where he
compelled the inhabitants to sell him a statue of the goddess Hestia,
the Greek equivalent of the Roman Vesta, goddess of the hearth,
which he intended to place in the temple of Concord; and shortly
after he returned to Rome in AD 2, walls and gates in the central
Italian city of Saepinum were erected in the names of himself and
Drusus. Some sources apparently claimed that Tiberius was exiled

45. Suet. *Tib.* 12.1. On his supporters in the east, see G. W. Bowersock, 'Augustus and
the east: the problem of the succession', in F. Millar and E. Segal (eds), *Caesar Augustus:
Seven Aspects*, Oxford: Oxford University Press, 1984, 169–88.

by Augustus on the grounds that he had been plotting against Gaius and Lucius, and, although this is certainly improbable given the attempts Augustus made to prevent him from leaving, and may well be the result of later anti-Tiberian propaganda, it may originate in his dislike of the position which resulted from the increasing focus on the two boys.[46]

Despite these problems within the imperial family, the work of dealing with the empire continued: an inscription from Cyrene in north Africa shows Augustus issuing four edicts in 7 or 6 BC, dealing both with a particular case that had been sent to him and with the structure of law courts in the province of Cyrenaica, allowing the Greek inhabitants the choice of a jury consisting entirely of Roman citizens or of equal numbers of Greeks and Romans; and another instance which happens to have survived is a letter sent by Augustus in 6 to the island of Cnidus, in which he rules on a murder charge which the authorities on the island had referred to him.[47] When this letter was written, Augustus was already consul designate for the following year, and in 5 BC he entered office as consul for the twelfth time, having not held the consulship since he had stood down in 23. The reason he held the consulship now was, so Suetonius tells us, for the introduction into public life of Gaius Caesar, and, given the celebrations that attended this, this is no doubt correct; but it is worth noting that the same year also saw the reintroduction of the election of suffect consuls taking office after the elected consuls stood down, a practice that had last been used in 12 BC, the year that Agrippa died. One such suffect might have been expected, since Augustus himself held office only in the early part of the year, but in 5 there were three. From now to the end of Augustus' reign the election of suffect consuls was to be the norm, with exceptions only in 3 BC and AD 14. It appears that in 5 BC the need to provide a mechanism for the honouring of members of the Roman establishment outside the imperial family had again been recognised; and the departure of Tiberius might well have been the motivating factor for this change.[48]

---

46. Dio Cass. 55.9.6–7; *EJ* 79.
47. Cyrene: *EJ* 311, edicts 1 to 4. Cnidus: *EJ* 312 and R. K. Sherk, *Roman Documents from the Greek East*, Baltimore: Johns Hopkins University Press, 1969, no. 67.
48. R. Syme, *The Augustan Aristocracy*, Oxford: Oxford University Press, 1986, 86.

The coming of age of Gaius and Lucius Caesar and the high point of Augustus' reign, 5–2 BC

If Augustus felt that he had been deserted by one member of his family from the generation after his own, he certainly demonstrated his determination to promote the two boys whom he had selected as its foremost members in the next. It was as consul that he brought his son Gaius down to the Forum, probably on the feast of the Liberalia (17 March[49]), which was the day on which customarily boys of about his age took off the *toga praetexta* with its purple border, worn while a boy, and put on the plain white *toga virilis*, the sign of manhood; and Augustus marked the celebration by the grant of a hand-out to the Roman plebs of 60 denarii each, the equivalent of a year's grain distribution.[50] The symbolism of the day was, as so often in Augustus' hands, a combination of the traditional and the new. Gaius was a citizen and entered as such on the census roll, but he was hardly an ordinary one. Augustus records in the *Res Gestae* that the senate immediately decreed that Gaius should take part in the councils of state (the *consilia publica*). This was in itself less remarkable than it sounds, as Augustus had already allowed sons of senators (and no others) to wear on their tunics the broad purple stripe (*latus clavus*) that was otherwise the mark of a senator, and to attend senatorial meetings.[51] In Gaius' case, however, much more was implied. In the following year Augustus convened a meeting of a council to deal with the succession to the kingdom of Judaea, following the death of Herod the Great and the competing claims of his sons. Gaius was a member of this group, along with senior figures from the senate, which divided the kingdom between the three claimants. This was the first time Gaius was involved in this way, but there is no reason to believe that it was the last.[52] Moreover, he was elected by the people to serve as consul in five years time, out of respect, so Augustus records, for the *princeps* himself. On his acquisition of the rights and duties of a citizen, Gaius also became eligible for military service and, as a son of a senatorial family, a member of the equestrian order. Augustus had specified that

49. Ovid, *Fasti* 3.771–90.

50. Aug. *RG* 15.2. See A. E. Cooley, *Res Gestae Divi Augusti*, Cambridge: Cambridge University Press, 2009, 172.

51. Suet. *Aug.* 38.2. On Augustus' ruling in 18 BC, see above, p. 118.

52. Josephus, *BJ* 2.25, *AJ* 17.229. On the situation in Judaea and the outcome of the *consilium*, see E. M. Smallwood, *The Jews under Roman Rule from Pompey to Diocletian*, Leiden: Brill, 1971, 105–13.

holders of the *latus clavus* should be given command of a unit of cavalry when they began their military careers. He had paid especial attention to those in the equestrian order who held the privilege of being awarded a 'public horse' (*equus publicus*), an honour which had its origins in the early Republic, when the *equites* were indeed the cavalry of the city's army, and he revived the practice of annual parades on horseback, held on 15 July in the Forum, in the course of which *equites* were examined for their physical and moral suitability for continued membership. He appointed three assistants to advise him in this process, to whom the power of the censors (*censoria potestas*) was delegated.[53] Although the award of a public horse might be expected for a senator's son, once again the case of Gaius was clearly exceptional. Permission was given for him to be the leader of one of the six squadrons into which the *equites* were divided for the annual parade; and, more significantly, he was acclaimed unanimously by the *equites* as *princeps iuventutis* (leader of the youth), and presented with a silver shield and spear.[54] This title was highly honorific and, as so often, highly ambiguous. The word *iuventus* (youth) might refer to young men in general or, as was implied by this title, given by the equestrian order, to those *equites* under the age of thirty-five who were reckoned as capable of active military service and who voted in the electoral assembly (*comitia centuriata*) in voting units called the *iuniores*.[55] The use of the word *princeps* was still more ambiguous and still more significant. As a complimentary description, *princeps iuventutis* had been used by Cicero when referring to young aristocrats whom he wished to flatter;[56] but the use of the term *princeps* by Augustus had by now given the word a new connotation, and it is clear from both literary and epigraphic sources that *princeps iuventutis* was intended to mark Gaius (and later his brother Lucius) as Augustus' successor.[57]

53. Suet. *Aug.* 38.3–39. F. G. B. Millar, *The Emperor in the Roman World*, London: Duckworth, 1977, 279–82. On the parade (*transvectio*), Dionysius of Halicarnassus, *Antiquates Romanae* 6.13.4; Livy, 9.46.15; Pliny, *HN* 15.4.19; Tacitus, *Ann.* 2.83. On his assistants, Suet. *Aug.* 37; *EJ* 209.
54. *Aug. RG* 14.2; Dio Cass. 54.9.9.
55. See P. M. Swan, *The Augustan Succession: An Historical Commentary on Cassius Dio's Roman History Books 55–56 (9 BC–AD 14)*, Oxford: Oxford University Press, 2004, 90.
56. Cic. *2 Verr.* 1.139; *Sulla* 34; *Vatin.* 24.
57. Ovid, *Ars am.* 1.194, describes Gaius as *nunc iuvenum princeps, deinde future senum* ('now *princeps* of the young, for the future of the elders'). See too the cenotaph of Gaius at Pisa, which describes him as *iam designatum iustissimum ac simillumum parentis suis virtutibus principem* ('already designated *princeps*, most just and most like

Nor was the significance of this missed throughout the empire: the city of Sardis, in the province of Asia, sent an embassy to Augustus to announce their rejoicing on the day that they received the glad tidings that Gaius had assumed the white toga, which they celebrated with sacrifices and the wearing of crowns and white clothes; and the small town of Conobaria in the Spanish province of Baetica swore an oath of loyalty to Augustus and to his son Gaius (described as *princeps iuventutis*, consul designate and priest), to his other son Lucius and to his grandson Agrippa Postumus.[58] It is noticeable that the name of Tiberius does not appear on this list.

Our information on the other events of 5 BC and on the three years that follow is scanty, due to a gap in the text of Dio Cassius, which is incomplete from this point on and, in the resulting lacunae, depends upon citations and epitomes from later sources.[59] It does not, of course, follow that nothing of note happened, but inevitably much less is known. Certainly the normal work of administering the empire went on. The inscription from Cyrene mentioned above[60] includes anther edict from Augustus, dated to 4 BC and sent to all the provinces, introducing a decree of the senate on the recovery by communities or individuals of monies improperly seized. This appears to be an alternative to a full-scale trial in the extortion court (*quaestio de repetundis*) and, following approval by a full meeting of the senate, would involve an investigation by five senators, who were to reach their conclusions within thirty days, with the plaintiff being allowed to call witnesses only from Italy, and then only five in the case of a claim from an individual and ten in the case of a community. The advantages of this process, from the point of view of the provincials, was (as the decree makes clear) that it avoided the lengthy trial which was required by the *quaestio* and the bringing of witnesses long distances to Rome; but it also meant that the recovery would be no more than simple restitution, rather than the severer penalties of the full process, and would mean that an erring provincial governor would be tried by other senators rather than by a jury made up mostly of non-senators. It could also only be used when the

his father in his virtues') (*EJ* 99, lines 12–13). On Augustus' use of *princeps*, see above, p. 89.

58. Sardis: *EJ* 99. Conobaria: J. González, 'The first oath *pro salute Augusti* found in Baetica', *Zeitschrift für Papyrologie und Epigrafik* 72 (1988), 113–27.

59. See F. G. B. Millar, *A Study of Cassius Dio*, Oxford: Oxford University Press, 1964, 1–4; Swan, *The Augustan Succession*, 36–8.

60. See p. 149. For the text of the fifth edict and a commentary, see also Sherk, *Roman Documents*, no. 31.

individual being complained of was not being accused on a capital charge. In effect, this was making available to provincials a civil law process, which might well be quicker and easier than the criminal process of the *quaestio*, and it is clear from both Augustus' edict and the wording of the senatorial decree that this was being presented as a move which would be welcome to the provincials. What the provincials thought of it is, of course, unknown.

Much more is known of the events of the year 2 BC, and not only because a fragment of Dio records some of them. Augustus was consul again, for the thirteenth and (as it turned out) last time, wishing, as he had three years earlier, to hold the office when he brought his son, in this case Lucius Caesar, down to the Forum for the ceremony of enrolling him as a full citizen at the age of fourteen.[61] The same pomp and circumstance attended Lucius' assumption of the *toga virilis* as had that of Gaius, and he too was made *princeps iuventutis* and designated to be consul when he reached the age of nineteen. The only difference in their lists of titles and honours was that Lucius was made a member of the college of augurs while Gaius had become a member of the college of priests (*pontifices*).[62] As with Gaius' celebrations, Augustus marked the occasion by distributing 60 denarii a head to the plebs in Rome.[63]

This time, however, the coming of age of the young Caesar was set in the context of two other Augustan celebrations, each of great significance. On 5 February (the Nones in the Roman calendar) Augustus was acclaimed as *pater patriae* ('father of the fatherland') by the senate, the equestrian order and the whole Roman people. The importance that he attached to this is clearly shown by the place he accords it in the *Res Gestae*: it is the last entry in this record of his achievements, the high point of his account, which begins with his raising an army in 44 at the age of nineteen to 'liberate the *res publica* from the domination of the faction' which had assassinated his adoptive father.[64] Suetonius tells us that Augustus was first approached by a delegation from the plebs to offer him the title while he was at Antium (modern Anzio, on the coast of Latium);

---

61. Aug. *RG* 14.1–2; Suet. *Aug.* 26.2; Dio Cass. 55.9.10.
62. For Lucius' titles, see *EJ* 65 (Rome, an inscription of 3 BC, when he was already augur, anticipating his other honours); *EJ* 67 (Mytilene); *EJ* 68, lines 6–8 (Pisa, following his death).
63. Aug. *RG* 15.4. See Cooley, *Res Gestae*, 172–3; and below, pp. 160–1.
64. Aug. *RG* 35.1; cf. *RG* 1.1. For the date of the acclamation, Ovid, *Fast.* 2.119–44; *Fast. Praenest.* (*Inscr. Ital.* 13.2.119 and 407).

he refused it, but was subsequently acclaimed in the theatre in Rome by masses of people, all wearing laurels wreaths, and then was addressed by the senior senator, Valerius Messala, in the senate house. Suetonius claims to give Messala's actual words, in which, on behalf of the whole senate, he prays for good fortune and divine favour to rest on Augustus and his house, for thereby they believe they are praying for the perpetual happiness of the whole *res publica*. Augustus, with tears in his eyes, responds that, now he has achieved what he had prayed for, what more can he ask the gods than that he retain the approval of the senators to his life's end.

The new title was not at this date an official designation, any more than Augustus had been before 27 BC, though both became part of the titles of the emperors who followed. *Pater patriae* had been used of great saviours of the state, such as Marcus Furius Camillus, the successful general of the early fourth century BC, and Marcus Marius, after his defeat of the invading Cimbri in the late second century; it was even used of Cicero after the suppression of the Catilinarian conspiracy of 63. Most particularly it was used of Romulus, the first king and legendary founder of the city.[65] The word *pater* had already been applied to Augustus himself, as the saviour and new founder of Rome, and Ovid, in his passage in the *Fasti* on the Nones of February, makes this point and explicitly compares Augustus and Romulus (to the credit of the former).[66] Though it carried no additional legal or constitutional powers, the acclamation in 2 BC was heavy with significance in a typically Augustan way: Augustus, as *pater patriae*, was the saviour and re-founder of Rome and, as the father of his country, due both the respect and obedience that Romans gave to their *paterfamilias* within their own families. No wonder, then, that he saw it as the crowning glory of his long career; and the prayer of Valerius Messala for Augustus and his house carries with it, especially in the year in which Augustus' second son reached manhood, the promise of continued glory and dominance.

The other major celebrations in this year echoed similar themes. On 12 May, the temple of Mars Ultor was dedicated in the new Forum Augustum. The Forum had taken a long time to build and had been opened for use as a place where law suits and other business related to the courts could be carried out before

---

65. See the discussion in Cooley, *Res Gestae*, 273–5.
66. Ovid, *Fast.* 2.119–44.

the completion of the temple, which was to be its focal point.[67] The building stood on a high podium, facing into a space flanked on either side by two colonnades, of which that on the left, looking towards the temple, contained statues of Aeneas, shown rescuing his aged father and young son from the ruins of Troy, and statues of members of the Julian family through the ages of the Republic; while that on the right contained a statue of Romulus, first king of Rome, carrying the arms of an enemy chief whom he had slain in battle, and statues of the great men of Roman history, who had won triumphs over Rome's enemies and thereby, in Suetonius' words, raised the power (*imperium*) of the Roman people from small beginnings to greatness.[68] In the temple itself stood the statue of Mars, with Venus, mother of Aeneas and so of the whole Julian family, alongside him, and probably also that of Divus Julius, the deified father of Augustus; and below, in the Forum itself, was placed a statue of Augustus in a four-horse chariot, voted for him by the senate and bearing the inscription 'PATER PATRIAE'. It was here that the Roman standards, recovered from the Parthians in 20, were finally lodged, and here too the names of the provinces where he had been victorious were inscribed in shining letters. The whole ensemble was regarded by the elder Pliny as one of the three greatest architectural achievements of the city or indeed of the whole world.[69] Its intention was to display the military glory of the Roman people, and in particular of their *pater patriae*, and the importance of the Julian family within that context, and to do so with great magnificence. These two themes were implicit in the god to whom the temple was dedicated: Mars Ultor (the Avenger) was the god to whom Augustus had vowed a temple at the battle of Philippi forty years before if he were able to revenge the assassination of his adoptive father, Julius Caesar. In this respect, the dedication was a mark of his righting the wrong inflicted

67. Suet. *Aug.* 29.1; Macrob. *Sat.* 2.4.9. There is disagreement in the sources about the actual date of the dedication: Ovid, *Fast.* 5.545–98, places it on 12 March, while Dio Cass. 60.5.3 has it on 1 August. Ovid, a contemporary, is probably right (see C. J. Simpson, 'The date of dedication of the temple of Mars Ultor', *Journal of Roman Studies* 67 (1977), 91–4); for doubts, see Swan, *The Augustan Succession*, 95–6.
68. Suet. *Aug.* 31.5: qui imperium p. R. ex minimo maximum reddidissent. On the Forum and its statues, see P. Zanker, *The Power of Images in the Age of Augustus*, Ann Arbor: University of Michigan Press, 1988, 201–3 and 210–15.
69. Venus: Ovid, *Tr.* 2.296. Divus Julius: see Beard et al., *Religions of Rome*, 1.199–200 and 331–3. Augustus' chariot: Aug. *RG* 35.1. Parthian standards: Aug. *RG* 29.2; Ovid, *Fasti* 5.579–94 (see above, pp. 108 and 110–11, nn. 96 and 103–5). Names of provinces: Vell. Pat. 2.39.2. See Pliny, *HN* 36.102.

on his family; but it was also showing this as part of the glorious progress of Rome, which, so the ensemble implies, depended on the predominance of the *gens Iulia*. So, as Ovid puts it in his entry for 12 May in his *Fasti*, Mars, not satisfied with avenging the death of Julius Caesar, had continued by securing the recovery of the standards from the Parthians, to overcome the shame that their loss brought to the Roman people.[70]

The Forum and its temple were intended not to be merely a memorial of past glories but also to provide a setting within which Rome's continuing military dominance and influence over foreign powers would be kept before the eyes of the people. It was in the temple of Mars Ultor that the senate was to meet to discuss wars and to determine the award of triumphs, and from there commanders were to set forth for their provinces and to receive the *ornamenta triumphalia*, should they return victorious. It was there too that leaders of barbarian peoples were made to swear oaths that they would remain in good faith and peace with Rome. The ritual by which those coming of age were enrolled in the lists of those eligible for military service was transferred here from the Forum Romanum, a change which was particularly notable in the year in which Lucius Caesar had assumed the *toga virilis*; and the censors, who kept the lists, were to drive a nail into the temple at the close of their tenure of office every five years, a practice which recalled the ancient rite whereby in earlier centuries a nail had been driven each year into the temple of Jupiter on the Capitoline.[71] The cult and the temple of Mars Ultor, the first temple of Mars to be dedicated within the sacred boundary of the city, with its strongly Julian overtones, was taking over some of the roles which had previously been those of Jupiter, to whose temple the triumphal processions had always gone, and indeed still did, on the rare occasions when a full triumph was celebrated. The new temple in the new Forum combined, in a way typical of the Augustan age, tradition and innovation, displaying the imperial regime and the imperial house as the continuation and fulfilment of the destiny of Rome.[72]

As befitted so important a ceremony, the dedication was accompanied by spectacular games, gladiatorial combats, animal hunts

---

70. Ovid, *Fast.* 5.569–98.
71. Dio Cass. 55.10.2–5; Suet. *Aug.* 21.2 and 29.2. On the *ornamenta triumphalia*, see above, pp. 111 and 137. On the nails in the temple of Jupiter Capitolinus, see Livy, 7.3.5–8, and S. P. Oakley, *A Commentary on Livy, Books VI–IX*, vol. 2, Oxford: Oxford University Press, 1998, 73–6.

(260 lions were slaughtered in the Circus Maximus and 36 croco-diles in the Circus Flaminius, which was flooded for the purpose), and a mock naval battle in a specially constructed artificial lake on the far side of the Tiber. Gaius and Lucius were put in charge of the games in the circuses, and Agrippa Postumus also participated in the equestrian exercise of the Troy game. These games, named the *ludi Martiales* in honour of Mars Ultor, were to be celebrated every year and the organising of them henceforth was to be undertaken by the consuls, the highest magistrates of the city.[73]

This year was clearly intended to be one in which the achieve-ments of Augustus' reign and the promise of future greatness for Rome under the control of his house were paraded before the world. It was a singular irony, and one which did not escape many of our ancient sources, that it was now that Augustus faced a major scan-dal within his own family. At some point towards the end of the year his daughter Julia, the mother of Gaius and Lucius and still the wife of Tiberius, was deported to the small island of Pandateria (modern Ventotene, off the Italian coast, north of Ischia), and was accom-panied by her mother, Augustus' previous wife, Scribonia. Julia was accused of outrageous sexual practices and in particular of adultery with a string of aristocratic Romans, headed by Iullus Antonius, the son of Marcus Antonius and Fulvia, who had been brought up by Octavia, Augustus' sister and Antonius' widow.[74] Iullus was there-fore himself close to the imperial house, and had held the consulship in 10 BC. He was either put to death or, according to Velleius, committed suicide. Other adulterers were exiled. Augustus is said to have been unaware of his daughter's promiscuity, or at least unwill-ing to believe it until it became too flagrant to ignore; but eventually in a rage he informed the senate. The ancient sources give different reasons for his anger and for his action against Julia and her lovers. Some claim that Iullus and Julia were plotting a coup, intending to murder Augustus and replace him with Iullus; some that he was appalled that his own daughter was flouting the laws that he had himself passed on marriage and adultery.[75] The accusations of

---

72. On the significances of the Forum Augustum, see K. Galinsky, *Augustan Culture*, Princeton: Princeton University Press, 1996, 197–213.
73. Aug. *RG* 22; Dio Cass. 55.10.6–8; Vell. Pat. 2.100.2. On the Troy game, see above, p. 131.
74. See above, pp. 66 and 73.
75. Vell. Pat. 2.100.2–5; Suet. *Aug.* 652–3; Dio Cass. 55.10.12–15 (Iullus aiming at monarchy); Seneca, *Ben.* 6.32.1–2 (against Augustus' legislation); Tacitus, *Ann.* 3.24.2

treason and murder might account for the speed and severity of
Augustus' action, though it is far from clear what the plotters might
have been intending to do if they were successful, not least because
Augustus' intended heirs were evidently Julia's children; but in any
case the damage done to the picture, so carefully presented since
at least the time of the *ludi saeculares* fifteen years earlier, of the
imperial family as a model of unity and moral propriety was almost
equally disastrous. Augustus was now over sixty and, in Roman
terms, officially an old man (*senex*); and it was only a few months
ago that he had been acclaimed *pater patriae* (father of the fatherland). Such behaviour by his own daughter made a mockery of that
title; and there were other signs that the upper classes in the city were
following Julia's example rather than her father's laws. The first two
books of Ovid's parody of a didactic poem, *Ars amatoria*, which in
the form we have them date from late in 2 BC or very early in the
following year, tell men how to pursue girls at games in the circus
and in particular at the mock naval battle which formed the high-
light of the celebrations for the dedication of the temple of Mars
Ultor.[76] Even if there was no serious attempt to overthrow the
princeps himself, the new Rome that he had spent years to construct
was under attack, and from within his own family. Tiberius was still
absent on Rhodes, and only heard of Julia's banishment when he
was informed that a bill of divorce in his name had been authorised
by Augustus.[77] Though he may well have been glad, as Suetonius
claims, at the news of the divorce, it meant that, although still the
princeps' stepson, he was no longer his son-in-law, and the focus of
Augustus' policy for the imperial family was still more resolutely on
the young Gaius and Lucius.

One change in the organisation of those in the emperor's
entourage has been associated with the accusations of conspiracy
which attended the disgrace of Julia. It was in this year that
Augustus appointed for the first time two equestrian officers,
Quintus Ostorius Scapula and Publius Salvius Aper, to act as prefects

---

(allegations of offences against religion and *maiestas*); 4.44.5 (Iullus Antonius guilty of
adultery); Julia aiming at overthrow and assassination: Seneca, *Brev. vit.* 4.6; Pliny, *HN*
7.149. On Augustus' laws on adultery, see above, pp. 120–1.
76. Ovid, *Ars am.* 1.171–6. The date is given by this mention, immediately followed by
a reference to Gaius Caesar's imminent departure to fight the Parthians, which occurred
early the following year, under the protection of Augustus and Mars (1.177–228). See
R. Syme, *History in Ovid*, Oxford: Oxford University Press, 1978, 8–11.
77. Suet. *Tib.* 11.4–5.

of the Praetorian Guard, the body which at least since 27 BC had acted as his personal protectors. These prefects were thus responsible for Augustus' security and in charge of the only body of soldiers posted permanently in the immediate vicinity of the city, though at this stage only part of the whole body (three of the nine cohorts) was kept at Rome, with the remainder distributed to towns elsewhere in Italy.[78] The appointment of the two prefects may have been primarily an administrative matter, and the Guard with its commanders did not have the importance that it was to acquire after its concentration into a single camp under a single prefect, which occurred twenty-five years later; but the placing of the Guard's organisation in the hands of men responsible directly to Augustus rather than (as was probably the case previously) their being directly commanded by himself was presumably intended to improve their efficiency in time of need. The security of the *princeps* was more than ever crucial in the context of his increasing solitude in supreme power, in the aftermath of the death of Drusus and the departure of Tiberius and in view of the youth of his intended successors.

A law which was passed in the later part of the year in the names of two of the suffect consuls, Gaius Fufius and Lucius Caninius, harked back to the sort of concerns that had been seen in Augustus' legislation in 18 and 17. This sought to limit the number of slaves who could be manumitted in the will of their master on his death, the numbers being determined on a sliding scale, so that an owner of between 3 and 10 could free not more than half the total, between 11 and 30 a third, between 31 and 100 a quarter, and between 101 and 500 a fifth. The restriction did not apply to the owner of up to two slaves, and at the other end of the scale no one could free more than 100. Moreover, the slaves to be freed had to be listed by name, and be entered in the will in a form which made clear the priority of those listed. The intention was clearly to limit the number of those freed, but it is notable that the law applied only to manumission by means of a will and so did not apply to other methods of giving freedom to slaves by a master during his lifetime. This and the provision that only those named in a will could be freed suggest that there was a desire to allow manumission where there was a real relationship

78. Dio Cass. 55.10.10; cf. 53.11.5; Tacitus, *Ann.* 4.5; Suet. *Aug.* 49.1 On the Praetorian Guard and its prefects, see L. Keppie, *Colonisation and Veteran Settlement in Italy, 47–14 BC*, London: British School at Rome, 1983, 33–5; Millar, *The Emperor in the Roman World*, 122–31.

between master and slave but to limit it where there was a suspicion that the act was being done as a mere gesture of extravagant generosity, and one which would cost the owner himself nothing.[79] The motive, assuming that Augustus at least approved of the law, was probably to place a cap on such extravagances because of fears that excessive use of manumission might pollute the purity of the Roman people, since all slaves manumitted in this way became Roman citizens.[80] Distasteful as this may sound to modern ears, the growth of a foreign element in the population of Rome was seen as damaging the traditional virtues of Rome, and this applied especially to those from the Greek-speaking eastern parts of the empire, whence many slaves came.[81]

A further attempt to return to the old ways took place at about this time, though again (as with the legislation of 18 and 17) by means of new controls.[82] The distribution of free grain to the *plebs Romana* dated back to the late Republic, when it had been introduced by the radical tribune Publius Clodius in 58 BC. Julius Caesar had attempted to restrict the numbers eligible for these doles in 46 from 320,000 to 150,000 by means of an additional census of the *vici*; but by the time of Augustus' hand-out in 5 BC to mark the coming of age of Gaius Caesar, the numbers had grown again back to 320,000. By the time Augustus made a similar distribution for Lucius' celebration in 2 BC, he recorded the number as 'a few more than 200,000' and described the beneficiaries as 'the plebs who at that time were in receipt of public grain', rather than 'the urban plebs', who had received the hand-out three years before. This was achieved by means of another additional census, conducted *vicus* by *vicus* as had been done in 46. The oddly tentative language of the *Res Gestae* at this point, which contrasts with Augustus' usual practice of giving numbers of recipients in his account of his grants and hand-outs, suggests that 200,000 was perhaps not the final figure he was intending for the number of what became known as the *plebs frumentaria* and that he was aiming at 150,000, as Julius Caesar had done. In either case, the reduction is remarkable and marks a

79. Gaius, *Inst.* 1.42–6; Ulpian, *Tit.* 1.24; Paulus, *Sent.*, 4.14.1–4.
80. Suetonius, *Aug.* 40.3, states that this was the reason Augustus set a limit on manumission, which probably refers to this law.
81. The classic example is the outraged remarks by the satirist Juvenal (*Sat.* 3.58–125). See A. N. Sherwin-White, *Racial Prejudice in Imperial Rome*, Cambridge: Cambridge University Press, 1967, ch. 3.
82. See above, pp. 123–4.

determination to limit the size of the constituency of beneficiaries.[83] It may belong to the same set of ideas which we have seen in the passing of the *lex Fufia Caninia*.

Problems in the east and the deaths of Gaius and Lucius Caesar, 2 BC–AD 4

For the next few years the attention of our sources, such as they are, is not on Rome but on events in the east. The difficulties in Armenia, which Tiberius had, by his departure for Rhodes in 6 BC, refused to handle, had become worse. Artavasdes, a Roman replacement for the anti-Roman Tigranes and his sister, was removed with Parthian help and considerable Roman losses.[84] The situation had been made more problematic by the murder of Phraates IV of Parthia, the king who had handed back the standards to Rome in 20, by his illegitimate son and his son's mother, an Italian slave who had been sent as a gift by Augustus and whom Phraates had later married. The son became Phraates V, usually known by the diminutive form Phraataces, and, according to Josephus, married his mother, Musa, who appears on his coins with the title 'queen and goddess of the heavens'.[85] A bad-tempered exchange of correspondence about the control of Armenia between Phraataces and Augustus followed and seemed likely to lead to war. Augustus' response to this was to send Gaius, to whom proconsular *imperium* was given, along with a number of senior advisers. Augustus also provided Gaius with a wife, Livia, the daughter of Tiberius' dead brother Drusus, to add to his appearance of seniority, despite his youth. Gaius had already had some experience of military life, having been with the legions on the Danube shortly before he left for the east, but he was still only eighteen years old. It was his first major engagement with the practical business of the empire, and, had Tiberius not withdrawn to Rhodes, it would probably have been he who would have been sent. As it was, Tiberius' five-year grant of *tribunicia potestas* expired in this

83. Suet. *Iul.* 41.3; *Aug.* 40.2 and 42.3; Aug. *RG* 15.2 and 4; Dio Cass. 55.10.1. See G. E. Rickman, *The Corn Supply of Ancient Rome*, Oxford: Oxford University Press, 1980, 175–85.

84. Tacitus, *Ann.* 2.4. On the problems in 7, see above, p. 145.

85. Phraates and the standards: see above, p. 108. Phraataces: Josephus, *AJ* 18.40–2. The mother is called Thesmousa by Josephus, but coins from Parthia call her Musa (in Greek *Mousē*); see D. Sellwood, *An Introduction to the Coinage of Parthia*, 2nd edn. London: Spink and Son, 1980, type 58 (pp. 189–90).

year and was not renewed, a clear sign that he was not someone that Augustus would have considered.[86]

Gaius set off amid a chorus of good wishes and high expectation. Augustus himself prayed to the gods to give him the goodwill of Pompeius, the boldness of Alexander and his own good fortune to accompany him; the poet Antipater of Thessalonica asked that Herakles might make him invincible, Aphrodite happy in his marriage, Pallas Athene wise and Ares unflinching in battle, and also predicted easy victories over the Parthians and the expansion of the empire; while Ovid, in a long passage in the *Ars amatoria*, said much the same of his presumed defeat of the Parthians.[87] Gaius proceeded east, leaving his young wife in Rome, and stopped on Samos, where Tiberius came to meet him. The meeting was not an easy one, though proper formalities were observed, with Tiberius, who had now no other official position than the rather unspecific title of *legatus* which he had extracted from an unwilling Augustus, acknowledging Gaius' status. One of the group of advisers whom Augustus had sent to accompany Gaius, Marcus Lollius, the consul of 21 BC, was particularly hostile to Tiberius and stirred up others in the retinue against him. Some twenty years later Tiberius was to accuse him of having been an evil influence on the young Gaius and the originator of the young man's prejudice against him.[88]

Gaius proceeded slowly towards Syria and was therefore not in Rome when he entered his promised consulship the following year, AD 1. He visited Arabia en route, and may have conducted a campaign there.[89] His remit included the reinstatement of Artavasdes, who had been driven from the throne of Armenia, but events had already changed. Artavasdes had died of an illness and Tigranes took the opportunity of writing to Augustus, who, in the hope of avoiding a war with Tigranes' Parthian backers, advised him to go

---

86. Dio Cass. 55.10.17–21; Vell. Pat. 2.101.1. Livia: Tacitus, *Ann.* 4.40.

87. Plut. *Reg. et imp. apophthegm.* 207e; Antipater, poems 46 and 47 in A. S. F. Gow and D. L. Page, *The Greek Anthology: The Garland of Philip*, Cambridge: Cambridge University Press, 1968, 38–41; Ovid, *Ars am.* 1.177–228.

88. Vell. Pat. 2.101.1 (reading *qui* for *cui*, with A. J. Woodman, *Velleius Paterculus: The Tiberian Narrative (2.94–131)*, Cambridge: Cambridge University Press, 1977, 63 and 125); Suet. *Tib.* 12.2; Dio Cass. 55.10.19. Dio places the meeting in Chios. On Tiberius as *legatus*, Suet. *Tib.* 12.1. Lollius: Suet. *Tib.* 12.2 and 13.2; Tacitus, *Ann.* 3.48.2; on his previous career, see above, pp. 106 and 127.

89. So T. D. Barnes, 'The victories of Augustus', *Journal of Roman Studies* 64 (1974), 21–6, at 22–3; but see Swan, *The Augustan Succession*, 126–7, on the chronology of Gaius' time in the east. On Gaius in Arabia, see Pliny, *HN* 6.141; 6.160; 12.55–6; 32.10.

to Gaius in Syria with good expectations. Phraataces apparently decided that the appointment of Tigranes as king of Armenia with Roman support was enough for him to settle affairs with Rome, especially as Augustus agreed that his four half-brothers, the sons of his father Phraates IV and thus rivals for his throne, whom Phraataces had demanded should be returned to him, should be kept away from the east. A magnificent scene took place on an island in the river Euphrates, the boundary between Parthian territory and the Roman province, where the agreement was ratified, accompanied by banquets at which Gaius feted the Parthian king on the Roman side, with Phraataces subsequently returning the favour for Gaius on the Parthian bank.[90]

The intended results of this meeting, however, rapidly unravelled. Tigranes was killed in a local war and his sister, Erato, resigned the throne, which she had shared with her brother. Gaius entered Armenia with his army and Augustus decided to give Armenia to Ariobarzanes, king of Media Atropatene (modern Azerbaijan). This, however, was resisted by at least some Armenians, who had no wish to be ruled over by a Mede, and, with the support of the king of Parthia, offered resistance. In the process of installing the new ruler Gaius was wounded in September AD 3 at a fortress in Armenia, having been lured into consulting with its commander, who had promised to reveal secrets of the Parthian king, but who then attempted to kill Gaius with a sword-thrust. Gaius recovered initially, and he and Augustus received acclamations as *imperatores* for what was described by the latter in the *Res Gestae* as the successful suppression of a rebellion. Ariobarzanes was placed on the Armenian throne, but Gaius was still ill from the result of his wounding, and was also deeply grieved by the death of his younger brother Lucius, who had died at Massilia in August AD 2, on his way to Spain. For whatever reason, Gaius wrote to Augustus to ask permission to retire into private life and to remain in Syria. The *princeps* was, not surprisingly, very upset, but reported Gaius' wishes to the senate and urged him at least to come back to Italy. Gaius reluctantly left Syria on a merchant vessel, giving up all his powers and offices, and sailed for home; but on 21 February AD 4 he died at Limyra in Lycia.[91] Augustus was stricken with grief and

90. Dio Cass. 55.10.21 and 10a.4; Vell. Pat. 2.101–2. Velleius was present at this event, serving as a military tribune.
91. Aug. *RG* 27.2; Vell. Pat. 2.102.2–3; Dio Cass. 55.10a.4–10; Florus, 2.32. Tacitus,

across the empire the deaths of the two brothers were commemorated with monuments and posthumous honours.[92] Their remains were placed in the Augustan Mausoleum.

In a period of eighteen months Augustus' dynastic plans has collapsed. The two youths, whom he had described in a tender and playful letter to Gaius, written on the eve of his sixty-third birthday in September AD 1, as 'playing your part like true men and taking over the sentry post from me', were both dead.[93] He had to look elsewhere for a successor. In AD 4, having lost two adopted sons, he adopted two more, neither *ex hypothesi* his first choices. On 26 July he adopted Marcus Agrippa, the posthumous son of Agrippa and Julia and thus the younger brother of Gaius and Lucius; and also Tiberius Nero, his stepson.[94] Agrippa Postumus, as he is always known, was an obvious candidate as a replacement for his brothers, though Augustus later found him difficult if not dangerous, and he was in any case only just fourteen. Tiberius had of course damaged himself in Augustus' eyes by his withdrawal to Rhodes in 6 BC, but by this time he had been back in Rome for two years. Augustus had made it clear, despite pleas from Tiberius himself and from his mother Livia, Augustus' wife, that he would not countenance a return unless Gaius agreed to it. Suetonius suggests that Gaius' refusal was due to the influence of Marcus Lollius, which is likely enough, and his change of mind to Gaius' having fallen out with the latter. Velleius Paterculus, who was with Gaius at the time, recounts that, in the context of the great meeting between Gaius and Phraataces on the island in the Euphrates, the king informed him that Lollius was involved in some form of treachery, and that within a few days Lollius was dead, either by chance or by his own hand. It may well have been this which laid open the possibility of Tiberius'

Ann. 2.4.1, contrary to Dio, says that Ariobarzanes was welcomed by the Armenians, because of his splendid appearance. On Gaius' feelings on Lucius' death, Seneca, *Ad Polyb.* 15.4.

92. Aug. *RG* 14.1; Suet. *Tib.* 23; Seneca, *Controv.* 4 *praef.* 5. Monuments and honours: EJ 68 and 69 (Pisa); cenotaph for Gaius at Limyra: J. Ganzert, *Das Kenotaph für Gaius Caesar in Limyra: Architektur und Bauornamentik*, Tübingen: E. Wasmuth, 1984; J. Borchhardt et al., *Götter, Heroen, Herrscher in Lykien*, Vienna: A. Schroll, 1990, 88–92; honours recorded on the *Tabula Hebana* (EJ 94a, lines 4–11), their names to be inserted in the hymn of the Salic priests and the ten centuries involved in the election of consuls and praetors to be named after them. The dates of their deaths were recorded in local *fasti*: Lucius in *Fast. Ant. min.* (*Inscr. Ital.* 13.2.208) and Gaius in *Fast. Cupr.* and *Fast. Verul.* (*Inscr. Ital.* 13.1.245 and 13.2.165 and 413).

93. Gellius, *NA* 15.7.3.

94. Vell. Pat.2.103.3–104.1; Suet. *Aug.* 65.1, *Tib.* 15.2; Dio Cass. 55.13.2.

return to Rome, which was sanctioned, on the understanding that he was to have no future part in the business of the state; and when in AD 3 Augustus' powers were once again renewed for a further ten years, there was no mention of his stepson.[95] Tiberius abided by this limitation over the next two years. Once he had undertaken the ceremony of bringing his son Drusus down to the Forum to be enrolled as an adult citizen, he moved from his house on the Esquiline hill in the middle of Rome (once the property of Pompeius Magnus and then of Marcus Antonius) to another less conspicuous one in the gardens of Maecenas nearby; and when Lucius Caesar died later in the same year, he wrote a verse elegy on the subject.[96] But however well Tiberius had managed to establish better relations with his stepfather, the adoption of these two was not and could not be like that of Gaius and Lucius in 17 BC. Agrippa Postumus might be seen as a substitute for one of his dead brothers, but Tiberius was forty-five years old in AD 4, and his place in the succession process looks far more like that of the elder Agrippa before his death in 12 BC than that of Gaius and Lucius; that is, as the guardian of the next generation, should Augustus die before the younger members of the imperial family were old enough to assume the position he held. This is demonstrated by another move that Augustus arranged before the adoptions took place in July. Tiberius was made to adopt his nephew, Nero Claudius Drusus Germanicus, the elder son of his dead younger brother Drusus.[97] As a result, on Tiberius' adoption, Augustus gained two grandsons, Germanicus and Tiberius' own son Drusus. Germanicus was already married to Agrippina, who was not only the daughter of Agrippa and Augustus' now disgraced daughter Julia but also the sister of Gaius and Lucius Caesar and Agrippa Postumus, so their children would be descendants of Augustus himself. The similarity of Tiberius' position with that of Agrippa can be seen in the grant in AD 4 of *tribunicia potestas* for the next ten years, a power held only by Augustus himself since 23 BC and for five-year terms by Agrippa in 18 and 13 BC and by Tiberius in 6 BC.[98] This had

95. Suet. *Tib*. 13.2; Vell. Pat. 2.102.1 and 103.1. Augustus' renewal of powers: Dio Cass. 55.12.3.
96. Suet. *Tib*. 15.1. On the house of Pompeius, see Cic. *Phil*. 2.68; Vell. Pat. 2.77; Appian, *B Civ*. 2.126. Elegy on the death of Drusus: Suet. *Tib*. 70.2.
97. Suet. *Tib*. 15.2; Dio Cass. 55.13.2; *Inst. Iust*. 1.11.11.
98. Dio Cass. 55.13.2. Suetonius says that the period was only five years (*Tib*. 16.1), but Dio's account is supported by Augustus' own statement (*RG* 6.2) of the number of times he was granted a colleague in the *tribunicia potestas* by the senate. See also above, pp. 99–101, 116, 132 and 145.

not been enough ten years earlier to keep Tiberius from departing for retirement in Rhodes; but this time he was not only to be Augustus' second-in-command and the protector of his young intended successors. By his adoption he was himself given a place in the scheme, both as father of the *princeps'* adoptive grandsons and in his own right as adoptive son. Augustus had by this move re-established the imperial family, almost wrecked by the deaths of Gaius and Lucius, and given Tiberius a position that he was prepared to take up, especially after the trauma of what had become his exile in Rhodes. When, at the adoption ceremony, Augustus declared that he was adopting Tiberius for the good of the *res publica*, there can be little doubt that he meant it.[99]

Tiberius in Germany and Pannonia, 4–9 AD

No sooner had he become the adopted son of Augustus than Tiberius left Rome to return to Germany, where trouble had broken out again in the previous three years. Velleius Paterculus, who was on his staff as a commander of cavalry, gives an unsurprisingly glowing account of his arrival among the troops. Having entered Germany, he subdued once again the tribes between the rivers Rhine and Weser in a campaign which lasted into December, and set up winter quarters at the source of the river Lippe before returning temporarily to Rome.[100]

In Rome this year also saw an important piece of legislation on the manumission of slaves and two executive actions in areas which were more closely associated with the work of the censors. The *lex Aelia Sentia*, which bears the names of the two ordinary consuls of AD 4, followed the *lex Fufia Caninia* of five years before in limiting the conditions under which slaves could be manumitted.[101] Unlike the earlier law, this concerned all manumissions, not just those under the will of a deceased master. An age limit was placed on the master, who had to be over twenty, and on the slave, who had to be at least thirty, but in each case a council, made up in Rome of five senators and five *equites* or in the provinces of twenty *recuperatores*, who were Roman citizens, could allow the manumission if it approved the reasons for it. Otherwise slaves below the age of thirty who were freed did not become full citizens immediately but were given the

99. Vell. Pat. 2.104.1; Suet. *Tib.* 21.3.
100. Vell. Pat. 2.104–5; Dio Cass. 55.28.5.

status of 'Latins', with freedom and some rights (based on those held by Latin allies of Rome in Italy before the extension of Roman citizenship in the 80s BC); these were later referred to as Junian Latins, since their position was defined by a *lex Iunia* of uncertain date, but probably Augustan.[102] Citizenship could be gained subsequently if a child was born from a marriage with a Roman woman or another Latin. Manumissions which were intended to defraud the master's creditors were also forbidden; and slaves who had been punished for criminal acts, either by a master or by the state, were permanently debarred from citizenship and placed in a status (or rather non-status) of *dediticii*, which had previously applied to foreign enemies who had surrendered but not subsequently been given any other place in the structure of alliances. Such bad characters shared with the Junian Latins the inability to make a will but were also required to live at least a hundred miles from Rome, and they were in effect free but stateless.[103] The focus of the legislators was clearly on manumissions conducted in Rome itself, as the limitation of *dediticii* shows; but its requirements were not restricted to the process of manumission alone. The freedman was not to show ingratitude to his *patronus* (his former master) and, though there is no evidence as to the penalties or the occasions for the charge in the original law, this was increasingly elaborated in the centuries that followed.[104] As often, there is no sign of a statutory provision of this sort under the Republic, where it was probably one of the rights of the *paterfamilias*, and was only now incorporated into law.

It was also at this time that Augustus conducted another review of the membership of the senate, using a committee of senators to undertake the task, with three being chosen by lot from a list of ten who had been approved by himself. This was similar to but much less complex than the process he had adopted in 18 BC for his second review (the first having been in 29 BC), no doubt because of the collapse of the previous method which led to his having to take on the business himself.[105] The review has been seen as an attempt

101. Dio Cass. 55.13.7; Gaius, *Inst.* 1.13–41; Ulpian, *Tit.* 1.11–15. On the *lex Fufia Caninia*, see above, pp. 159–60.

102. On the date of the *lex Iunia*, see A. N. Sherwin-White, *The Roman Citizenship*, 2nd edn, Oxford: Oxford University Press, 1973, 332–4.

103. Gaius, *Inst.* 1.25–27; Ulpian, *Tit.* 20.14.

104. Ulpian, *Dig.* 40.9.30; Paul, *Dig.* 50.16.70. See W. W. Buckland, *The Roman Law of Slavery*, Cambridge: Cambridge University Press, 1908, 422–7.

105. Dio Cass. 55.13.3. This is probably the third review of the senate referred to in Aug. *RG* 8.2 (so Rich, *Cassius Dio*, 215; contra A. H. M. Jones, 'The censorial powers

to secure the senate by expelling those who might be opposed to Tiberius, and it is true that Dio links Augustus' decision to conduct it with his having settled the matter of the succession with the adoption of Tiberius and Tiberius' adoption of Germanicus.[106] However, Dio also says that not many senators were removed from the list, either by declaring themselves no longer eligible or by being forcibly erased, and this perhaps suggests that it was done because it was so long since the last full review of 18 BC and perhaps also because of Augustus' unwillingness to cause antipathy from the senatorial class during his promotion of his young sons, Gaius and Lucius.

The other piece of business, mentioned only by Dio, was a census. Augustus does not include this in his account of the censuses he conducted, given in the *Res Gestae*, even though Dio's description sounds to be of a full, formal, censorial census, including the ceremony of the *lustrum* at the end.[107] In any case, this was not an ordinary census: Dio says that it excluded all those living outside Italy and anyone whose property was less than 200,000 sesterces, that is, half the census qualification of the equestrian order. The reason Dio gives is that Augustus was afraid that those excluded might be disturbed if they were included and go into revolt. The motive for this census (assuming that Dio is right that it took place at all) is far from clear. It has been associated with the creation of a fourth group from whom jurors were drawn (*decuria*) to add to the already existing three, made up of senators and *equites*. This consisted of men who had a census rating of at least 200,000 sesterces (and hence were called *ducenarii*) and dealt with cases involving smaller amounts of money.[108] The identical level of the census qualification is suggestive, though it may be that the legal reform was the consequence of the partial census rather than vice versa. Another explanation is that this was a preparation for the new tax introduced by Augustus two years later to fund retirement payments for veteran soldiers, though it is not clear why this should lead to a census only in Italy.[109] Neither of these, however, seems to

of Augustus', in *Studies in Roman Government and Law*, Oxford: Blackwell, 1968, 21–6, at 22). For the review of 18 BC, see above, pp. 116–18.

106. Dio Cass. 55.13.3; Levick, *Tiberius*, 51.

107. Dio Cass. 55.13.4–6; cf. *RG* 8.2–3 and Suet. *Aug*. 27.5. On the *lustrum*, see above, p. 82.

108. Suet. *Aug*. 32.3; Jones, *Studies in Roman Government and Law*, 23 and 41.

109. P. A. Brunt, *Italian Manpower 225 BC–AD 14*, Oxford: Oxford University Press, 1971, 115 n.4; W. Eck, *Die staatliche Organisation Italiens in der hohen Kaiserzeit* (*Vestigia* 28), Munich: C. H. Beck, 1979, 125 n. 62. On the tax, see below, p. 172.

fit with the full-scale *lustrum* which Dio refers to, or to his insistence that Augustus used the proconsular *imperium* to conduct it. This sounds like a misrepresentation of the way in which Augustus used consular *imperium* in 29 and 8 BC to conduct full censuses, and casts doubt on Dio's whole account.[110] He may have attached the details of the other censuses to the much more restricted reassessment that took place in AD 4.

In the next year, Tiberius continued his campaign in Germany. Velleius, never missing an opportunity to exalt Tiberius, gives a picture of the universal success of his operations, with the establishment of Roman control of the whole of Germany up to the Elbe and the arrival of the fleet, which had sailed through the North Sea and down the river to connect with the land forces. This was undoubtedly a major logistical achievement, though the north German coastline was not quite as unknown as Velleius suggests: Tiberius' brother Drusus had sailed along the coast while he was campaigning in Germany between 12 and 9 BC, and had also reached the Elbe, as had a subsequent commander in Germany, Lucius Domitius Ahenobarbus, who in AD 1 had undertaken operations up to and across the Elbe.[111] As the events of the following year showed, Tiberius' securing of this huge territory between the Rhine and the Elbe was intended to serve as preparation for an assault on the Marcomanni, who had migrated from the valley of the Main into Bohemia in about 8 BC, under pressure from the campaigns of Drusus and Tiberius, and had, under the rule of their leader Maroboduus, established a powerful presence there.[112] For the time being Tiberius returned to Rome at the end of the season, once he had led his troops into their winter quarters.

In Rome the year had begun badly, with the Tiber flooding again, and with a corn shortage, accompanied by earthquakes and an eclipse of the sun. It was, however, in this year that Agrippa Postumus was admitted to the *iuvenes* and thus became a full citizen, as had happened for his two brothers Gaius and Lucius in 5 and 2 BC respectively.[113] The contrast between this occurrence and the

---

110. See above, pp. 82–4 and 141.
111. Vell. Pat. 2.106–9. On Drusus' voyage, see Suet. *Claud.* 1.2; Tacitus, *Germania* 34.2; on his campaigns in Germany, see above, pp. 136–7 and 138. On Domitius Ahenobarbus, Dio Cass. 55.10a.2; Tacitus, *Ann.* 4.44.2; Suet. *Nero* 4. It is probably to Drusus' voyage that Augustus refers at *RG* 26.4 (so C. Nicolet, *Space, Geography and Politics in the Early Roman Empire*, Ann Arbor: University of Michigan Press, 1991, 87).
112. Vell. Pat. 2.108–9. See above, p. 143.
113. Dio Cass. 55.22.3–4. On Gaius and Lucius, see above, pp. 150–2 and 153.

earlier two is more remarkable than the similarities. This year, unlike those of the introduction of Gaius and Lucius into public life, Augustus did not take the consulship; Agrippa Postumus was not made *princeps iuventutis*, was not pre-elected to the consulship and did not receive any of the other honours that had accompanied the first two's coming of age. Indeed Agrippa was two years older than his brothers when the ceremony, such as it was, took place. The difference between his status and that of his brothers can only have been made more noticeable by the passing of a law by the two consuls of AD 5, Lucius Valerius Messalla Volesus and Gnaeus Cornelius Cinna Magnus, which commemorated Gaius and Lucius by instituting ten new voting units (*centuriae*) in the *comitia centuriata*, the assembly which elected the consuls and praetors, which were to cast their votes first and to determine the candidates who were to be elected. These were called the *centuriae Caesarum*. This change was intended to give permanent recognition to the dead brothers, and was certainly still functioning fifteen years later.[114] The establishment of such an honour stands in marked contrast to the low-key treatment of Agrippa Postumus. That snub to Postumus highlighted in turn the importance of Tiberius in the dynastic intentions of Augustus. Whatever those who would have preferred another young Caesar in the model of Gaius or Lucius might have hoped after the adoptions of the previous year, it must now have been clear that the emperor was not putting his expectations on a young man still in his teens at a time when he himself was approaching his sixty-eighth birthday.

The year also saw two other incidents which revealed problems and discontents in quite different parts of the structure of the life of the Roman state. A vacancy had occurred in the college of the Vestal Virgins, which required Augustus, as *pontifex maximus*, to draw up a list of twenty girls between the ages of six and ten, with no physical defects and with both parents still alive, from whom one would be chosen by lot. On this occasion senators, from amongst whose families the Vestals were usually drawn, proved unwilling to put their daughters forward as candidates, despite Augustus' assertion that, had one of his granddaughters been of the right age, he would have added her name. This was a serious matter for the *princeps*. The Vestals were an ancient and highly significant part of

114. The *lex Valeria Cornelia* is attested in the later bill which gave similar honours to the dead Germanicus in AD 20 (M. H. Crawford (ed.), *Roman Statutes*, London: Institute of Classical Studies, 1996, 1.507–43).

the religious establishment, and he enhanced their status in various ways, including at some point setting aside special seats for them at the theatre. To ensure that there was a complete list of twenty candidates in this year, he set aside the usual requirement that the parents should also not be former slaves, though in the event it was not one of these who was chosen.[115]

The other problem was more pressing. Dio records that soldiers were angry with the small size of payments they received on discharge from service and refused to serve beyond the period of sixteen years that had been specified by Augustus when he set up the system of payments on discharge in 13 BC.[116] The matter was critical, both because of the major offensive being planned in Germany and because a large number of men who had been recruited after the large demobilisations of 14 BC had passed the date at which their service should have ended; they were probably kept on active service, under a process called being *sub vexillo* ('under a standard'), which made it possible for veterans to continue as soldiers for some years.[117] The response to this potentially damaging development was to adjust further the terms of service for soldiers. The sum they were to be given at discharge was to be 12,000 sesterces for ordinary soldiers and 20,000 for members of the Praetorian Guard; but at the same time the period of service was increased to twenty years for the former and sixteen years for the latter. The decision, taken formally by the senate but doubtless under the advice of the *princeps*, was inevitable, but the cost was substantial, and Augustus proposed to the senate that revenues should be sought to fund, as both Dio and Suetonius imply, both the pay and the end-of-service payments for the soldiers.[118]

The problem of identifying resources sufficient to cover these costs ran on into the following year (AD 6). Augustus set up a separate institution, to be called the military treasury (*aerarium militare*), under the control of three ex-praetors, chosen by lot and serving for three years, into which he transferred a sum of money in the names of himself and Tiberius. In the *Res Gestae* he states that this was 170,000,000 sesterces, paid in this year out of his own funds, and

115. Dio Cass. 55.22.5; Suet. *Aug.* 31.3, 44.3. See Beard et al., *Religions of Rome*, 1.193–4. On the regulations for the appointment of Vestals, see Gellius, *NA* 1.12.1–12.
116. Dio Cass. 55.23.1. On the arrangements in 13 BC, see above, pp. 131–2.
117. See L. J. F. Keppie, 'Vexilla veteranorum', *Papers of the British School at Rome* 41 (1973), 8–17.
118. Dio Cass. 55.24.9; Suet. *Aug.* 49.2.

Dio records that he undertook to pay more annually, though there is no indication that he actually did so. Augustus also accepted gifts from foreign rulers and from cities, though he refused those proffered by private individuals.[119] All this, however, was far too little to cover the expected costs: at this date there were twenty-eight legions under arms. each of between 5,000 and 6,000 soldiers, of which only 14,000 could have been provided with their retirement benefit by the money given by Augustus in AD 6. A regular source of income was essential, and Augustus invited members of the senate to suggest ways in which this might be done. Unsurprisingly, there was no agreement in the proposals that came as a result. In the end he himself established at least two sources: the revenue from a tax of 1 per cent on sales by auction (*centesima rerum venalium*) was assigned to the *aerarium militare*; and in addition (and much more controversially) he instituted a new tax of 5 per cent on inheritances (*vicesuma hereditatium*), which was levied on all bequests other than those left to close members of the family. Though this seems not to have been applied to the very poor, it was a radical and intrusive tax, which affected huge numbers of individuals and required the opening and investigation of wills by officials across the empire.[120] That Augustus was prepared to undertake such a far-reaching change in order to provide for the post-retirement conditions of the army despite the discontent of senators and others shows how significant the soldiers and their attitudes were. The process he had put in place in 13 BC to make the military a fully professional body, loyal to the state and to its leader, remained central to the emperor, and its importance was about to be demonstrated still more clearly.

Tiberius began the year by consecrating the rebuilt temple of Castor and Pollux in the Forum in the names of himself and his deceased brother Drusus on 27 January. The cost had been met from booty from Germany, where Tiberius and Drusus had campaigned together, and the appropriateness of a dedication in the name of the two brothers to the divine brothers who were patrons of the city was noted by Ovid in his entry in his poem on the Roman calendar for that day.[121] Tiberius returned to Germany to begin the campaign

119. Dio Cass. 55. 25.1–6; Aug. *RG* 17.2. On the *centesima rerum venaliun*: Tacitus, *Ann.* 1.78.2.
120. F. G. B. Millar, *The Roman Empire and its Neighbours*, London: Duckworth, 1981, 91.
121. Dio Cass. 55.27.4; Suet. *Tib.* 20; Ovid, *Fasti* 1.705–8; *Fast. Praenest.* (*Inscr. Ital.* 13.2.116–17, 403–4).

against Maroboduus, carefully arranged the previous year. The intention was for Tiberius himself to bring the five legions based in Illyricum up to the Danube, to be joined by forces under Gaius Sentius Saturninus from the army based on the Rhine in the territory of the Marcomanni; but before the two armies could meet, news reached Tiberius of a serious revolt which had broken out in Illyricum itself. It had begun in Dalmatia when the governor of Illyricum, Valerius Messalinus, attempted to raise a contingent of local troops to accompany him to join Tiberius in Germany, a task made more difficult because of grievances about the taxes that had had to be paid since the settlement of the area by Tiberius in 10 BC.[122] Those who gathered for this purpose were stirred up by a leader called Bato from the tribe of the Desidiates, based near modern Sarajevo, and overcame the Romans who attempted to control them. No sooner had Dalmatia been roused to revolt than another insurrection began in the north of the province in Pannonia, led by another man by the name of Bato, who belonged to the Breuci from the valley of the river Save. This group attacked the Roman base at Sirmium, and were only prevented from taking it by the intervention of the governor of the neighbouring province of Moesia, Aulus Caecina Severus, who defeated them at a battle on the river Drave. Further south, however, the Desidiate Bato succeeded in attacking Salonae, a port on the Adriatic, and, despite himself being wounded there, sent forces down the coast, ravaging the region as far as Apollonia on the border with Macedonia and even into Macedonia itself. At Apollonia, despite an initial reverse, the insurgents succeeded in inflicting a defeat on the Romans who had been sent against them.[123]

At Rome, panic broke out. Augustus in the senate said that if action were not taken the enemy might be within sight of the city within ten days; all veterans were called up, freedmen were recruited to the legions, senators and members of the equestrian order were required to promise their services and Tiberius was to be the commander in the war. Later, Suetonius was to describe the war as the most serious threat since the Carthaginians.[124] Tiberius meanwhile

---

122. See above, p. 138.

123. Vell. Pat. 2.110; Dio Cass. 55 29. On the Pannonian wars in general, see E. Koestermann, 'Der pannonisch-dalmatische Krieg 6–9 n. Chr.', *Hermes* 81 (1953), 345–78; D. Dzino, *Illyricum in Roman Politics, 229 BC–AD 68*, Cambridge: Cambridge University Press, 2010, 137–55.

124. Vell. Pat. 2.110.6–111.2; Suet. *Tib.* 16.1.

made peace with Maroboduus and, abandoning the assault on the Marcomanni and sending Valerius Messalinus ahead of him, marched the Illyrian army back to the province from which he had brought them earlier. To protect Italy from the invasion of which those in Rome were so fearful, he based himself at Siscia in the upper valley of the Save, and awaited the reinforcements due from the capital. Messalinus, with one under-strength legion, was successfully checked in open conflict by the Desidiate Bato, but managed to recover sufficiently to mount an ambush and put the enemy to flight. At this point Bato joined forces with his Breucian namesake, thereby constructing a formidable alliance, along with a third leader named Pinnes. The two Batos established themselves on Mount Alma, some 15 kilometres to the north of Sirmium. They were harassed by a contingent of Thracians, under the command of their king Rhoetometalces, who had been brought by Caecina Severus, but Severus himself was unable to dislodge them, and when he had to return to Moesia, which was being threatened by raids from Dacians and Sarmatians, they were able to continue their attacks on Roman allies in the area, undisturbed by Tiberius and Messalinus, who remained in Siscia. It was probably only late in the year that the promised reinforcements arrived from Rome, brought by Velleius Paterculus, who later was to write the history of these events and who, after having been elected quaestor for the following year, was commissioned by Augustus to undertake this task. The following year, in place of his expected quaestorian functions, Augustus was to send him back to Illyricum as a staff officer, with the title *legatus Augusti*, to serve under Tiberius.[125]

The abandonment of the campaign in Germany and the revolt in Illyricum were not the only problems that Augustus faced in the wider empire in AD 6. In Palestine, where the kingdom of Herod the Great had been divided between his three sons ten years earlier, one of them, Archelaus, appointed ethnarch of Judaea, Samaria and Idumaea, was accused of misgovernment by a deputation of his subjects, supported by complaints from his two brothers. Augustus summoned him to Rome and, after depriving him of his ethnarchy, banished him to Vienna (modern Vienne) in Gallia Narbonensis. His territory was taken into Roman control, under the governorship of an equestrian official, and Publius Sulpicius Quirinus, the governor

125. Vell. Pat. 2.111; Dio Cass. 55.30.

of Syria, undertook a census there as well as in Syria.[126] Dio also records under this year other wars which took place about this time: Sardinia was overrun with bandits, to the extent that for some years an equestrian military commander governed the island, which had been designated as one of the people's provinces in 27 BC,[127] and Dio also mentions troubles with banditry in Isauria, a mountainous area in southern Asia Minor, which developed into warfare, and the suppression by Cossus Cornelius Lentulus, the proconsul of the province of Africa, of a long-lasting rebellion by the Gaetulian tribes against Juba II, the king of Mauretania, who had been installed by Augustus in 25 BC.[128] The expansion of Roman power across the Mediterranean region as well as into Germany and the Balkans was putting a major strain on the resources available to the emperor.

Meanwhile Rome was also suffering. Severe famine affected the city, caused apparently by crop failures in the regions from which grain was usually shipped. Emergency measures were put in place: gladiators and slaves who were up for sale were moved out of the city (as were all foreigners except doctors and teachers), the courts went into recess and senators were allowed to leave (a temporary change was introduced with regard to the quorum required in the senate for the passing of decrees). Two former consuls were appointed to supervise and ration the grain and bread supplies, and Augustus is said to have provided an extra corn dole to those who were on the list to receive it, a measure that he repeated in the following year. He even contemplated abolishing the corn dole, because the importation of grain had discouraged farmers in Italy from growing it. The famine must have continued at least until September, since he forbade the public banquets which usually marked the celebration of his birthday on 23 September; and it was only after the shortage lessened that gladiatorial games in honour of Tiberius' brother Drusus could be held, in the names of his sons Germanicus and Tiberius Claudius Nero (the future emperor Claudius), fifteen years after he had died in Germany.[129]

126. Strabo, 16.2.46; Josephus, *BJ* 2.111, 117–18; *AJ* 17.342–4, 18.1–4; Dio Cass. 55.27.6; *EJ* 231. See Smallwood, *The Jews under Roman Rule*, 114–19, 144–5.
127. Dio Cass. 55.28.1. On the state of Sardinia, see Strabo, 5.2.7, and S. L. Dyson, *The Creation of the Roman Frontier*, Princeton: Princeton University Press, 1985, 259–63; on the allocation of provinces in 27 BC, see above, p. 87.
128. Dio Cass. 55.28.3–4. On Cossus' victory in Africa, see also *EJ* 43; Vell. Pat. 2.116.2; Florus, 2.31.40; Orosius, 6.21.18. On Juba II, see above, p. 95.
129. Dio Cass. 55.26.1–2; Suet. *Aug.* 42.3. On the repetition of the appointment of grain commissioners, Dio Cass. 55.31.4.

As if the famine were not enough, serious fires broke out in Rome, which destroyed several parts of the city. Augustus had given the responsibility for fire precautions to the *magistri* of the fourteen regions of the city when he had set them up in 7 BC, but now he instituted a new body of freedmen, called the *vigiles*, under an equestrian prefect, initially (according to Dio) as a temporary measure, but then retained to deal with the recurrent threat.[130] They were divided into seven cohorts, each to cover two of the fourteen *regiones*, and were distributed at stations across the city and also acted as the nearest thing Rome had to a police force, so that the *praefectus vigilum* had jurisdiction in cases of petty crime. In the following year another new tax was introduced of 2 per cent on the sale of slaves, the revenue from which was to provide pay for the *vigiles*.[131]

There were other troubles in Rome apart from the outbreak of fires. Dio reports that discontent resulting from the famine, the tax on inheritance and the losses sustained in the fires led to plans for revolution, with fly sheets being posted round the city at night. It was rumoured that the person responsible for this was a certain Publius Rufus, but there was a suspicion that others were behind him. An investigation was mounted, with rewards promised for information, but this only exacerbated the situation. Only once the grain scarcity had been dealt with did the disturbances calm down. There were also problems with the elections for the following year, as appears from a note Dio places later in his account, that Augustus had to designate all the magistrates himself because of electoral strife.[132] Although Dio does not make the connection (and the famine and the fires are perhaps an adequate explanation), some modern scholars have argued that these demonstrations are to be linked with a struggle about the successor to Augustus within the imperial house, between on the one hand Tiberius and his supporters and on the other those who were promoting the claims of young Agrippa Postumus, particularly Julia, Augustus' granddaughter and Postumus' sister.[133] What is clear is that Agrippa Postumus, either in AD 6 or early the following year, was rejected by Augustus.

---

130. Dio Cass. 55.26.4–5; Strabo, 5.3.7; Suet. *Aug.* 30.1; Paul, *Dig.* 1.15.1 and 3. O. F. Robinson, *Ancient Rome: City Planning and Administration*, London: Routledge, 1992, 106–10; W. Nippel, *Public Order in Ancient Rome*, Cambridge: Cambridge University Press, 1995, 96–8. See above, p. 144.
131. Dio Cass. 55.31.4.
132. Dio Cass. 55.27.1–3; 34.2.
133. So Levick, *Tiberius*, 54–61; but see Syme, *Augustan Aristocracy*, 115–27. See further, below, pp. 179–80.

In a notably severe move, the *princeps* disowned his adopted son, returning him to the family of the Vipsanii and removing him to the town of Surrentum (modern Sorrento) on the Amalfi coast, south of Naples; he was later in AD 7 transferred to the island of Planasia, between Corsica and the Italian coast, and a decree of the senate ordered that he should remain there until he died. Suetonius states that the reason for this was his sordid and violent temperament (*ingenium sordidum ac ferox*), and other sources describe him as mentally imbalanced: it can be no accident that *ferocitas* was a reason that could be cited for the act of disowning a child. As a consequence he lost not only his place in the imperial family but also the wealth that he had inherited from his father Agrippa, which was given to the newly established *aerarium militare*.[134]

The reason for this radical change of attitude by Augustus towards a young man whom only two years before he had adopted as his son along with Tiberius is not clear. It is unlikely that it was simply Postumus' waywardness and bad temper, though that seems to be the formal reason given, and is reflected in the highly hostile sources. A passing note in Suetonius records that a plebeian named Junius Novatus circulated a letter 'in the name of the young Agrippa' which was scathingly critical of Augustus, and Dio claims he spoke ill of Livia as a stepmother.[135] It may well be that he saw himself as the natural successor to the position that his two elder brothers had held, and resented the way in which he was denied the rapid and spectacular promotion that they had had and the evident intention of Augustus to make Tiberius his successor, to be followed by Germanicus. If this was the case, Postumus would have been not only interfering with the policy of the *princeps* but also undermining the image of the imperial house as a unified and model family, which Augustus had done so much to disseminate, not least in the adoptions of AD 4.[136]

So it was Germanicus, rather than Agrippa Postumus (as had apparently been expected), who as quaestor took reinforcements, consisting of freedmen as well as of free-born citizens, to Tiberius at Siscia early in AD 7.[137] Tiberius cautiously moved against the enemy,

---

134. Vell. Pat. 2.112.7; Suet. *Aug.* 65.1 and 4; Dio Cass. 55.32.1–2 (cf. on *ferocitas* Quint. *Decl. min.* 259 and 279). For a different view of the rejection of Postumus, see Shelagh Jameson, 'Augustus and Agrippa Postumus', *Historia* 24 (1975), 287–314.
135. Suet. *Aug.* 51.1; Dio Cass. 55.32.2.
136. See above, pp. 164–6.
137. Dio Cass. 55.31.1 and 32.1.

avoiding direct contact and wearing them down by depriving them of supplies. This was a prudent strategy, though Augustus for one seems to have thought victory over the rebels could be achieved more quickly.[138] Germanicus contributed to the process by harassing and defeating the Mazaei, to the south of Siscia. A large force consisting of five legions under the command of Caecina Severus from Moesia and Marcus Plautius Silvanus, the governor of Galatia-Pamphylia, together with cavalry supplied and led by Rhoeto-metalces, the king of Thrace, advanced into the area later in the year but were nearly destroyed en route, having been ambushed and surrounded by enemy forces. They succeeded in fighting their way out of a desperate situation and getting through to join up with Tiberius. He now had an immense force of ten legions at his disposal. Of these he seems to have taken the new arrivals to strengthen the important position at Sirmium, so that when Caecina had to return again to Moesia, Silvanus remained with the two legions that he had brought. Tiberius returned to his base at Siscia and, leaving his *legati* (including Velleius Paterculus) in command there, went back as usual to Rome.[139]

Tiberius' policy of attrition paid dividends in the next year (AD 8). By the summer the Pannonians in the north were so reduced by famine and disease that the Breucian Bato handed over Pinnes, one of the other leaders of the revolt, and he and his followers laid down their arms at the river Bathinus (perhaps the Bosna, in modern Bosnia and Herzegovina). This was not, however, the end of the war. Bato, who was rewarded by the Romans by being recognised as the leader of the Breuci, was captured and killed by the Desidiate Bato, at which the revolt sprang to life again, and was suppressed by the action of Plautius Silvanus. The surviving Bato abandoned the northern Pannonian area and withdrew to Dalmatia in the south, while the Romans returned to their winter quarters at Siscia.[140] Tiberius did not return as usual to Rome at the end of the campaigning season, but remained with his troops until the following spring, when he did return to report on the progress of the

---

138. This is the most likely interpretation of Dio's remark at 55.31.1.
139. Vell. Pat. 112.3–6, 113.1–114.3; Dio Cass. 55.32.3–4. R. Syme, 'Some notes on legions under Augustus', *Journal of Roman Studies* 23 (1933), 14–33, at 26–7; Dzino, *Illyricum*, 150–1.
140. Vell. Pat. 2.114.4; Dio Cass. 55.33.1, 34.4–5.

conflict to the emperor, leaving his forces under the command of his legate, Marcus Aemilius Lepidus.[141]

Augustus, once again, had not had a good year. Dio, in a passage disrupted by yet another of the manuscript lacunae which break into his account of these years, depicts him as worn down by the physical weariness of old age (he was now seventy years old) and consequently involving himself less in the public business of the state. He still heard legal cases, accompanied by counsellors, at a tribunal on the Palatine, but passed to a group of three ex-consuls the hearing of embassies from cities and kings, which, unless the matters raised had to be considered by the senate or the emperor, they were empowered to deal with themselves. He no longer attended elections, instead commending candidates by posting notices. As for the senate, he absented himself even when they were acting in a quasi-juridical fashion. He did, however, venture as far as Ariminium to consult with Tiberius on the progress of the Pannonian war.[142]

What must have caused Augustus particular grief in this year was yet another fissure in the already troubled imperial family. His granddaughter Julia, born to his daughter Julia and Marcus Agrippa, was banished to the island of Trimerus, one of an archipelago of small islands off the coast of Apulia in the Adriatic Sea. The grounds were adultery with a senator, Decimus Iunius Silanus, who was not punished by a court ruling but who, having been informed that he no longer enjoyed the friendship of the emperor, retired into a voluntary exile. Julia herself was less fortunate. Unlike Silanus, who was permitted to return to Rome in AD 25, she remained on her island until her death twenty years later, though supported by clandestine financial assistance from the emperor's wife, Livia; moreover a child born to her after her exile was, on Augustus' orders, neither acknowledged nor allowed to be reared, and he demolished the country palace Julia had built for herself. In his will he specifically excluded her from burial in the Mausoleum which housed the ashes of the emperor's family.[143] The savagery of Augustus' reaction has led some modern scholars to posit a deeper problem than simply the

141. Dio Cass. 56.1.1.
142. Dio Cass. 55.33.5–34.3. On embassies, see Talbert, *Senate*, 412. Dio assumes that the senate acted as a court, as was the case in his own time, but see J. S. Richardson, 'The senate, the courts, and the *SC de Cn. Pisone patre*', *Classical Quarterly* n.s. 47 (1997), 510–18.
143. Suet. *Aug.* 65.1 and 4, 72.3, 101.4. Return of Silanus: Tacitus, *Ann.* 3.24; death of Julia: Taitus, *Ann.* 4.71.

question of adultery and to propose opposition to his favouring Tiberius as against the true Julian family, represented by Agrippa Postumus, Julia's brother.[144] This view is strengthened by the appearance of Julia's husband, Lucius Aemillius Paullus, in a list of conspirators given by Suetonius, where he is associated with one Plautius Rufus, who is often identified with the Publius Rufus who was responsible for inciting rebellion against Augustus by a campaign of fly posters in Rome two years earlier.[145] There may well have been resentment on the part of Julia and those around her at the treatment of Agrippa Postumus, but the theory of a conspiracy underlying the exile of Julia herself is weak. The gap between the disturbances of AD 6 and her banishment seems too long to account for a close connection between the two, and it was only in 8 that another of Augustus' step-grandchildren, Tiberius Claudius Nero (the future emperor Claudius), was required to dissolve his betrothal to Aemilia Lepida, the daughter of Paullus and Julia. Moreover Paullus himself was not put to death, as might have been expected if he had been involved in such a conspiracy, but was still alive until AD 14.[146] The mere fact of yet another case of immorality within the imperial family, following that of her mother Julia ten years before, once again flouting the laws that he himself had promoted, was enough to account for Augustus' rage. It is no surprise that at about the same time, Ovid, who had earlier paraded himself as the poet of liberated sexuality, was banished by the emperor to the Black Sea town of Tomis, whence he never returned.[147]

Tiberius' return to Rome in the early spring of AD 9 was accompanied by the pomp and ceremony which were usually reserved for the re-entry of Augustus himself to the city. The games which were put on by the consuls at the close of the ceremonies were, however, disturbed by a demonstration by members of the equestrian order, objecting to penalties imposed on those who were unmarried and had no children by the *lex Iulia de maritandis ordinibus*, the law that Augustus had promulgated in 18 BC, and perhaps to new proposals, modifying the *lex Iulia*, which the emperor had proposed and which resulted soon after. Augustus, indignant at this, summoned an assembly in the Forum, at which he separated the unmarried and the

---

144. This view is clearly presented by Levick, *Tiberius*, 54–61.
145. Suet. *Aug.* 19.1; Dio Cass. 55.27.3. See above, p. 176.
146. Suet. *Claud.* 26.1; *ILS* 5026. Syme, *Augustan Aristocracy*, 121–7; Swan, *The Augustan Succession*, 183–4.
147. See above, pp. 157–8. On Ovid's exile, see Syme, *History in Ovid*, 215–29.

married men into two sections, and delivered to each a long speech, urging the former to marry and produce offspring. He further exemplified this by bringing forward the sons of Germanicus, who had returned with Tiberius from the Pannonian war, and seating them on his own and on their father's laps.[148] Later in the year a revised law on marriage was passed, in the names of the suffect consuls in office in the latter part of the year, Marcus Papius Mutilus and Quintus Poppaeus Secundus. As in the case of the *lex Iulia*, it is difficult to determine exactly what were the changes to the earlier law made at this time because in our legal sources the two are regarded as a single body of law. It has been suggested recently that the incapacity of the unmarried to inherit, a penalty imposed under the *lex Iulia*, was extended to those who had no children, who were allowed to take only half of any inheritance left to them by anyone who was not a close relative;[149] and Dio states in this context that Augustus permitted some women to inherit amounts in excess of 100,000 sesterces, which had been forbidden under the *lex Voconia*, dating from the second century BC, and granted the rights of married women with children to the Vestal Virgins.[150] It also appears that, under the new law, the periods of exemption from incapacity to inherit allowed to women following divorce or the death of a husband were increased from those laid down in the *lex Iulia* (six months and a year respectively) to eighteen months and two years.[151] Tacitus indicates that this law was regarded as especially severe and Dio that it increased rewards to those with children, both of which suggest that there were other provisions of which we know nothing. It may be that Augustus had to modify his intended changes to the *lex Iulia*, as Suetonius suggests, but the tone of the speeches Dio puts in his mouth does not suggest that these were substantial; and it is also likely that the new penalties of incapacity, which will have resulted in forfeited inheritances being passed to the treasury, made

---

148. Dio Cass. 56.1.1–9.3; Suet. *Aug.* 34.2, *Tib.* 17.2. In his life of Tiberius, Suetonius seems to have conflated this return of Tiberius with his later entry into the city after the final conclusion of the war later in the year (Swan, *The Augustan Succession*, 224–5). On the *lex Iulia*, see above pp. 118–20. The speech given to Augustus by Dio (56.2.1–9.3) is, of course, Dio's composition.

149. Swan, *The Augustan Succession*, 232–4. Gaius, *Inst.* 2.286–6a and (probably) 2.111, distinguishes the position of the unmarried, imposed by the *lex Iulia*, from that of the childless, resulting from the *lex Papia Poppaea*.

150. Dio Cass. 56.10.2.

151. Ulpian, *Tit.* 14.

further resources available to the state, much needed to fund the
prolonged war in Pannonia and Dalmatia.[152]

It was to that war that first Germanicus and then Tiberius
returned in the late spring and early summer of AD 9. Germanicus
moved, with varying success, against a number of fortified places in
the mountains of Dalmatia. Tiberius seems to have advanced inland
into modern Bosnia, where he was joined by his legate, Lepidus, who
had undertaken a difficult march from Siscia through hitherto
unconquered country, ravaging and subduing it as he went. Tiberius
launched a three-pronged attack on the tribes of the region, one led
by Lepidus and a second by Plautius Silvanus from Sirmium in the
north, while he himself, accompanied by Germanicus, set of in
pursuit of the Desidiate leader, Bato. Tiberius eventually caught up
with Bato at the fortified and inaccessible site of Andetrium, not far
from Salonae on the Adriatic coast. After besieging the place,
Tiberius reduced Bato to asking for terms, but the others in the fort
refused to support Bato and he slipped away, abandoning the
remainder of those holding the fort. Tiberius then launched an
attack which, after a difficult and hard-fought struggle, succeeded.
Those who fled from the fortress were hunted down in the forests
that surrounded it.[153] While Germanicus, aided by Gaius Vibius
Postumus, probably governor of a new province of Dalmatia, spent
time clearing up a number of remaining points of resistance, Tiberius
made initial provisions for the settlement of the area, including
accepting the surrender of Bato, who, although he was to appear in
Tiberius' Illyrian triumph three years later, was spared his life to live
in honourable retirement in Ravenna.[154]

The long and costly war was over. Tiberius returned to Italy,
where Germanicus announced the successful conclusion of the
conflict in Rome. Augustus and Tiberius were both voted salutations
as *imperatores* and the celebration of triumphs; Germanicus was
awarded the *ornamenta triumphalia*, along with other generals who
had taken part in the war, Messalla Messalinus, Marcus Lepidus,
Plautius Silvanus and Gaius Vibius Postumus. In celebration of the
success of the imperial house, Germanicus was given the rank of
praetor and permission to stand for the consulship before he reached

---

152. Tacitus, *Ann.* 3.28; Dio Cass. 56.10.1; Suet. *Aug.* 34.
153. Vell. Pat. 2.115; Dio Cass. 56.11–14 (with Swan, *The Augustan Succession*, 215–45).
154. Dio Cass. 56.15–16; Suet. *Tib.* 20; Ovid, *Pont.* 2.1.43–6.

the normal age; and Drusus Caesar, Tiberius' own son, was admitted to meetings of the senate and to be counted ahead of ex-praetors once he was elected to the quaestorship.[155] The sense of victorious jubilation lasted no more than five days. News reached Rome from Germany that the commander of the Roman army there, Publius Quinctilius Varus, and his three legions had been wiped out by a well-planned assault, carried out by a huge military force of Germans, previously believed to be allies.

The Varian disaster and the withdrawal from Germany, AD 9–12

Varus had probably been in Germany since AD 6 or 7, in succession to Sentius Saturninus, who had commanded the Roman troops on the Rhine and was bringing them to meet Tiberius' own forces for the invasion of Bohemia when the Illyrian revolt broke out. The Germans had given no trouble during the period of the war and the sources give a picture of Varus as a civilian administrator, inept when it came to military matters and too ready to assume that his remit was to impose the structures of a Roman province on a people already pacified. This is too simplistic a view, both of the situation in Germany and of the career and character of Varus. He had previously been a successful governor of both Africa and Syria, and had shown himself ready to intervene with force when necessary. As for Germany, recent excavations have shown that before AD 9 military stations had been established not only along the Rhine but also eastwards, especially along the lines of the rivers Lippe and Main; and a civilian settlement, complete with forum building and a remarkable gilded equestrian statue, has been found at Waldgirmes, near Lahnau in Hesse, close to the river Lahn.[156] The overthrow of Rome's presence in Germany, when it came, was masterminded by a man who himself represented the extent to which Roman ways had been adopted by at least the upper echelons of German tribal society. Arminius, as the ancient sources call him, a young noble of the Cherusci, had become not only a Roman citizen as a result of his participation in earlier campaigns but even a member of the

155. Dio Cass. 56.17.1–3. Generals honoured: Vell. Pat. 2.112.2, 115.3. 116.2; Ovid, *Pont.* 2.2.85–90; *EJ* 200.
156. On Varus, see Syme, *Augustan Aristocracy*, 313–28. On Augustan sites in Germany, see Colin Wells, 'What's new along the Lippe: recent work in north Germany', *Britannia* 29 (1998), 457–64; Armin Becker, 'Lahnau–Waldgirmes: Eine augusteische Stadtgründung in Hessen', *Historia* 52 (2003), 337–50.

equestrian order; he was trusted by Varus and often in his company. It was this Arminius who engineered, along with others, a plot to drive the Romans out of Germany and secretly negotiated with other German leaders to secure their support. Although the story leaked out and was reported to Varus, he refused to believe it and allowed himself and his army to be lured into dense woodland in the territory of the Cherusci, to deal with a revolt which Ariminius had arranged. There they were ambushed by the forces of Arminius, who had left Varus shortly before, saying he would assemble local troops to support him, and after a running battle lasting four days in pouring rain, the Romans were effectively exterminated after a final struggle at Kalkriese, north of the modern town of Osnabruck. Varus committed suicide and several of his officers with him.[157] When the Germans found Varus' body, they disfigured it with further wounds and Arminius had its head cut off and sent to Maroboduus, no doubt to encourage him to join them in the revolt. Maroboduus, however, had the head sent to Rome, where it received decent burial.[158]

The Roman losses were greater than any since the terrible defeat suffered by Crassus at the hands of the Parthians at the battle of Carrhae in 53 BC, and in Rome there were fears of a great German invasion like those of the Cimbri and the Teutones in the closing years of the second century BC. Augustus is said to have refused to shave or cut his hair for months after the news reached Rome and sometimes to have struck his head against a door, crying out, 'Quinctilius Varus, give me back the legions!'[159] The situation on the Rhine was serious and potentially desperate. Lucius Asprenas, Varus' nephew, who was the commander of the other two legions in Germany, moved swiftly to prevent the revolt spreading to the area west of the Rhine, and, inevitably, Tiberius was despatched to deal with the danger of the loss of parts of Gaul as well as that of Germany. He was to remain there for three more years.[160] The sources tell us little of what he did, not helped by another gap

157. Vell. Pat. 2.117.1–120.6; Dio Cass. 56.18.1–24.5; Suet. *Aug.* 23.1–2. On the site of the final battle, see the review by Wells, 'What's new along the Lippe'.
158. Vell. Pat. 2.119.5.
159. Suet. *Aug.* 23.1–2; Dio Cass. 56.23.1.
160. There is some uncertainty about the year in which Tiberius returned to Rome to celebrate a triumph at the end of his campaigning in Germany, but this probably occurred in AD 12 (see G. V. Sumner, 'The truth about Velleius Paterculus: prolegomena', *Harvard Studies in Classical Philology* 74 (1970), 257–97, at 274 n. 107).

in Dio's text. Tiberius left Rome early in AD 10, after dedicating on 10 January the temple of Concordia Augusta in the names of himself and his brother Drusus, as he had promised seventeen years before.[161] Once with the army, he settled and reinforced the Rhine frontier and had at his disposal a force consisting of eight legions, more than had been based there at any time before.[162] At Rome, Augustus instituted severe measures in an attempt to raise recruits, compelling those who were unwilling to volunteer by threats of disenfranchisement or even death. He also took the precaution of sending away the Germans who served as his personal bodyguard and ordering Gallic and German civilians to leave the city.[163] Although soldiers recruited at this time are to be found in the armies of the northern frontier shortly after this, it is clear that Tiberius' force in AD 10 was largely made up of legions diverted from other provinces of the empire.[164] It is probable that he did not attempt to cross the Rhine until the following year, when, with Germanicus on his staff once again, he ventured a short distance into German territory. They avoided any direct conflict but did remain there until the autumn, celebrating Augustus' birthday on 23 September with horse races, before returning to their bases.[165] In AD 12, after another year's campaigning about which nothing is known, Tiberius returned to Rome, where on 23 October he celebrated a triumph, not, however, over the Germans but for the ending of the Pannonian war three years earlier.[166] Whatever the intentions of Augustus had been when he sent Tiberius back to the Rhine after the disaster of the destruction of Varus' legions, the result was no more (and no less) than the stabilisation of frontier.[167]

161. See above, p. 145.
162. The eight legions are listed by Tacitus, *Ann.* 1.37, writing of the mutinies that followed Augustus' death in AD 14.
163. Dio Cass. 56.23.1–4; Suet. *Aug.* 49.1.
164. Syme, 'Some notes on legions', 28–31. On urban recruits in Germany in AD 14, see Dio Cass. 57.5.4; Tacitus, *Ann.* 1.31.4.
165. Vell. Pat. 2.120.1–2, 121.1; Suet. *Tib.* 18 and 19; Dio Cass. 56.24.6, 25.2–3. Velleius' account suggests that Tiberius crossed the Rhine as soon as he arrived, which Dio denies (see Swan, *The Augustan Succession*, 275).
166. Vell. Pat. 2.122; Suet. *Tib.* 20; Ovid, *Pont.* 2.1, 2.2, 3.3.85–92; *Fast. Praenest.* (*Inscr. Ital.* 13.2.134–5, 524–5). See above, n. 160.
167. C. M. Wells, *The German Policy of Augustus: An Examination of the Archaeological Evidence*, Oxford: Oxford University Press, 1972, 241–5.

Augustus' last years, AD 11–14

Meanwhile in Rome there was still work to be done by the now aged emperor, and much of it reflected the strained and soured atmosphere between him and the upper classes in the city which had been evident for some years. In AD 11 Augustus allowed sixteen praetors to hold office, rather than the ten which he had established as a norm in 23 BC, under pressure from the senatorial class and from an unwillingness to offend any of them. In the same year a ban was imposed on the foretelling of death by astrologers, despite Augustus' apparent disinclination to keep such matters secret (he is said to have published the details of the position of the stars at the time of his birth in an edict); but this must be related to attempts to determine when the emperor, now in his seventy-third year, would die. He also permitted members of the equestrian order to participate in gladiatorial combat because a previous order forbidding them from doing so was so widely ignored. On the other hand, he issued a prohibition on provincial governors receiving honours from those they governed either during their tenure of office or within sixty days of its termination, an attempt to avoid the use of such bestowals to frustrate charges of maladministration being brought; it had the additional advantage of imposing control on the giving of such honours to those outside the imperial house, and thereby reducing the freedom of self-promotion by senators.[168]

The advancement of the next generation of the imperial family also continued. In AD 11 Drusus Caesar, Tiberius' son, became quaestor, as had been anticipated two years earlier.[169] He was twenty-three years old. In the following year Germanicus became consul without having previously held the praetorship, and remained in office for the whole year. He was responsible as consul for the traditional games in honour of the god Mars, though they were disrupted by another flooding of the Tiber as a result of which the Circus Maximus was unusable. Horse races took place instead in the Forum of Augustus and Germanicus put on a second set of games, including the slaughter of 200 lions, later in the year. Nothing else of note is recorded for his period of office, other than that he appeared

---

168. Dio Cass. 56.25.4–8. On the previous history of bans on performance as gladiators, see Barbara Levick, 'The *senatus consultum* from Larinum', *Journal of Roman Studies* 73 (1983), 97–115, at 105–8. On the ban on provincial governors receiving honours, see G. W. Bowersock, *Augustus and the Greek World*, Oxford: Oxford University Press, 1965, 119.
169. Dio Cass. 56.25.4. See above, p. 183.

as an advocate in the law courts; but clearly his consulship was seen by Augustus, now only too aware of his increasing age, as an opportunity once again to put forward his intended successors. In the year of Germanicus' consulship Augustus reinforced this by writing a formal communication to the senate, commending Germanicus to them and the senate to Tiberius. This message with its markedly dynastic intent was read not by Augustus himself, who could no longer make himself heard, or by his quaestor (the *quaestor Caesaris*), whose task it would normally have been, but by Germanicus himself. Augustus was withdrawing steadily from the public gaze, but he was determined to make his intentions for the future clear.[170] The dedication of the Basilica Iulia in the Forum, begun by Julius Caesar, almost completed by Augustus when it was burned down, and now dedicated in the names of Gaius and Lucius Caesar, can only have emphasised the significance of the dynasty.[171]

Augustus also took more extreme measures to prevent what he regarded as scurrilous writings, ordering the burning of books and the punishment of some authors. Dio, who records this, does not mention any writers by name and still less suggests that they were composing works against Augustus or his family, but the first person to suffer the destruction of books by fire is said by the elder Seneca to have been the free-speaking advocate and historian Titus Labienus; and it may be that it was also now that another aggressive and clever advocate, Cassius Severus, who is said to have defamed both men and women with his immoderate slanders, was tried and condemned under the *maiestas* law, which dealt with offences against the state. Labienus committed suicide and Severus was exiled first to Crete and then to the desolate island of Seriphos in the Aegean.[172] The use of the *maiestas* law in Severus' case may indicate that the imperial family was involved but, if so, who and how are quite unclear. What is apparent, however, is that Augustus was becoming less rather than more tolerant of such unacceptable freedoms as he grew older. At the same time he also tightened the conditions under which exiles could live after being removed from

---

170. Dio Cass. 56.26.1–3. On the role of the *quaestor Caesaris*, see Ulpian, *Dig.* 1.13.
171. Dio Cass. 56.27.5; Suet. *Aug.* 29.4. Augustus states in the *Res Gestae* that the Basilica was not completed when he wrote (*RG* 20.3), which suggests either that he did not revise this part of the document before he died, or that the Basilica was not finished when it was dedicated (see Cooley, *Res Gestae*, 194).
172. Dio Cass. 56.27.1. Labienus: Seneca, *Controv.* 10. *praef.* 5–9. Cassius Severus: Tacitus, *Ann.* 1.72.3; 4.21.3. For the uncertain dating of Severus' condemnation, see Swan, *The Augustan Succession*, 287.

Rome. No exile who had been condemned by being refused fire and water (the traditional form of exile when imposed by a court) should be permitted to live on the mainland or on any island less than fifty miles from it, with the exception of Cos, Rhodes, Samos and Lesbos, all being off the Aegean coast of the province of Asia. Exiles were also forbidden to cross the sea, possess more than one merchant ship capable of carrying a thousand amphorae and two oared ships, or have more than twenty slaves or freedmen or property worth more than 500,000 sesterces.[173] The intention was to ensure the intended severity of the penalty was not avoided, and here again Augustus is seen as growing harsher in his treatment of those who had not complied with his notion of how Rome should be or how a Roman should behave. As Dio puts it, despite the infirmities that prevented him from appearing in public, for the rest he continued to attend to business.

Tiberius' departure from the German campaigns did not mean they were over. In AD 13, the year after his consulship, Germanicus was appointed to command the eight legions on the Rhine, with the intention (or at least the announced intention) of revenge for the loss of Varus' legions.[174] In Rome preparations were being made for a different handover of power. The *imperium* of Augustus was due for renewal, and was accepted with the usual show of reluctance on the part of the *princeps*. At the same time Tiberius was given *imperium* equivalent to that of Augustus, which covered all the provinces that were named as Caesar's and was greater than that of the proconsular governors of such public provinces he might enter. His *tribunicia potestas*, which had been granted for the second time in AD 4 after having lapsed in 1 BC while he was in Rhodes, was also renewed.[175] Tiberius was now at last in the position that Marcus Agrippa had occupied in 13 BC, the year before his death.[176] Second only to Augustus himself, he was acknowledged as co-ruler of the Roman Empire. The context in which this happened, however, was different from that of twenty-six years before. Then, had the *princeps* died and Agrippa succeeded, his intended successors, Gaius and Lucius Caesar, would have been young boys. In AD 13 Germanicus had

173. Dio Cass. 56.27.2–3. See Barbara Levick, 'Poena legis maiestatis', Historia 28 (1979), 358–79, at 376–9.
174. Tacitus, Ann. 1.3.5–6; Vell. Pat. 2.123.1; Strabo, 7.1.4.
175. Dio Cass. 56.28.1; Tacitus, Ann. 1.54–71; Vell. Pat. 2.121.1; Suet. Tib. 21.1. See Ferrary, 'The powers of Augustus', 125–8.
176. See above, pp. 132–3.

already held the consulship, and Drusus Caesar was given permission to become consul two years later without previously being praetor, just as had been the case for Germanicus.[177] Moreover, in AD 13 the *princeps* was inevitably nearer to death. He asked that the senatorial subcommittee, which prepared business for the senate and for many years had acted as his advisory body, should be enlarged to include Tiberius, Germanicus and Drusus and be given powers to pass resolutions which would have the same status as decrees of the full senate.[178] The reason Dio gives for this, that he was no longer able due to his age to attend the senate except on rare occasions, is no doubt part of the explanation, but the inclusion of his adopted son and grandsons suggests that he was planning for a smooth transition after his death.

Not that he was only concerned with the aftermath of his demise; he might have been old but he was still involved in the transaction of public affairs and had not lost his ability to manipulate others. Further opposition to the 5 per cent inheritance tax which provided revenue for the *aerarium militare* looked set to become serious; Augustus wrote to the senate, instructing them to find an alternative source of income for the fund. He took the precaution of concealing his own view and ensured that neither Germanicus nor Nero Drusus expressed an opinion on the subject, which might have been interpreted as his. The result of the views he gathered was that the senators were prepared to envisage any tax rather than the one in place, so the *princeps* proposed one on land and buildings, and the process of assessing the property of both individuals and cities began immediately. The outcome was the collapse of the opposition to the 5 per cent levy on inheritances. Once again, as with the establishment of the tax in AD 6, Augustus had outflanked those who objected to it.[179]

Late in the year a census of all Roman citizens was undertaken by Augustus and Tiberius, the latter having been given the power to act by a law proposed by the consuls; it was completed with the ceremony of the *lustrum* on 11 May the following year. In the *Res Gestae* Augustus records that the total number of citizens registered was 4,937,000, an increase of 874,000 since the census of 28 BC and

---

177. Dio Cass. 56.28.1.
178. Dio Cass. 56.28.2–3. See J. Crook, *Consilium Principis: Imperial Councils and Counsellors from Augustus to Diocletian*, Cambridge: Cambridge University Press, 1955, 14–15.
179. Dio Cass. 46.28.4–6. On the introduction of the tax, see above, p. 172.

(more remarkably) of 704,000 since that of 8 BC.[180] The likely reason for these large increases is the addition to the citizen body resulting from the enfranchisement of provincials and freedmen; but the motive behind the conduct of the census at this time and the publishing of the figures at the completion of the *lustrum* will have been at least in part the same as it had been in 28 BC: a demonstration of the power and strength of the Roman people and its *res publica*. It is a notable parallel that as in 28 BC it was Agrippa who was Augustus' colleague in carrying out the census, so in AD 14 that role was played by Tiberius.[181]

Shortly after Tiberius was dispatched to Illyricum, being accompanied by Augustus as far as Beneventum, taking a roundabout route which included a stay on Capri and attendance at an athletic competition in Naples, established in his honour. From Beneventum Tiberius proceeded to the region he had left in AD 9. There is no indication that there was any specific task allotted to him; Velleius says that he was to 'strengthen by peace what he had subdued by war'. His function sounds to be like that of Agrippa in and after 23 BC: to act as the deputy for the *princeps* in an area of particular concern.[182] Whatever the intention in sending him to Illyricum, nothing came of it. Augustus, after he left Tiberius, went to an old family property at Nola in Campania. There he became increasingly ill, and Tiberius was recalled. The sources disagree as to whether Tiberius reached Augustus before, on 19 August, he died.[183]

The first thing that Tiberius did while still at Nola was to write to all the legions and provinces throughout the empire to inform them of Augustus' death. Although he was careful not to write as *princeps* (he had not at this stage been given the name of Augustus by the senate), he was, under the arrangements put in place in the previous year, certainly in a position to issue such a communication to the commanders in 'Caesar's provinces'; but if Dio is correct, he also wrote to all the provinces, which would include the 'public provinces', administered by former consuls. The letter may have been no more than a means of passing on the news of his adoptive father's death; but in taking this upon himself Tiberius was already

180. Aug. *RG* 8.4; *Fast. Ostiens. (Inscr. Ital.* 13.1.184–5); Suet. *Aug.* 97.1, *Tib.* 21.1.
181. On the Augustan census figures, see Brunt, *Italian Manpower*, 113–20. On the census of 28 BC, see above. pp. 82–4.
182. See above, pp. 98–9.
183. Vell. Pat. 123.1–2; Tacitus, *Ann.* 1.5.3–4; Suet. *Aug.* 97.1–100.1; Dio Cass. 56.29.2–31.1.

acting as Augustus' successor, however careful he may have been about the proprieties.[184]

From Nola, Tiberius escorted Augustus' body back to Rome, the corpse being carried by the leading men of various cities along the route and from Bovillae, in Latium, by members of the equestrian order.[185] On the day after the procession reached the city, Tiberius, using his tribunician power, summoned the senate. There were two main items of business: the reading of Augustus' will and the arrangements for his funeral. The will, which had been written a year and four months before his death and deposited with the Vestal Virgins, revealed that his heirs were Tiberius, to whom two-thirds of his estate was left, and his widow, Livia, who was to have the remaining third; both were to take his name. Livia was adopted into the Julian family and given the name Augusta; Tiberius was given the cognomen Augustus, with all that that implied, by Augustus himself, the only person in a position to do so. Augustus' secondary heirs, who would only inherit if the primary heirs did not, were Drusus Caesar (who would have taken one third) and Germanicus and his three sons, who would have had the remainder. Augustus also left 40,000,000 sesterces to the Roman people and 3,500,000 to the Roman plebs, with 1,000 each to the members of the Praetorian Guard and 300 to each of the legionaries. He also specified that neither his daughter Julia, whom he had banished to the island of Pandateria in 2 BC (though he later allowed her to live on the mainland at Rhegium), nor his granddaughter Julia, removed permanently to Trimerus in AD 8, should be buried in the Mausoleum on the Campus Martius.[186] One other person was not mentioned at all. Agrippa Postumus' name did not appear. He had been murdered on the island of Planasia, to which he had been exiled by Augustus some seven years previously, immediately after the death of the *princeps*. Suspicion inevitably focused on Tiberius and his mother, Livia, and was fomented by a story that, a few months before his death, Augustus had visited Postumus and that a reconciliation was imminent.[187] The story is hard to credit: Augustus had made plentiful

---

184. Dio Cass. 57.2.1. Tacitus, *Ann.* 1.7.5, notes that from the beginning he sent letters to the armies as though he had already attained the principate.
185. Dio Cass. 56.31.1; Suet. *Aug.* 100.2, *Claud.* 6.1.
186. Meeting of the senate and reading of the will: Tacitus, *Ann.* 1.8.1–5; Suet. *Aug.* 100.2–3, 101.1–4, *Tib.* 23, 70.3; Dio Cass. 56.31.2–33.6. On the elder Julia, see above, p. 157, and Tacitus, *Ann.* 1.53.1; Suet. *Aug.* 65.3; Dio Cass. 55.13.1; on the younger Julia, see above, p. 179.
187. Tacitus, *Ann.*1.5–6; Dio Cass. 56.30.2.

preparations for the smooth transfer of power to Tiberius and there is no sign in anything else he did in his last months to suggest that he had changed his mind. There was danger enough, however, in the continued existence of Postumus for someone to want him dead. Tacitus mentions Gaius Sallustius Crispus, a close associate of Augustus, and it was he too to whom Tiberius, some two years later, entrusted the task of suppressing a potential threat when a slave of Postumus, named Clemens, who had attempted to rescue his master just before the latter's death, presented himself as Postumus Agrippa, whose ashes he had stolen from Planasia, and gained considerable support.[188] In AD 14, however, Tiberius assured the senate that he had not ordered the killing of Postumus, and the matter went no further.

It was not only the will itself which was brought to the senate but also a series of other documents which Augustus had prepared as codicils. These included directions for his funeral; the text of his own account of his achievements, his *Res Gestae*, which were to be engraved on bronze tablets and set up at the entrance to the Mausoleum; and a summary of the military and financial state of the entire empire (with the names of the imperial freedmen and slaves from whom details could be obtained).[189] These brought together the results of his work as *princeps* as he would have it remembered and enabled its continuation in other hands.

The second item of senate business, the arrangements for Augustus' funeral, resulted in a series of proposals from the senate elaborating his own directions, most of which Tiberius refused; but the event, which followed shortly after, was nonetheless remarkable, as was only to be expected. Mindful of the disorder which had attended the last great funeral in the city, that of Julius Caesar in 44 BC, Tiberius had troops on the streets to control the crowds and insisted that the cremation should take place on the Campus Martius outside the city walls, near the Mausoleum in which Augustus would be buried, rather than in the Forum. It was in the Forum, however, that the ceremony began. The funeral bier, a couch made of gold and ivory with coverings of gold and purple, concealed the coffin in

---

188. Tacitus, *Ann.* 2.39–40; Suet. *Tib.* 25.1.
189. Suet. *Aug.* 100.4; Dio Cass. 56.33.1–6. Suetonius mentions these three rolls, whereas Dio adds a fourth, with advice to Tiberius and the senate, one part of which, the advice not to enlarge the empire, appears also in Tacitus (*Ann.* 1.11.4) as part of the third of Suetonius' rolls, which (according to Tacitus) Tiberius produced during the senatorial debate following Augustus' funeral.

which the body lay, with a wax image of the *princeps*, dressed in the costume of a *triumphator*, open to view. This was carried by the magistrates who had been elected for the following year down from Augustus' house on the Palatine hill, where his body had been laid out, to the Forum. Two other images of Augustus were also brought out, one a golden statue which had stood in the senate house, the other showing him in a triumphal chariot, together displaying his achievements in both military and civilian spheres. Behind the bier came a procession of images of his ancestors (Julius Caesar's being omitted as he was now one of the gods) and then of other prominent Romans (beginning with Romulus, the founder of the city, and including Pompeius Magnus), with representations of all the nations Augustus had brought in to the empire. When the procession arrived from the Palatine, the bier was placed on the rostra at one end of the Forum in front of the temple of Concord, where Drusus Caesar, as one of the deceased's nearest male relatives, gave the traditional eulogy; Tiberius then gave another, concentrating on Augustus' achievements as *princeps*, from the new rostra at the other end of the Forum, in front of the temple of Divus Julius. From there the bier was carried on the shoulders of senators through the gate by which triumphal processions entered the city (the *porta triumphalis*)[190] out to the Campus Martius, where the body was laid on a pyre. A procession of priests circled it, followed by members of the equestrian order and cavalrymen and foot soldiers from the Praetorian Guard, who threw the triumphal decorations that Augustus had awarded them onto the pyre. It was then lit by centurions and (according to Dio) an eagle was released, to signify the ascent of his soul to heaven. After the ceremonies had been completed, most people left, leaving Livia and a number of the most prominent members of the equestrian order, who kept vigil at the pyre for five days, after which they gathered Augustus' bones and interred them in the Mausoleum.[191]

The senate convened again shortly after the funeral, on

---

190. On the *porta triumphalis* and the problems of its identity, see Mary Beard, *The Roman Triumph*, Cambridge, MA, and London: Harvard University Press, 2007, 96–101.

191. Tacitus, *Ann.* 1.8.3–6; Suet. *Aug.* 100.2–4; Dio Cass. 56.34.1–42.4. Dio's account is the fullest, including his version of Tiberius' eulogy, but is coloured by his experience of later imperial funerals (which may account for the mention of the eagle). See Swan, *The Augustan Succession*, ad loc.

17 September.[192] There Augustus was declared to be a god, like his father, Julius Caesar; and the senators then moved on to discuss the matter of the succession. Tacitus[193] paints a memorable scene in the senate, in which Tiberius presents the task of governing the empire as Augustus had done as being beyond him and says that so great a burden should not be placed in the hands of one man when so many distinguished men were available. To strengthen his point, he produced the document which Augustus had appended to his will, giving details of the finances and military deployments across the empire. Although many senators obsequiously insisted that Tiberius alone was capable of undertaking all this work, he still insisted, until the matter was brought to a head: a question was posed by the senator Gaius Asinius Gallus as to which part Tiberius would take, and when the emperor appeared offended, he explained that he was simply pointing out that the *res publica* was an indissoluble whole; in Tacitus' words, a single body which could only be governed by a single mind.[194] Tiberius disliked Asinius Gallus, not least because it was he who had married Tiberius' wife Vipsania, whom he had been compelled to divorce in order to marry Julia in 11 BC, but in the end he gave way to the entreaties of the senate.

In practice there was no debate to be had. Tiberius already possessed the *imperium* of a *princeps*, given to him the previous year, and the *tribunicia potestas*. The decree of the senate on the same day had made him, as Augustus had been, *divi filius*, son of the deified one.[195] Tiberius had all the powers and the titles that Augustus had had: the transition worked as no doubt Augustus had planned that it should. In so far as there was a problem, it was the absence of Augustus, whose skill at handling the senate had remained unsurpassed and totally effective to the end of his life. That was something which Tiberius, whose career had been predominantly as a highly successful general, had never developed, and never did. In September AD 14, however, the senate was in no state to propose anything that was contrary to the evident wishes of Augustus within days of his funeral, even when being handled by his less adept successor.

Ironically it was among the very soldiers that Tiberius had led

---

192. The date is given in the *Fast. Amit.* and *Fast. Ant.* as that on which heavenly honours (*honores caelestes*) for Augustus were decreed by the senate (*Inscr. Ital.* 13.2, 192–3, 209, 510).
193. Tacitus, *Ann.* 1.11–14
194. Tacitus, *Ann.* 1.12.2–3; Dio Cass. 57.2.6.
195. See Levick, *Tiberius*, 75–81; Ferrary, 'The powers of Augustus', 125–9.

over the past decade that trouble broke out. Legions both in Pannonia and on the Rhine frontier mutinied on hearing of Augustus' death.[196] These revolts were serious, resulting in the case of the Rhine legions in threats to Germanicus and his family and in the deaths of many legionaries, but the origins of both seem to have been complaints about levels of pay and conditions of service. Moreover the Pannonian mutiny was led by one Percennius, who had been a cheer-leader in the theatre and almost certainly one of the soldiers conscripted in AD 9 in the desperate attempt to find recruits in the aftermath of the slaughter of Varus' legions; and others enrolled at the same time were active in the rebellion on the Rhine.[197] Although the German legions are said to have tried unsuccessfully to persuade Germanicus to seize power in opposition to Tiberius, the roots of their unrest, as with the Pannonians, lay in the problems caused by Augustus' expansive foreign policy and his inability to raise the manpower and the cash required to sustain it. It is perhaps not surprising that one of the pieces of advice for Tiberius that Augustus included in a final codicil to his will was that the empire should be extended no further.[198] Although by mid-October both mutinies had been defused and suppressed, the fact that they happened at all showed the dangers that might too easily occur.

If his acclamation as *pater patriae* in 2 BC was intended to mark the high point of Augustus' reign as *princeps*, the difficult sixteen years that followed before his death in AD 14 revealed the underlying problems that he did not and perhaps was not able to foresee or prevent. In the empire, the revolts in Illyricum and Germany showed the fragility of the military control that was exercised over a greatly expanded area, and the financial demands required to maintain an army large enough to support that control. In the sphere of social and moral reform, the changes that he had made to shore up the status of marriage and to enhance the position of free citizens as opposed to slaves by means of new laws and new courts came under pressure from those who found such restrictions irksome. Perhaps most notably, his exaltation of the imperial family and his plans for the succession, which at the beginning of 2 BC had seemed brilliantly

196. Vell. Pat. 2.125.1–5; Tacitus, *Ann.* 1.16–49; Suet. *Tib.* 25.13; Dio Cass. 57.4.1–6.5. See Levick, *Tiberius*, 71–4; Robin Seager, *Tiberius*, London: Eyre Methuen, 1972, 58–74.
197. Tacitus, *Ann.* 1.16.3, 31.4; Dio Cass. 57.5.4. On the conscriptions of AD 9, see above, p. 185.
198. Tacitus, *Ann.* 1.11.4; Dio Cass. 57.33.5.

secure, despite the loss of Agrippa ten years earlier, were undermined by the deaths of Lucius and Gaius Caesar in AD 2 and 4, by the disgrace and exile of his daughter Julia later in 2 BC and of her daughter Julia ten years later, and by the events that led to the renunciation of Agrippa Postumus. The years after the high point of 2 BC were not easy for the ageing *princeps*, and one of the lessons that might be learned was that, unlike the consuls of the Republic, an emperor could not go into a peaceful and honourable retirement; but the remarkable fact is that the new Rome that Augustus had fashioned did not disintegrate under the pressures that assailed it, and that the regime that he had created was passed on to his adopted son with such relative ease. That is not the least of the achievements of Augustus, which it now remains to discuss.

CHAPTER 6

The achievements of the divine Augustus

Among the documents that were produced at the meeting of the senate, shortly after the arrival of the procession bearing Augustus' body to Rome from Nola, was his own account of what he had accomplished, with instructions that it should be inscribed on bronze tablets and be set up in front of the Mausoleum in which his remains were to be laid.[1] It was not the only such inscription to be exhibited there: decrees in honour of his sons Gaius and Lucius Caesar were already in place, and were to be joined by another in honour of Germanicus, after his death in AD 19.[2] None of these tablets has survived, but that of Augustus was copied, along with a version in Greek, onto the walls of the temple of Rome and Augustus at Ancyra (modern Ankara), capital of the province of Galatia in Asia Minor, and substantial amounts of this remain intact; two other partial texts have been discovered from the same province, one of the original Latin (from Antioch in Pisidia) and one of the Greek (from Apollonia). The heading of the Latin text from Ancyra describes it as a copy of the *Res Gestae Divi Augusti*, the achievements of the divine Augustus.[3] It is with this document, his own presentation of what he had succeeded in doing, that an assessment of Augustus must begin.

---

1. Suet. *Aug.* 101.4; Dio Cass. 56.33.1. See above, p. 192. Dio says the tablets were to be placed 'in front of his shrine', which must be an error (P. M. Swan, *The Augustan Succession: An Historical Commentary on Cassius Dio's Roman History Books 55–56 (9 BC–AD 14)*, Oxford: Oxford University Press, 2004, 316).
2. See *Tabula Siarensis* fr. (b), col. I, lines 5–7, in M. H. Crawford (ed.), *Roman Statutes*, London: Institute of Classical Studies, 1996, 516.
3. For the sites and the manner of display of these inscriptions, see the excellent edition, translation and commentary by Alison E. Cooley, *Res Gestae Divi Augusti*, Oxford: Oxford University Press, 2009, 3–18. Cooley's edition is now the best resource for English speakers, though the briefer edition, translation and commentary by P. A. Brunt and J. M. Moore, *Res Gestae Divi Augusti: The Achievements of the Divine Augustus*, Oxford: Oxford University Press, 1967, is still useful. For a full scholarly edition, see also J. Scheid, *Res Gestae Divi Augusti: Hauts Faits du Divin Auguste*, Paris: Les Belles Lettres, 2007.

Augustus' account: the *Res Gestae Divi Augusti*

The *Res Gestae* as we have it ends with an appendix, summarising the expenditure Augustus made in donations to the Roman plebs and veteran soldiers, the buildings he erected in Rome and various other signs of his generosity, but this is not, as is the rest of the text, in the first person and does not represent itself as being from Augustus' own hand. The end of the main text reads, 'When I wrote these things I was in my seventy-sixth year', which certainly sounds as if it was meant to indicate that the whole of the preceding document had been produced after his seventy-fifth birthday on 23 September AD 13.[4] The last events mentioned which can be dated are the grant of *tribunicia potestas* for the thirty-seventh time, which will have taken place in late June or early July AD 14, and the completion of the census, conducted by Augustus and Tiberius, which took place on 11 May AD 14.[5] Most modern scholars who have examined the question of the date of composition have found it hard to believe that Augustus could have been writing the *Res Gestae* as late as this and have argued that the basic text was written by 2 BC, with additions being made later, including (in the case of the references to the year AD 14) by Tiberius after Augustus' death; and some have developed a theory of complex layers of its structure.[6] Most recently, Alison Cooley has restated the case for believing that it was indeed put together in the last months or even weeks of Augustus' life, perhaps under the pressure of the omens recorded by Suetonius that he was about to die.[7] While it is true that much less is said about the period after 2 BC, this is explicable, given the increasing problems that he faced in the later years of his reign. At the least there is no reason to doubt that, whenever the material that makes up the *Res Gestae* was compiled, the final version was what Augustus, as he approached his death, wished to hand on as his own account of what he had achieved.

The document we have was clearly put together with care, however it came to be constructed. Augustus begins abruptly with the statement that at the age of nineteen (that is, in 44 BC), on his

4. Aug. *RG* 35.2: Cum scri]psi haec, annum agebam septuagensu[mum sextum].
5. Aug. *RG* 4.4; 8.4. For the date of the grants of *tribunicia potestas*, see Dio 53.32.3–5, with the note of J. W. Rich, *Cassius Dio: The Augustan Settlement (Roman History 53–55.9)*, Warminster: Aris and Phillips, 1990, 169. On the census of AD 13–14, see above, pp. 189–90.
6. For a brief exposition of the arguments, see Brunt and Moore, *Res Gestae*, 6.
7. Cooley, *Res Gestae*, 42–3.

own private initiative and at his own expense, he gathered an army with which he set free the state (*res publica*), which was oppressed by the domination of a faction, for which in the following year he was honoured by the senate, admitted to its membership and entrusted along with the consuls with the safety of the *res publica*; and that when the consuls had both fallen in battle, the people made him consul and triumvir for the establishment of the *res publica*. After this brief and highly selective account of the events which followed the assassination of Julius Caesar, he records that he drove into exile those who had killed his father through trials in the courts and then defeated them twice in battle when they made war on the state, thus claiming for himself the victories over the 'Liberators', Cassius and Brutus, at Philippi in 42 BC, though the chief credit for these lay with Marcus Antonius (*RG* 1–2).[8] He then moves away from a purely chronological account to a listing of the wars, both civil and foreign, that he had conducted, emphasising not only his successes but also the generosity with which he treated the vanquished; and records the large number of soldiers who served under him and the rewards he gave them, in terms of land on which to settle and financial gifts (*RG* 3). He then records the triumphs and *ovationes* that he was awarded, the numerous occasions on which he refused triumphs offered by the senate, and the 890 days of thanks-givings to the gods that they decreed for his victories, concluding this section with a note that, at the time he wrote, he had been consul thirteen times and was in the thirty-seventh year of his *tribunicia potestas* (*RG* 4).

This reference, which reads like a dating, forms a bridge to the next section (*RG* 5–7), which deals with powers he had been offered at various times (as dictator, perpetual consul and sole curator of laws and morals), all of which he had refused as being magistracies inconsistent with the custom of the ancestors (*mos maiorum*), instead accepting only a temporary post in charge of the corn supply (*curatio annonae*) to relieve a corn shortage, and using the *tribunicia potestas* to enact his social legislation in 18 and 17 BC. He underlines the non-monarchical nature of the tribunician power by noting that on five occasions he was granted by the senate a colleague at his own request (Agrippa in 18 and 13 BC, Tiberius in 6 BC, AD 4 and AD 13, on each occasion for five years). He rounds off this section by listing the positions he has held: *triumvir* for the

---

8. On the two battles at Philippi, see above, p. 41.

establishment of the state for ten consecutive years and leader of the senate (*princeps senatus*) for forty, up to the day he was writing; *pontifex maximus*, augur and a member of five other religious bodies (several of which, though he does not mention this, he revived or created himself).

Next he moves to reforms he introduced which affected the make-up of the citizen body itself. First the increase in the members of the patricians, ordered by the senate and people; next his three revisions of the roll of the senate; and then his three censuses of the Roman people, once with Agrippa as his colleague (in 29/28 BC), a second time on his own (in 8 BC) and finally, with his son Tiberius Caesar (in AD 13/14). For each of these three censuses the numbers of citizens is given, to the nearest thousand, showing the growth of the size of the Roman people. The section ends with a reference to the many exemplary practices of the ancestors that he reintroduced by new laws proposed in his own name, and to the many such examples he set himself for transmission to the generations to come.

These achievements were marked, as the next chapters show, by religious honours, decreed by the senate. Vows for his health, accompanied by sets of games. were to be undertaken every five years by the consuls and by the priestly colleges, and all citizens, both as individuals and as communities, joined in the prayers (*RG* 9). His name was added by the decree of the senate to the ancient (and incomprehensible) hymn, sung twice yearly by the Salii, a priesthood which claimed its foundation in the reign of Numa, the second of the kings of Rome, as they danced through the streets of the city to keep Rome safe in its wars; his person was declared sacrosanct by law (a protection provided by religious sanction for tribunes of the plebs while in office) and he was given the tribunician power for as long as he lived. He refused to take the post of *pontifex maximus*, the highest priesthood in the city, while Lepidus (not mentioned by name) was still alive, though the people offered it to him, but after, once Lepidus was dead, was elected by a multitude of a size previously unseen in Rome, who poured into the city from the whole of Italy for the voting (*RG* 10). When he returned in 19 BC from the east, having secured the Roman legionary standards from the Parthian king, the senate dedicated an altar to Fortuna Redux, at which the priests and the Vestal Virgins made an annual sacrifice on the anniversary, and the day was named the Augustalia; and when he returned from Spain and Gaul in 13 BC, it decreed the altar of Pax Augusta on the Campus Martius, with similar annual sacrifices (*RG* 11–12). The

gates of the shrine of Janus, which were closed only when throughout the whole of the empire of the Roman people peace had been
achieved by victories, were shut by decree of the senate three times
while he was *princeps*, though this had previously occurred only
twice since the foundation of the city (*RG* 13).

After this great list of religious honours, Augustus records the
civic marks of distinction given to his two sons Gaius and Lucius
Caesar, designated as consuls at the age of fourteen by the senate and
people (an office to be taken once they were nineteen) as an honour
to Augustus himself, admitted to the councils of state and each
hailed by the equestrian order as *princeps iuventutis*. These two were
snatched from him by Fortune while still young. The clear implication is that, had they lived, they would have achieved far more. As
it was, the honours given to them reflected the esteem in which their
adoptive father was held.

He then turns to the immense sums he had paid out from his
own funds to the Roman plebs, both in donations of cash and in
distributions of grain, and the expenditure on land for the settlement
of his veterans, both in Italy and in the provinces; he was, he notes,
the first founder of military colonies to pay for the land on which
they were placed. He also assisted the treasury (*aerarium*) with his
own money on four occasions, in addition to the huge sum he
provided in AD 6 to support the setting up of the military treasury
(*aerarium militare*) to give retirement benefits to veteran soldiers
(*RG* 15–18).

He continues the theme of his gifts to the people of Rome with an
astounding list of the buildings he erected in the city (*RG* 19) and of
those which he restored (including the aqueducts, though omitting
the still greater contribution by Agrippa to this work) (*RG* 20). He
ends this section with the building of the temple of Mars the Avenger
and the Forum of Augustus, paid for with booty resulting from the
spoils from Philippi, and the theatre of Marcellus, named for his
nephew and husband of his daughter Julia who died in 23 BC. Also
from the proceeds of booty he made dedications in the Capitol and
the temples of the divine Julius, Apollo (on the Palatine, next to his
own house), Vesta (probably the shrine in his own house, dedicated
after he became *pontifex maximus*) and Mars the Avenger, costing
him about one hundred million sesterces (*RG* 21.1–3). The temple
on the Capitol was a frequent recipient of such dedications; the
others were all closely connected with Augustus himself. To emphasise his own commitment to these sites, he concludes this section

with a note that in 28 BC, following his great triple triumph after the victory at Actium, he returned 35,000 pounds of gold which had been sent to him by the municipalities and colonies of Italy in recognition of his victories, and refused to accept similar payments, made each time he was acclaimed as *imperator* following another victory (*RG* 21.3).

He then lists an equally astounding number of games and spectacles he put on in Rome, both in his own name and in those of his (adopted) sons and grandsons: gladiatorial shows of unprecedented scale, athletic displays and animal hunts, and including the Saecular Games in 17 BC and the first set of *ludi Martiales*, which annually marked the dedication of the temple of Mars the Avenger, in 2 BC; he concludes with the mock naval battle, staged in a specially constructed artificial basin on the far side of the Tiber on the same occasion, which involved thirty warships and many smaller vessels, and 3,000 men, in addition to the rowers (*RG* 22–3).

To this roll of buildings and displays given to the city, he adds a note of dedications to the gods, both those he restored after his victory at Actium to temples in all the cities of the province of Asia which had been removed by Marcus Antonius (referred to here as 'the enemy against whom I had prevailed') to fund his campaign; and those which Augustus gave to the temple of Apollo at about the same time, paid for by his removal of some eighty silver statues of himself, probably presented by cities from the Greek east (*RG* 24). This brings him back briefly to the chronological survey with which he had begun his account in the first two sections of the document. In the next section (*RG* 25), he tells how he rid the seas of pirates in a war in which he returned to their masters 30,000 captured slaves, who had deserted to take up arms against the *res publica*. This is his version of the struggle against Sextus Pompeius, which came to an end with the defeat of Pompeius at the battle of Naulochus in September 36 BC; as usual, his opponent in not named. He follows this by recording that the whole of Italy swore an oath of allegiance to him and demanded that he be commander in the war which culminated in the victory at Actium; and that the western provinces of Gaul, Spain, Africa, Sicily and Sardinia all swore the same oath. Moreover, as he states, some seven hundred members of the senate served under him in this campaign, of whom eighty-three had already been or were subsequently made consuls up to the time of writing, and about one hundred and seventy priests.

Augustus' message at this point is plain. It was he who was the chosen leader of Rome and the Roman west against its enemies. There is no indication here that what was involved was a civil war. The point is made crystal clear by what follows. He records how he has enlarged the bounds of all the provinces adjoining peoples who were not subject to Roman rule; he has pacified the Gallic and Spanish provinces as well as Germany, all the area abutting the Ocean from Gades (modern Cadiz) to the mouth of the Elbe; he has pacified the Alps and his fleet has sailed the coastline east from the Rhine, territory unvisited by Romans before this time, and received ambassadors from the peoples there, seeking his friendship and that of the Roman people; his armies have extended into to Arabia and Ethiopia (*RG* 26); he has brought Egypt under the control of the Roman people; in Armenia, where he could have set up a province, he established a series of kings; and he recovered all the provinces in the east, having already recovered Sicily and Sardinia, seized during the slave war (*RG* 27). This is a most impressive list, even allowing for the fact that the eastern provinces mentioned were those held by Marcus Antonius before Actium, and Sicily and Sardinia were controlled by Sextus Pompeius. These Roman opponents in the civil wars (again unnamed) are simply included in the catalogue of foreign enemies that he had subdued.

From here he moves to the consequences of his successes in expanding the power of the Roman people across the world. He lists the provinces around the Mediterranean in which he has founded colonies for veteran soldiers, in addition to the twenty-eight in Italy (*RG* 28); and then records the recovery of Roman legionary standards lost by previous commanders in Spain, Gaul and Dalmatia, and in particular the restoration by the Parthians in 20 BC (*RG* 29). It is probably the mention of Dalmatia that leads him to add at this point the conquest of the Pannonians by Tiberius in 12 to 9 BC, though he omits the Pannonian and Dalmatian revolts which occupied Tiberius and Germanicus from AD 6 to 9 (*RG* 30). He rounds off this account of the global reach of Rome's empire by listing embassies sent by kings in India, and from the Bastarnae, the Scythians and kings of the Sarmatians, Albanians, Iberians and Medes, which petitioned for friendship (*RG* 31), and then the kings of Parthia, the Medes, the Adiabeni, the Britons, the Sugambri and the Marcomanni and Suebi who sought refuge with him (*RG* 32.1); he adds that Phraates, king of Parthia, sent his sons and grandsons as a pledge of his friendship, and that, while he was *princeps*, many other peoples who had never previously had relations with Rome experienced the good faith of the Roman people (*RG* 32.2–3). It was from him that both the Parthians and the Medes received kings (*RG* 33).

As climax to this display of the power and influence of Rome under his leadership, he records two moments which he clearly sees as most significant in this account of his achievements. They are worth citing in full.[9]

> In my sixth and seventh consulships [28 and 27 BC], after I had put an end to civil wars, although by everyone's agreement I had power over everything, I transferred the state (*res publica*) from my power (*potestas*) into the control of the Roman senate and people. For this service, I was named Augustus by senatorial decree, and the door-posts of my house were publicly clothed with laurels, and a civic crown was fastened above my doorway, and a golden shield was set up in the Julian senate house; through an inscription on this shield the fact was declared that the Roman senate and people were giving it to me because of my valour, clemency, justice and piety. After this time I excelled everyone in influence (*auctoritas*), but I had no more power (*potestas*) than the others who were my colleagues in each magistracy.
>
> When I was holding my thirteenth consulship [2 BC], the senate and equestrian order and people of Rome all together hailed me as father of the fatherland, and decreed that this title should be inscribed in the forecourt of my house and in the Julian senate house and in the Augustan forum under the chariot, which was set up in my honour by senatorial decree. When I wrote this I was in my seventy-sixth year. (*RG* 34–5)

It is with these two points in his long career that Augustus chose to end his account, and both the choice of these two and the manner in which he presents them say much about the picture he wishes to give of his achievements. First and most obvious, he is noting how at these two moments he was honoured in an exceptional way by the whole body of the people of Rome, the senate, the equestrian order and the people. These were the constituted elements of the Roman state and it was they who acknowledged what he had achieved. This, and not his great victory over Marcus Antonius and Cleopatra at the battle of Actium or his effectual establishment of a dynastic monarchy, was what he marked out as the defining characteristic of his life's work; and his respect for the constitutional structures which Augustan Rome inherited from its past is clearly marked out by the

---

9. Aug. *RG* 34–35. I give the translation of Alison Cooley.

way in which he presents these events. He was named Augustus not because (as was indeed the case) he was in 27 BC given by the senate the control of the armies and the major military provinces but because he had transferred the business of the state from his power to the control of the senate and people; and he is careful to point out that, although he exceeded all others in *auctoritas*, he had no more power in the magistracies he held than each of his colleagues. All this indeed underlies the whole structure of the document: the first words of the *Res Gestae* state that at the age of nineteen he had mustered an army at his own personal decision and his own personal expense, with which he had freed the *res publica* from the oppression of a faction (*RG* 1.1); the last paragraph presents him, in his seventy-sixth year, acknowledged as Father of the Fatherland (*Pater Patriae*) by whole of the Roman people in their various constituted bodies (*RG* 35.1–2).

Of course the *Res Gestae* is not an unbiased description of the reign of Augustus. It is better described as a masterpiece of 'spin'. A prime example of this is the claim in the passage quoted above that, although he excelled everyone in influence (*auctoritas*), he had no more power (*potestas*) than the others who were his colleagues in each magistracy (*RG* 34.3). This sentence is designed to show that it was his extra-constitutional *auctoritas*, based on the regard in which he was held, which was the foundation of his position and that in terms of the constitution he was in the same position as other Roman notables. It is true, in that his influence was immense and that, when he held the consulship, the other consul of the year was formally his equal. It ignores, however, the pattern seen throughout his reign of the separation of the powers and functions of magistracies and other offices from the offices themselves: in 29/28 BC he, along with Marcus Agrippa, conducted the census through a grant of *censoria potestas*, though they were not censors, and the same seems to have been the case with the other censuses he undertook in 8 BC and AD 13/14 by virtue of his consular power;[10] from 23 BC onwards, he held the *tribunicia potestas* without being a tribune of the plebs;[11] and also from 23 BC he held consular *imperium*, which, along with further honours given four years later, enabled him to appear as the equivalent of a consul both within and outside Rome,

---

10. See above, pp. 82–4. See also J.-L. Ferrary, 'The powers of Augustus', in J. Edmondson (ed.), *Augustus*, Edinburgh: Edinburgh University Press, 2009, 90–136, at 104–6. For the later censuses see Aug. *RG* 8.3–4 and above, pp. 141 and 189–90.
11. See above, pp. 99–101.

even when not holding the consulship.[12] Thus even in the constitutional sphere he was far more powerful than all others, precisely because he was not holding offices. What Augustus records in this sentence cannot be faulted in terms of the accuracy of what he writes, but the impression it gives tells less than half the truth.

In his account of events overseas he also sometimes presents versions which are at odds with what we hear from other sources. Thus his brief record of invasions of Arabia and Ethiopia in the 20s BC suggests, though it does not state, that his armies were militarily successful and the invasions resulted in the incorporation of these lands into the Roman empire, whereas our narrative sources indicate that the former was a dismal failure and that there was no military presence established in Ethiopia;[13] and his report of the recovery of the standards from the king of Parthia claims that he compelled their return, implying a military victory, though it was by diplomacy that this was achieved.[14] Other matters were, not surprisingly, omitted altogether: there is no mention of the difficult war in Pannonia and Dalmatia of AD 6–9 or of the disastrous loss in Germany of three legions by Quinctilius Varus in AD 9.

The focus of the whole document is firmly on Augustus himself. Not only, as we have noted, does it begin with him at nineteen years of age and end in his seventy-sixth year, but apart from the consuls, whose consulships are given to mark the dates of years, no other Romans are named except for members of his family: his adopted sons Gaius and Lucius Caesar; his nephew and son-in-law Marcellus; his stepson, son-in-law and finally adopted son Tiberius; and Marcus Agrippa, his son-in-law and father of Gaius and Lucius. Even Julius Caesar is not named, but is referred to simply as 'my father'. As to his enemies and opponents in the period of the civil wars, none is mentioned by name: Brutus and Cassius are referred to as the murderers of his father who took up war against the *res publica* (*RG* 2); Sextus Pompeius is not mentioned at all, and the war in which he was involved is represented as against pirates and slaves (*RG* 25.1); of his two former colleagues in the triumvirate, Marcus Antonius is 'he against whom I had waged war' (*RG* 24.1) and Lepidus 'he who had taken the opportunity of civil unrest to appropriate' the post of *pontifex maximus* (*RG* 10.2). The contrast

12. See above, pp. 99–102 and 111.
13. Aug. *RG* 26.5. See above, p. 95.
14. Aug. *RG* 29.2. See above, pp. 102–3 and 108.

with the long lists of the names of foreign kings who had come to him as suppliants or whose kingdoms he had rearranged or established (*RG* 27.1, 32 and 33) is marked. The implicit message is that in Rome the legitimate authority lay with those who are named: the consuls and the family of the *princeps*.

Implication is the means by which Augustus presented himself in the *Res Gestae*. Earlier he had written thirteen books of an auto-biography down to the end of the wars against the Cantabri in Spain, in which he was involved in 26 and 25 BC, which survives only in citations and reworkings in other sources.[15] Despite the fragmentary nature of what we have, it is clear what sort of work this was. Repeatedly he rebuts accusations made by his opponents about the low class of his family, about cruel and illegal savagery and about his disappearance from the field of combat during the battle of Philippi.[16] The autobiography was a defensive polemic against the propaganda of his enemies, written in the aftermath of Actium, when he still felt the need to restore his reputation after the damage done to it in the turbulent years of the civil war. There is nothing defensive about the *Res Gestae*: by the time it was completed, the record (as Augustus presented it) spoke for itself and his greatness was implied in every section.

Augustus among the gods

There are other ways in which the *Res Gestae* works by implication and thereby conceals (at least for a modern reader) as much as it tells. One such is the relation of the *princeps* to the religion of Rome and its impact on the city and the empire.[17] Augustus does record the great number of earlier temples, often seriously dilapidated, which he restored or rebuilt (*RG* 19.2; 20.4), as well as the new buildings which he added to the city, notably the temples of the Deified Julius in the Forum, of Apollo on the Palatine, of Jupiter the Thunderer on the Capitol and of Mars the Avenger in the Augustan Forum. What

---

15. Suet. *Aug.* 85.1. The fragments can be found in H. Malcovati, *Imperatoris Caesaris Augusti Operum Fragmenta*, 5th edn, Turin: Paravia, 1969, 84–97.
16. See Z. Yavetz, 'The *Res Gestae* and Augustus' public image', in F. Millar and E. Segal (eds), *Caesar Augustus: Seven Aspects*, Oxford: Oxford University Press, 1984, 1–36, at 1–3.
17. See especially John Scheid, 'To honour the *princeps* and venerate the gods: public cult, neighbourhood cults, and imperial cult in Augustan Rome', in Edmondson, *Augustus*, 275–309.

these lists do not reveal is the extent to which the massive amount of building and the scale of the new construction, often overshadowing earlier temples, will have displayed to the inhabitants of the city the close relationship of their leader and their gods. Even when (as he sometimes did) Augustus carefully omitted his name from a building that he had restored (*RG* 20.1), there could be no doubt who was the patron of the temple, or conversely on whom the patronage of the gods rested. In the case of the temple of the deified Julius, the connection with its dedicator, the son of the deified (*divi filius*), was particularly obvious. The close links between the religious activities of the districts of the city, the *vici*, and the imperial family will have had the same effect; and the inclusion, by a senatorial decree in 30 BC, of a libation offered to his *genius*, his personal spirit, at all banquets, both private and public, brought a ritual which was usually practised within private households for the well-being of the *paterfamilias* into the lives of all the citizens of Rome.[18]

Augustus was closely associated with the divine, but in the city itself there was no temple which marked him as a god. The nearest Rome came to such an acknowledgement were such entities as *Pax Augusta* (the altar of which stood in the Campus Martius, decreed by the senate in 13 BC and dedicated in 9 BC); and the naming of the festival which marked the dedication of the altar of Fortuna Redux as the Augustalia, rather than after the goddess whose altar it was, was an unprecedented honour for a mortal human (*RG* 11 and 12.2). Otherwise it was his *genius* or (as in the case of an altar dedicated by Tiberius in Rome at some point after his adoption in AD 4) his *numen* (divine power) which was honoured.[19] Outside Rome matters were different. Dio records that in 29 BC, following the battle of Actium, permission was given by Caesar (not yet named Augustus) to the cities of Ephesus and Nicaea, the leading cities of the provinces of Asia and Bithynia respectively, to dedicate sacred precincts to Rome and to his father, Divus Julius, laying down that resident Roman citizens should honour these gods; but adding that the Greek population could also dedicate precincts to himself, in Pergamum for Asia and in Nicomedia for Bithynia. Pergamum was also given authority to institute sacred games 'to honour his temple'. Dio notes that this was a practice which continued under later

18. On the *vici*, see above, pp. 144–5. On the libations to his *genius*, see Dio Cass. 51.19.7 with Scheid, 'To honour the *princeps*', 295.
19. *Fast. Praenest.* for 17 January (*Inscr. Ital.* 13.2.115). *Numen*, unlike *genius*, was an attribute of gods rather than of mortals.

emperors, with regard not only to the Greeks but to all other subject peoples; and that in Rome and Italy no emperor dared to do this, however worthy they might be, divine honours being delayed until after their deaths.[20] This was true for Rome under Augustus, but in Italy, especially in areas further away from Rome, local communities went beyond this. In 2 BC the Greek city of Neapolis (Naples) set up sacred games, as had the Pergamenes, 'to Augustus himself', games which took place every four years, and which Augustus attended in AD 14 just before his death;[21] and at Cumae in Campania a list of religious feasts, all relating to events in Augustus' career and set up towards the end of his reign, specifies the thanksgivings (*supplicationes*) that should be given to various gods on each of the days mentioned, but that on one, Augustus' birthday on 23 September, both a thanksgiving and a sacrifice are to be made to Augustus himself.[22] These are examples of what appears to have been a much more widespread phenomenon of local cults in Italy, often involving the colleges of freedmen called *Augustales*.[23] Such recognitions of Augustus as a god were, like those recorded by Dio in Asia and Bithynia, the initiatives of the local communities, though it must be assumed that they did not go against the wishes of the emperor; on the contrary, his presence at the games in Naples shows that he not only approved but enjoyed this display of public adoration.

In the rest of the Roman world the forms that the cult took were varied. In the Greek-speaking east, where the worship of rulers was known from the time of the Hellenistic kings and had extended to Roman generals and governors during the Republic (and to Marcus Antonius in the 30s BC), the pattern was based on the religious practice of the city which proposed the honours, and the most important sites were usually to be found in the provincial capitals, as in the cases that Dio mentioned.[24] In areas of the west, the Romans themselves established altars. Lucius Sestius, suffect consul in 23 BC after Augustus' abdication as consul that year, set up three altars to Augustus in north-west Spain, probably in 19 BC,[25] and altars were

---

20. Dio Cass. 51.20.7–9; Suetonius (*Aug.* 52) makes the same point, emphasising Augustus' refusal to accept such honours in Rome.
21. Dio Cass. 55.10.9, 56.29.2; Suet. *Aug.* 98.5; Strabo, 5.4.7.
22. *ILS* 108.
23. So the temple of Rome and Augustus at Terracina (*EJ* 121); *Augustales* at Nepet in Etruria (*ILS* 89).
24. S. R. F. Price, *Rituals and Power: The Roman Imperial Cult in Asia Minor*, Cambridge: Cambridge University Press, 1984.
25. Pomponius Mela, 3.13; Pliny, *HN* 4.111; Ptolemy, *Geographia* 2.6.3; see G. Alföldy,

established at Lugdunum (modern Lyons) by his stepson Drusus in 10 BC [26] and at Cologne, in the territory of the Ubii, probably shortly after.[27] In 2 BC Lucius Domitius Ahenobarbus reached and crossed the Elbe with Roman forces and set up an altar to Augustus.[28] These altars were the signs of Roman victories and the (presumed) pacification of the areas around, but they were also indications of the divinity of the individual who led them from far-off Rome and that of his family. The effect can be seen in a story, reported by Velleius, of an elderly German who crossed the Elbe in a dug-out canoe in AD 5 to see and touch Tiberius, whom he regarded as a god.[29] An altar was also set up to Augustus during his lifetime in Tarraco, the leading city of Hispania Citerior: a story, told by Quintilian in his instructional work on oratory, relates that the citizens of the city announced to the *princeps* that a palm tree had sprung up on his altar, to which he replied, with his accustomed wit, that it showed how often they burnt offerings on it.[30]

It was in the years following Actium that the fastidious distinction which Dio notes between Rome and the provinces was put in place. Still in the early 20s BC coins minted in Rome showed the victor as Apollo, Jupiter and Neptune; and the original intention for the great temple of the Pantheon which Agrippa built in the Campus Martius was for a statue of Augustus to be placed inside, along with those of the other gods. By the time the temple was consecrated in 25 BC, the *princeps* had made sure that the statues of himself and Agrippa would appear outside it, with that of the deified Julius inside.[31] The care Augustus took to avoid being regarded as a god in Rome itself (and his reticence in the *Res Gestae*, intended in the first instance for display in Rome, about his divine status elsewhere) is no doubt due to his desire not to transgress the boundaries of what was acceptable there, as his adoptive father, Julius Caesar, had done, and connects with his insistence that, in the constitutional sphere, he did not have

---

Fasti Hispanienses: senatorische Reichsbeamte und Offiziere in den spanischen Provinzen des römischen Reiches von Augustus bis Diokletian, Wiesbaden: Franz Steiner, 1969, 133.

26. See above, p. 138.
27. Tacitus, *Ann.* 1.37; 1.57.
28. Dio Cass. 55.10a.2.
29. Vell. Pat. 2.107.
30. Quint. *Inst.* 6.3.77. The altar with its palm is shown on coins from Tarraco from the early years of Tiberius, when the city was given permission to erect a temple to the deified Augustus (*RPC* I, nos 218, 221, 225 and 231). On the temple: Tacitus, *Ann.* 1.78.
31. Coins: see A. Burnett, *Gnomon* 55 (1983), 563–5. Pantheon: Dio Cass. 53.27.2–3.

more power in office than any other of the magistrates. Like that claim, this reticence about his divinity conceals much of the reality. There were no doubt some, especially among the political classes in Rome, who took offence at the religious honours he had acquired, and Tacitus records the complaint that he had left nothing to the gods when he wanted to be worshipped with temples and statues with divine attributes by the priests.[32] This remark is not (and was not intended to be) an accurate account of Augustus' practice, especially in Rome; more importantly it is unlikely that it reflected the ideas of the mass of the population of the city or of the various areas of the empire. For them the association of the emperor with the gods, whether through their patronage of him or by his being one of them, marked his extraordinary power and status.

Along with the temples to the gods, both new and restored, the centre of Rome bore witness to the *princeps* in other buildings of more secular character, and in the redesign of the whole set of structures around the Roman Forum, the new Forum of Augustus and the extraordinary collection of temples and monuments in the Campus Martius.[33] Augustus not only transformed the appearance of the public buildings of the city (the basis of his famous remark that he found a Rome built of brick and left it made of marble[34]), but with the help of Agrippa and others provided it with new sewers, aqueducts and gardens. The social as well as the architectural setting of the city provided the context within which the superhuman nature of the *princeps* might be assumed, even if not explicitly displayed.

Augustus and Augustan literature: patronage or control?

In another sphere, that of Latin literature, this was a period of remarkable development and flourishing. Vergil produced his *Eclogues*, modelled on Hellenistic pastoral poetry, in the early 30s BC; the *Georgics*, which use archaic and Hellenistic Greek models of didactic poems to sing the praises of farming and bee-keeping, in the early 20s, date from after the battle of Actium in

---

32. Tacitus, *Ann.* 1.10.6.
33. See P. Zanker, *The Power of Images in the Age of Augustus*, Ann Arbor: University of Michigan Press, 1988, esp. chs 3 and 4; N. Purcell, 'Rome and its development under Augustus and his successors', in A. K. Bowman, E. Champlin and A. Lintott (eds), *The Cambridge Ancient History*, 2nd edn, vol. X, *The Augustan Empire, 43 BC–AD 69*, Cambridge: Cambridge University Press, 1996, 782–811.
34. Suet. *Aug.* 28.3; reported also by Dio (Dio Cass. 56.30.3–4), who relates it to the strength of the empire rather than to the appearance of the city.

31 BC; and his great epic, the *Aeneid*, was left almost completed at his death in 19 BC. The earliest poems of Horace, probably written in the late 40s or early 30s after his participation on the losing side in the battle of Philippi, are some of those included in his *Epodes*, patterned on the iambic verse invectives of archaic Greek poetry, though others in the collection date from after Actium (for instance *Epodes* 1 and 9); this points to a publication date of around 30 BC. At about the same time he produced his *Sermones* (generally known as the *Satires*), written in conversational hexameter verse, following the model of the second-century BC Latin satirist Lucilius, though not employing the savage tone or the attacks on public figures that the latter was known for. In the 20s, Horace turned to lyric metres, producing the first three books of his *Carmina* (usually referred to in English as the *Odes*) in 23 BC. He was commissioned by Augustus to write the *Carmen saeculare*, which was sung by a choir of boys and girls at the Saecular Games in 17 BC.[35] Shortly after that a fourth book of *Carmina* appeared; and, probably before this, two books of *Epistulae*, letters in hexameter verse, each published separately, and a poem, also in hexameters, about the composition of poetry, the *Ars poetica*. Propertius' first book of poems in elegiacs, consisting almost entirely of love poetry, probably appeared in 28 BC, with his second book, also largely of love poems, two years later, and books 3 and 4, in which he deals with other subjects to a greater extent and claims to be writing as a Roman Callimachus, following the most learned and intricate of the poets of Hellenistic Alexandria, seem to date to 23 and 16 BC respectively. The two books of elegiac verse by Tibullus, containing predominantly love poems, addressed to his mistresses Delia (in book 1) and Nemesis (in book 2), as well as a boy named Marathus (also in book 1), seem to date from the mid- and late 20s BC, and he is reported to have died in 19 BC. Tibullus and Propertius were younger than Vergil and Horace, who were roughly coevals of Augustus himself. Ovid, the youngest of the Augustan poets, was not born until 43 BC. His earlier poems are variants on the tradition of elegiac love poetry – the *Amores* (of which the collection in three books which we have are a second edition, produced after 16 BC) being, or at least presenting themselves as being, about the love affairs of the poet; the *Heroides*, which are letters from mythological heroines to absent husbands and lovers; the *Medicamina facei femineae*, a mock-didactic piece on

35. See above, p. 125.

women's cosmetics, of which only the first hundred lines survive; the *Ars amatoria*, another mock-didactic poem, in three books, which describes how to find and win a lover, set in contemporary Rome; and the *Remedia amoris* ('Remedies for Love'), which (almost as a rebuttal of the *Ars amatoria*) gives advice on how to get out of a love affair. The *Remedia amoris* was produced at some point between 1 BC and AD 2, and was the last of Ovid's love poems in elegiac metre. Instead he turned to the hexameters of epic verse and produced a poem in fifteen books, the *Metamorphoses*, a collection of stories culled from mythology and drawn from an immense range of sources, relating to supernatural changes of shape. This was the last work he completed before his expulsion from Rome by Augustus in AD 8.[36] He had by then begun and half-completed his *Fasti*, a work on the feasts included in the Roman calendar, written once again in elegiacs, which he appears to have edited to some extent while in exile at Tomis on the Black Sea, though never finished. From there he also wrote five books of poems to his wife and other unnamed friends in Rome about the woes of his banishment to so inhospitable and distant a place, the *Tristia* ('Sorrows'), including one to Augustus which takes up the whole of the second book and presents an appeal for clemency and a defence of his poetic career; and he followed these with four books of verse letters, the *Epistulae ex Ponto*, on similar themes. He died, still at Tomis, in the early years of Tiberius' reign.

This brief catalogue shows the amount of Latin poetry which was produced in these years, and of course much more was written by authors whose poems have not survived at all or only in fragments. It also demonstrates the extent of innovation, both in the adoption and adaptation of archaic and Hellenistic Greek poetry, and (particularly in Ovid) in experimentation with different genres of poetry to produce new effects. Thus Ovid, in the first poem in the first book of his *Amores*, tells (in a line which carries reminiscences of the beginning of Vergil's *Aeneid*) how he was setting about producing a poem on arms and violent warfare in epic hexameters when Cupid, the god of love, stole a metric foot from the second line, turning the metre into the elegiac verse of the Latin love poets, and ordered him to write love poems instead. Such innovation and the sheer quantity and quality of the poetry make the 'Augustan' period a high point in Latin literature. The question that remains for the examination of

36. See above, p. 180.

the achievements of Augustus is in what sense this remarkable group of writers and the work they produced was 'Augustan' in more than a chronological sense. Were they writing under the influence, the patronage or the direction of the emperor?

That some at least of the earlier of these poets were members of a group associated with Gaius Maecenas, a close associate of the young Caesar from the earliest days onwards,[37] is not in doubt. His name appears in the poems of Vergil, Horace and Propertius, and the fact that this is not in their earliest productions suggests that he had picked them out as a result of the promise they showed. Vergil addressed his *Georgics* to Maecenas, mentioning him near the beginning of each of his four books (*G.* 1.2; 2.41; 3.41; 4.2). Horace similarly writes the first poem in the *Epodes*, and the first book of the *Sermones*, the *Carmina* and the *Epistles* to him (*Epod.* 1.1; *Sat.* 1.1.1; *Carm.* 1.1.1; *Epist.* 1.1.3), and he is mentioned frequently in all these, especially the *Sermones* and the *Carmina*; and the second book of Propertius' elegies is also written to Maecenas. He was clearly an influential friend and supporter of these men through the 30s and 20s BC, and Horace's account of a journey to Brundisium (*Sat.* 1.5) shows Maecenas travelling with Horace, Vergil and a number of other literary men. It is only in passing that Horace mentions that Maecenas and Lucius Cocceius Nerva, who was also with them, were on important state business, which was the attempted reconciliation of the young Caesar with Marcus Antonius in 38 BC.[38] Horace had been introduced to Maecenas by Vergil and another poet, Lucius Varius Rufus, a friend of Vergil and another member of the party who went to Brundisium, and became part of Maecenas' circle some nine months later.[39] The nature of this grouping and the relationships between Maecenas, Caesar (later Augustus) and the poets in Maecenas' circle have long been a matter of debate among scholars.[40] Close relationships between the rich and powerful and poets had been frequent in the Republic and continued throughout this period: Gaius Asinius Pollio, who, despite his earlier support for Antonius and his Republican sympathies, was a major figure in

37. See above, p. 24.
38. Hor. *Sat.* 1.5.27. See above, pp. 51–2.
39. Hor. *Sat.* 1.6.45–62.
40. See for example J. Griffin, 'Augustus and the poets: *Caesar qui cogere posset*', in Millar and Segal, *Caesar Augustus: Seven Aspects*, 189–218; P. White, *Promised Verse: Poets in the Society of Augustan Rome*, Cambridge, MA: Harvard University Press, 1993.

Rome down to his death in AD 4 and was responsible for the first public library in the city in the Atrium Libertatis, was the dedicatee of Vergil's fourth *Eclogue* and is addressed by Horace in one of his odes;[41] and Marcus Valerius Messalla Corvinus was associated with a number of the poets of the time, including Horace and Vergil, and especially Tibullus and Ovid, neither of whom was supported by Maecenas.[42] These were great men, with the influence and wealth to attract and support poets and others, and the interest in literary matters to wish to do so. Predominant in all these respects, however, were Caesar Augustus and Maecenas. They had both political power and financial resources beyond the reach of others. The case of Horace, of whom a brief biography by Suetonius survives and whose poetry is more autobiographical than most, shows how their interaction with a poet worked. Horace's background was not distinguished (his father was a freedman from the Apulian town of Venusia) but was reasonably prosperous, and, after a good education in Rome, he had joined the army of Brutus as an officer (*tribunus militum*) and was on the losing side at Philippi. He managed to get back to Rome, where he held a post in the treasury as a *scriba*. After his meeting with Maecenas and his subsequent joining the group of poets which surrounded him, Horace became known to Caesar, who liked him and later asked him to join his personal staff to assist with is correspondence. Although Horace refused, Augustus continued to count him as a friend and gave him substantial gifts. Augustus commissioned from him the *Carmen saeculare* for the Saecular Games of 17 BC; and, according to Suetonius, who quotes the letters between the two, Augustus also, after reading the *Sermones* and (probably) the first book of *Epistles*, complained in a friendly style that he did not appear in these works, which resulted in the first poem in Horace's second book of *Epistles* being addressed to him. Augustus could influence the work that poets produced, but it appears that it was possible to refuse or at least modify a request. In his epistle to Augustus, Horace duly acknowledges Augustus' greatness and superiority over all others but then moves on to dilate on the (to Horace) unfair preference

41. Library: Suet. *Aug.* 29.5; Pliny, *HN* 7.115, 35.10. Verg. *Ecl.* 4.12; Hor. *Carm.* 2.1.14.
42. Horace: Hor. *Sat.* 1.10.29 and 85; *Carm.* 3.21; *Ars P.* 371. Vergil: Servius on Verg. *Aen.* 8.310; Seneca, *Suas.* 2.20. Tibullus: Tib. 1.1.53–4; 1.3.1–4 and 55–6; 1.5.31–4; 1.7, 2.1.31–6; 2.5.119–20. Ovid: Ovid, *Tr.* 4.4.3–6 and 27–34; *Pont.* 1.7.27–30; 2.2.1 and 97–8; 2.3.69–78; 3.5.7.

given to the ancient poets over those of the present. Suetonius also tells of Augustus' desire, after the first three books of the *Carmina* appeared, that Horace should write to celebrate the victories of his stepsons Tiberius and Drusus over the Vindelici in 15 BC,[43] which resulted in the fourth book. It is true that book 4 of the *Carmina* includes a poem about Drusus' campaign (*Carm.* 4.4) and a second (*Carm.* 4.14) which describes the feats of the two brothers, but the emphasis in the second is firmly on Augustus himself, and the last three stanzas have no mention of either Tiberius or Drusus but list Augustus' victories over peoples across the Roman world.[44] At the beginning of Vergil's third *Georgic*, the poet writes that while at the moment he must fulfil Maecenas' orders to write on the raising of livestock, he will soon erect a temple which will display Caesar's great triumphs, a poem on his fiery wars, beginning with his ancestors.[45] This was not what the *Aeneid* was, but it contains some of the same themes. Propertius was urged by Maecenas to compose an epic but declined to write on the great themes of Thebes and Troy, arguing that he should stick to love poems, though he might try something on Jupiter and the Titans, or the beginnings of Roman history or even, on Maecenas' instructions, the more recent wars, the Parthians, Perusia and the defeat of Antonius.[46] In the event he never wrote an epic, though he produced elegiacs in praise of Italy and grieving the death of Marcellus in the same book in which his reply to Maecenas appeared, and his last book included a series of poems on Roman *aetia* (origins) in the style of Callimachus and one on the victory at Actium.[47]

All this seems to be a series of suggestions or proposals which come from Maecenas (and perhaps therefore from Augustus), and which the poets concerned can adopt, modify or refuse at will. Of course the suggestions from such a source have rather more force than those from others. Horace, speaking of a singer who would neither keep quiet when asked nor sing when wanted, writes that Caesar could have compelled him, but makes it clear that he did not.[48] That is the picture that Horace wanted to present in the

43. See above, p. 128.
44. See the interpretation by White, *Promised Verse*, 127–32.
45. Verg. *G.* 3.1–48.
46. Prop. 3.9. See Ovid, *Am.* 1.1, for another refusal to move from love poetry to epic.
47. Italy: Prop. 3.22. Marcellus: 3.18. Roman *aetia*: 4.1, 2, 4, 6 (on the temple of Apollo on the Palatine and Actium), 9 and 10.
48. Hor. *Sat.* 1.3.1–19.

30s BC when this was written, but it does seem that, especially in his later years, Caesar might take a stronger line. Ovid's expulsion from Rome in AD 8 was, as he himself states, the result of a poem and an error.[49] The 'error', though apparently well known, was not something he could speak about, but the poem was clearly the *Ars amatoria*: both, it appears, angered the *princeps*, and Ovid's books were withdrawn from public libraries in Rome.[50] He was not the only writer who was punished for what he had written. Dio records that in AD 12 Augustus ordered the burning of pamphlets attacking certain individuals, and this seems to have included the works of the old-fashioned but effective advocate and historian Titus Labienus and the clever but famously savage orator Cassius Severus.[51] By this time, of course, Maecenas was long dead (he died in 8 BC, shortly before Horace), and he seems to have withdrawn from involvement in public affairs well before that. It may well be that it was he who maintained an easy relationship between Augustus and the poets, and the tone of the letters that the emperor wrote to Horace, preserved in Suetonius' life of the poet, suggests that. Although the poems from this period often relate to the policies and ideas that Augustus promoted and some sections which tell of his glory, it is not until later that such glorification becomes predominant, as in Horace's fourth book of *Carmina* and Propertius' poem on the victory of Actium in his last book, from which any mention of Maecenas has disappeared.[52] Augustus was clearly interested in what poets and others wrote, and could and did influence them; but, at least while Maecenas was closely involved, this seems to have been less a matter of work produced to order than of responses to the ideas and the ethos which emanated from above. Only in the period around and following the celebration of the Saecular Games did the tone of the suggestions (it appears) become more directive. Of course the negative reaction to work of which the *princeps* actively disapproved was a different matter, but this seems to belong to the latter years of his reign.

---

49. Ovid, *Tr.* 2.207: perdiderint cum me duo crimina, carmen et error.
50. Ovid, *Tr.* 3.1.65–74.
51. See above, p. 187.
52. Hor. *Carm.* 4.4, 5, 14 and 15. Prop. 4.6. Some scholars have argued that this poem by Propertius is an irreverent mocking of Augustus' victory, using an inappropriate Callimachean style (W. R. Johnson, 'The emotions of patriotism: Propertius 4.6', *California Studies in Classical Antiquity* 6 (1973), 151–80).

Beyond Rome: Italy and the west

Control over literary output, whether in verse or in prose, was in any case unlikely to have been a major concern of Augustus, however significant it seems to those who have studied the remarkable work of poets and others from this period. The readers of such work at the time will have made up only a small part of the populace of the empire or even of Rome, even if it did include members of the governing classes of the senatorial and equestrian orders; and it is worth noting that there is no mention of any poet or prose-writer in the *Res Gestae*, even the writers of the *Aeneid* or the *Carmen saeculare*. The intended audience for this document were clearly in the first instance those who would see it in the Campus Martius, in front of the Mausoleum, and the emphasis placed on his gifts to the Roman plebs and to the building and rebuilding of the city point in the same direction. Beyond Rome, it is particularly the population of Italy to which Augustus refers: it was they (followed by the provinces of the west) who swore allegiance to him of their own free will in the war which ended at Actium (*RG* 25.2); it was they who swarmed into the capital in unprecedented numbers to elect him *pontifex maximus* in 12 BC (*RG* 10.2); it was in Italy that he made the great majority of payments to towns for land on which to settle veterans (*RG* 16.1) and where he paid back in 28 BC the 35,000 pounds of gold which the Italian *municipia* and *coloniae* had sent in recognition of his triumphs, and did the same whenever they made similar contributions thereafter (*RG* 21.3).[53] In the years since the extension of Roman citizenship to Italy following the wars of the 80s BC, Italy had become steadily more homogenised from the collection of individual and quite distinct communities that it had been before, not least by the recruitment of soldiers into the Roman armies, and this had reached a pitch in the civil wars and the subsequent distribution of veterans throughout the peninsula.[54] Augustus played a direct part in this by dividing Italy into eleven *regiones*, a move which reflects on a larger scale his division of Rome itself.[55] The support he had, or claimed to have, from Italy by the late 30s BC was central to his presentation of himself as leader of the

53. See Cooley, *Res Gestae*, 39.
54. M. H. Crawford, 'Italy and Rome from Sulla to Augustus', in Bowman et al., *Cambridge Ancient History*, vol. X, 414–33; Edward Bispham, *From Asculum to Actium: The Municipalization of Italy from the Social War to Augustus*, Oxford: Oxford University Press, 2007.
55. Pliny, *HN* 3.46. See above, pp. 144–5.

Roman west against his enemy Antonius and the queen of Egypt. The prominent place which Italy and (to a lesser extent) the western provinces have in the *Res Gestae* is not surprising; and by contrast the inhabitants of the eastern provinces feature there hardly at all.[56] The propaganda of this self-assessment by Augustus, at once blatant and subtle, was aimed primarily at Rome, its senators, *equites* and people, and then the Latin-speaking inhabitants of Italy and the west.

The assessment of others: Tacitus

The *Res Gestae* is not the only estimate of the reign and achievements of Augustus to emerge from the Roman world of the early empire. The most arresting is that of Tacitus in the first ten chapters of the *Annales*, not only because of his hostile tone but also because he is clearly responding in some places to the claims made by Augustus in the *Res Gestae*.[57] In a pair of chapters which follow his description of the funeral of the *princeps* (*Ann.* 1.9–10), Tacitus writes that there was much talk about Augustus. The majority marvelled over various unimportant points, that he died on the same day on which he first received *imperium* as consul in 43 BC, and in the same house and the same room in which his father had expired; the number of times he had been consul, the thirty-seven years in which he held the *tribunicia potestas*, the number of acclamations he had received as an *imperator* (a victorious general), and the other honours, repeatedly bestowed or new, which he had received, all of which had been proudly listed in the *Res Gestae*. The more perceptive (*prudentes*) either praised or criticised him. Some argued that loyalty to his adoptive father and the needs of the state, in which he had no official position, drove him to civil war, and that he made many concessions to Antonius and Lepidus until his father's murderers were disposed of; and that after that the failings of both meant that there was no cure for the ills of the fatherland other than rule by one man; but he did not rule as a king or a dictator but established the state, using the title of *princeps*. Moreover he left an

56. Note the ways in which the translators of the Greek version of the *Res Gestae* had to add to and adapt the Latin original to make it understandable by a Greek-speaking audience (Cooley, *Res Gestae*, 26–30).
57. See Cooley, *Res Gestae*, 48–51. Tacitus was not the only author to use the text of the *Res Gestae* as a source. Scheid, *Res Gestae Divi Augusti*, lxiii–lxiv, lists six such passages from Suetonius' life of Augustus, most notably *Aug.* 43.1 (from *RG* 22.2).

empire bounded by the ocean or by long rivers, and the legions, the provinces and the fleets joined together in a close network. There was law given to protect the citizens, mildness shown to the provinces, and Rome itself was magnificently adorned. Force had been little used, and by it all others lived in peace and quiet.

All this could be seen as a précis of Augustus' own view of himself. On the other side, according to Tacitus, it was said that his duty to his father and the problems of the state were merely excuses: it was his lust for power which had led him to bribe veterans and raise an army, though only a private citizen, and an adolescent at that; he got hold of the power and status of a praetor by a senatorial decree (that is, not by election); and after the convenient deaths of the consuls Hirtius and Pansa (for which he was probably responsible), he took over their forces, extorted the consulship from an unwilling senate and then used the army he had been given to deal with Antonius against the state; the proscriptions of citizens and the distributions of land which followed were decried even by those who carried them out. To be sure, Cassius and Brutus were killed as the result of his family feud, but he should have put that aside for the sake of the state. He then beguiled and cheated Sextus Pompeius, Lepidus and Antonius with pretended friendships, the last losing his life as the result of his marriage to Octavia. No doubt peace followed, but even that was stained with blood by the military disasters of Lollius and Varus and the killings in Rome of Varro Murena, Egnatius Rufus and Iullus Antonius. As for his family life, he abducted Livia when she was not only the wife of Tiberius Claudius Nero but pregnant by him, and asked the college of *pontifices* the ludicrous question whether it was in order to marry her in this condition. The result had been that the state acquired a mother and the house of the Caesars a step-mother who was disastrous for both. Moreover he had assumed divine status with all its trappings, and even the appointment of Tiberius as his successor had been done to enhance his own glory in comparison to someone whose cruelty and arrogance he well knew.

Although Tacitus sets these two views alongside one another with no explicit comment (he ends with the note that nonetheless the burial of Augustus was duly performed and his deification decreed), the way in which they are presented makes it clear that he favoured the latter view. In the chapters which precede these, he has presented a picture of the civil wars leading to the emergence of one surviving leader of the Caesarians in a Rome where all who might oppose him were dead and the remainder prepared to submit to slavery for the sake of riches and honours offered by the new regime, while the soldiers were won over by gifts, the people of Rome by corn and everybody by the delights of peace and quiet. In the meantime Augustus himself accrued, little by little and without opposition, the functions of the senate, the magistrates and the laws. He attempted to secure the transmission of power to members of his family but, after the deaths of Gaius and Lucius Caesar, had to turn to Tiberius. At the time there were no wars, except in Germany, and no one left who had known the Republic. The only worry was that Augustus himself was ageing, and the malign influence of Livia, who had long been working to ensure that her son Tiberius succeeded, became dominant. Augustus' approaching demise led a few to talk about the blessings of freedom; more feared a return to war, and some hoped for it, but the great majority discussed the likely successors. Agrippa Postumus was too young and too wild, Tiberius well experienced but a typical Claudian, arrogant, potentially savage and given to hiding his intentions and his faults. And then there was the imperious Livia and the two young men, Germanicus and Drusus, who would oppress the state and afterwards tear it apart. Tacitus follows this grim prospect with an account of the banishment and death of Agrippa Postumus, placing the blame firmly at Livia's door.

Tacitus' account of these debates about Augustus takes the same materials that Augustus himself had used in the *Res Gestae* and interprets them negatively to show him as a skilled and opportunistic politician, quite capable of using deceit and force to seize and maintain his domination, and the earlier chapters confirm this view, with the addition of the deleterious results of the power of the imperial household, and in particular of Livia. Tacitus does not deny that many in the upper classes accepted Augustus, but puts this down to their servility in the earlier years and their ignorance of the liberties of the Republic later. This is a sobering corrective to the picture that Augustus provides in his own version of his achievements, even when it is borne in mind that Tacitus was seeing the first of the emperors through a lens shaped by those who followed, notably Tiberius and Domitian, to whom he was extremely hostile, regarding them as tyrants implacably opposed to his own senatorial class. The question he leaves is the same which he presented in the form of the two views attributed to the *prudentes*, the more perceptive evaluators of the career of the dying *princeps* in AD 14: how far can we accept Augustus' own account of himself in what is undoubtedly a tendentious document?

Augustus and Rome: some conclusions

For the purposes of this book, which, despite its inevitable focus on Augustus, is a contribution to the history of Rome and not a biography of its first emperor, another approach is required and a different question must be asked. In what ways was the Roman world different in AD 14 from what it had been when Julius Caesar was assassinated in 44 BC? And, to subdivide this short but eventful period a little, what changes had taken place by 30 BC, after the battle of Actium, and by 2 BC, the high point of Augustus' reign, the year in which he was named as father of the fatherland, *pater patriae*?

Pax Augusta: *peace after war*

The most obvious difference between the mid-40s BC and the time at which Augustus died was, as even the critical *prudentes* of Tacitus had to admit, the absence of war and its turmoils. The assassination of Julius Caesar came almost exactly a year after the defeat of the Pompeians at Munda, and just over a year later his adopted son, along with the consuls Hirtius and Pansa, was ranged against Marcus Antonius at Mutina. Later in 43 the march of Antonius, Lepidus and Caesar on Rome led to the establishment of the trium-virate and the horrors of the proscriptions and consequent confis-cations of property. The war against Brutus and Cassius ended with the battles of Philippi in October 42, to be followed in 41 by the struggle between the consul Lucius Antonius, Marcus' brother, and the siege of Perusia, ended only in the early months of 40. The uneasy and potentially explosive relations between the triumvirs, and especially between Caesar and Antonius, were patched up, but relations with Sextus Pompeius, though he too was temporarily reconciled with the triumvirs at Misenum in spring 39, had broken down by the year's end, and he was at war with Caesar from 38 to his eventual defeat in September 36 BC. Lepidus was removed from the triumvirate days later. The next five years saw the final break-down between Antonius, based in Alexandria with Cleopatra, whence he conducted his unsuccessful campaigns against Parthia, and Caesar, based in Rome but campaigning from 35 to 33 in Illyricum. In 32 BC 'the whole of Italy' swore allegiance to Caesar and the senate declared war on Cleopatra; the battle of Actium followed in September 31, and by August of the next year Caesar had captured Alexandria. Throughout these fifteen years war was ever present throughout the Mediterranean, even if military action was more sporadic, and it was war between Romans, not Romans and foreigners, however it might be dressed up as directed against slaves, pirates and an Egyptian foe.

The establishment of peace was a recurrent motif in Augustus' presentation of himself. Already after the defeat of Sextus Pompeius at Naulochus in 36 BC he was decreed a golden statue in the Forum which bore an inscription that he had restored by land and sea the peace which had long been disturbed;[58] the gates of the shrine of Janus were closed, so Augustus writes in the Res Gestae, on three occasions, of which one was certainly after Actium and a second at the end of the Cantabrian wars in Spain in 25 BC, to mark the fact, as he claims, that victories had secured peace by land and sea throughout the whole empire of the Roman people;[59] and the public cult of Pax (peace) was instituted, probably for the first time in Rome, when in 13 BC the senate decreed the altar of Pax Augusta, dedicated in 9 BC, celebrating the peace brought about by the princeps whose name the goddess bore.[60] The city was, of course, full of monuments recording Augustus' prowess as a military victor, most notably the Augustan Forum, with its temple to Mars Ultor (the Avenger), recalling the defeat of his father's assassins, its statues of past celebrators of triumphs and its list of the peoples he had conquered;[61] but, as his own note on the closing of the doors of Janus makes clear, military victory was seen as the cause not the antithesis of peace. In the same Forum of Augustus the province of Baetica in Spain erected a golden statue of him, with an inscription recording that, through his beneficence and perpetual care, he had pacified the province.[62] The ending of the civil wars with the victory over Antonius and Cleopatra and the defeat or disabling of foreign enemies was seen by Velleius, writing in the reign of Tiberius, as the creating of a peace on which all Augustus' other achievements were built; and that, especially in the earlier years of his reign, when those who remembered what had gone before were still alive, will have seemed an enormous and beneficial change.[63]

58. Appian, B Civ. 5.103.
59. Aug. RG 13; see Cooley, Res Gestae, 157–61.
60. Aug. RG 12.2. See above, p. 130. On the introduction of the cult of Pax, see A. J. Clark, Divine Qualities: Cult and Community in Republican Rome, Oxford: Oxford University Press, 2007, 159–60.
61. See above, pp. 154–6. On the list of conquered peoples, see Vell. Pat. 2.39.2.
62. EJ 42.
63. Vell. Pat. 2.89.3–4 (cited in full at pp. 76–7 above).

Optimi status auctor: *the monarch and the* res publica

A second change was the institution of a newly restored Roman society, built on the peace which was achieved after the victory at Actium, and of which the successful campaigns against foreign foes was a sign. When in the sixth book of the *Aeneid* Vergil describes Aeneas' visit to the underworld, he makes Aeneas' father, Anchises, show him the future of Rome in the persons of Romulus, Julius Caesar and lastly Augustus Caesar, who will bring back golden centuries (*aurea saecula*) to Latium, and goes on to list the lands and peoples that Augustus will bring under the power of Rome.[64] Augustus himself was proud of the closing of the gates of Janus three times while he was *princeps* but only twice before in the history of the city; and that he was the first ever to purchase with his own money lands for veterans in Italy and the provinces. He also asserted justifiably that the new laws he proposed had restored many of the exemplary practices of the ancestors, and that he himself had passed on many such examples to posterity for their imitation. He saw himself, as Suetonius records, as instituting the best possible state of affairs in a new Rome: *optimi status auctor*.[65] It was these exemplary practices that were celebrated in the Saecular Games in 17 BC, held in the midst of his social and moral legislation in 18 and 17 BC.[66] Such laws were not always popular or even successful. The law of 18 BC on marriage was the subject of demonstrations by objectors from among the equestrian order in AD 9, and was modified in some way then.[67] The sense that this was seen as a significant part of his work was, however, clear. Horace, at the beginning of his verse epistle to Augustus, produced at about the time of Augustus' moral legislation, writes that he would be acting against the public interest were he to waste Augustus' time by expecting him to read a long poem when he was taking on all alone such great burdens of business, defending Italy with armies, improving its morals and correcting them with laws.[68]

Horace's apology for troubling Augustus not only confirms the amount of work and the beneficial intentions of the *princeps*; it also displays the most fundamental change in the Roman world from the

64. Verg. *Aen.* 6.791–807.
65. Aug. *RG* 13 (Janus); 16.1 (purchase of land); 6.1–2 and 8.5 (moral legislation and exemplars). Suet. *Aug.* 28.2, citing an edict of Augustus.
66. See above, pp. 124–6.
67. See above, pp. 181–2.
68. Hor. *Epist.* 2.1.1–4.

period of the Republic, and even from the time of Julius Caesar. Augustus alone is responsible for the defence of Rome, the centre of that world, and for its morals and the laws that protect them. The *res publica*, the state, the business of the senate and people of Rome, was now in the hands of one man; and, though the same could be said of the dictatorship of Julius Caesar in 44 BC or even that of Sulla in the late 80s, this was now, under Augustus, a permanency (unlike that of Sulla) and accepted (unlike that of Julius). Augustus and his successors were monarchs, even when (as Augustus did with Agrippa and later Tiberius) they associated others with them in their rule. That did not mean that the *res publica* was no more, and already in 28 BC, before Augustus was granted that name, a coin, showing him seated on a consul's chair with a scroll in his hand and a voting urn at his feet, declared that he had restored the Roman people's laws and rights.[69] Unlike his adoptive father, Julius Caesar, who is said to have stated that the *res publica* was nothing, a mere name without body or form,[70] Augustus showed respect to the senate and the magistracies, and in his comparatively modest house and his mode of dress he associated himself with the other citizens of Rome, at least those of the senatorial class. He took care, as *princeps* (which might best be translated 'first citizen'), not to set himself apart, and in so doing established a pattern which shaped the style of the principate for his successors. In this, as in other ways, he might almost be seen as following the advice of his old mentor Cicero. In his relations with the senators, the equestrians and the people of Rome, on all of whom his ruling of the Roman world depended in different ways, this was undoubtedly useful; but no one can have been in any doubt that his behaving in such a way was his own choice, and the fact that he was able to make that choice showed him as sole ruler.[71] So too his restoration of the exemplary practices of the ancestors in 18 and 17 BC was an attempt to return to the upright morality of the Republican period (at least as perceived at the end of the first century BC), but it was to be achieved by the decidedly non-Republican means of the establishment of courts set up by the laws

69. J. W. Rich and J. H. C. Williams, 'Leges et iura p.R. restituit: a new aureus of Octavian and the settlement of 28–27 BC, *Numismatic Chronicle* 159 (1999), 169–213.
70. Suet. *Iul.* 77.
71. See especially A. Wallace-Hadrill, '*Civilis princeps*: between citizen and king', *Journal of Roman Studies* 72 (1982), 32–48; and, for the extent and speed with which his sole rule was recognised across the empire, F. Millar, 'State and subject: the impact of monarchy', in Millar and Segal, *Caesar Augustus: Seven Aspects*, 37–60. On Cicero, see above, pp. 36–7.

proposed by the *princeps*; and his claim not to have had more power than any of his colleagues in any of the magistracies he held conceals his unprecedented holding of so many and of other powers that were separated from magisterial office.[72] He is restoring and implementing Republican institutions but doing so as a monarch.

There were of course ways in which his status was more obvious. His departures from and returns to Rome were marked by deputations of the magistrates and senate, and when he came back after the successful recovery of the standards from the Parthians, though he may have avoided the deputation, he accepted a senatorial decree that an altar should be erected to Fortuna Redux (Fortune the Home-Bringer).[73] Indeed Suetonius states that he avoided entering and leaving the city except in the evening or at night in order to spare people the inconvenience of the ceremony.[74] Such rituals were not performed for ordinary citizens of however high a rank.

When he was in Rome, Augustus and those surrounding him inevitably formed a grouping of far greater significance than those about any other individual. His house on the Palatine, which, though modest in comparison to the palaces of later emperors, was a remarkable complex of buildings, including the temple of Apollo, libraries and a portico, and also, after he became *pontifex maximus* in 12 BC, the shrine of the goddess Vesta. Also on the Palatine were houses belonging to his friends (*amici*) and his freedmen, from which he sometimes watched the games in the Circus below the hill. These *amici* formed part of the wide and varied circle on whom Augustus could call for advice on matters of all sorts, whether judicial, political or personal. Unlike the senatorial committees which had prepared senatorial business and acted as an advisory body from early in his reign, the *amici* had no formal place in the structures of government, but could be used in arriving at decisions in matters of major importance.[75] Their significance lay in their closeness to the *princeps* rather than any rank they held, though many were major generals or important figures in the senate.[76] Closer still were the

72. See above, pp. 121 and 205–6.
73. See above, p. 110. On the ceremony, see R. J. A. Talbert, *The Senate of Imperial Rome*, Princeton: Princeton University Press, 1984, 70–2; W. K. Lacey, *Augustus and the Principate: The Evolution of the System*, Leeds: Francis Cairns, 1996, 17–56.
74. Suet. *Aug.* 53.2.
75. Senatorial committees: see above, p. 189. The work of a *consilium* of *amici* can be seen in the discussions of the future of Judaea after the death of Herod: see above, p. 150.
76. J. Crook, *Consilium Principis: Imperial Councils and Counsellors from Augustus to Diocletian*, Cambridge: Cambridge University Press, 1955, 21–36.

imperial freedmen and slaves, at least those who worked directly
with Augustus, such as the freedmen Polybius and Hilarion, who
were responsible for writing part of his will, and those whom he
mentioned in his account of the military forces and revenues of the
empire, who were in a position to provide details on these matters,
essential for the governing of the Roman world.[77] Such men, along
with the members of the imperial family, formed the core of what in
the century that followed would become the emperor's court.[78] As
with so many of the developments of the Augustan monarchy, the
origins of the court can be traced to the social and political patterns
of the upper classes of the late Republic. The use of the freedmen and
slaves of the household, the formal reception of friends in the early
morning, the attachment of intellectuals and literary figures to the
head of the family, and the summoning of family and others to
advise him on legal and other matters were all features of the great
and aspiring in the Republican period, and indeed continued to be
so thereafter. The difference between these institutions and those
which surrounded Augustus was not so much the patterns of behaviour as the size and scope of the emerging imperial court. It is not
certain whether Augustus classified his *amici* into categories with
different privileges of admission to him when they paid their visit to
him at the morning *salutatio*, but others did, and Seneca reports that
this had been had been introduced at Rome by Gaius Gracchus in
the late second century BC in imitation of courts of the Hellenistic
kings, to be followed shortly after by Marcus Livius Drusus, the
tribune of the plebs in BC 91. Augustus made it his practice to be
accessible at the *salutatio* to all senators, and only abandoned it at
the end of his reign due to his old age.[79] The fact that the whole
senate, not to mention many others who were numbered among his
amici, had such access marks the difference between the *princeps*
and the rest; and, of course, this is accounted for by the far greater

77. Suet. *Aug.* 101. On the slaves and freedmen in imperial service, see P. R. C. Weaver,
Familia Caesaris: A Social Study of the Emperor's Freedmen and Slaves, Cambridge:
Cambridge University Press, 1972.
78. A. Wallace-Hadrill, 'The imperial court', in Bowman et al., *The Cambridge Ancient
History* (2nd edn), vol. X, 283–308.
79. Seneca, *Ben.* 6.33.4–34.2; Dio Cass. 56.26.2–3. An inscription, from the reigns of
Augustus or Tiberius, which was recorded in the sixteenth century but is now lost,
records an *eques*, Gaius Caesius Niger, as having been *ex prima admissione*, which
would mean that he was among those first admitted at the *salutatio* (*ILS* 1320). Seneca
also remarks that Augustus filled his *cohors primae admissionis* from the camps of his
former enemies (*Clem.* 1.10.1). There is, however, no other evidence of such a system
under Augustus. On the *amici* of Augustus, see Crook, *Consilium Principis*, 31–6.

importance of decisions that were made in his house and the significance of the influence of anyone who might count as being close
to him.

Domus Augusta: *the imperial family and the dynastic succession*

Closest of all, both from the natural structures of any Roman household and because of the way in which Augustus promoted the
imperial house as a model of social policy and the executors of his
military strategy, were his own family. The women, notably his wife
Livia and his sister Octavia, were granted exceptional honours from
as early as 35 BC, and were presented as exemplars of feminine
virtue; they were also significant figures in the politics of the time,
Octavia as Antonius' abandoned wife and Livia as Caesar Augustus'
wife and the mother of Tiberius and Drusus;[80] and his daughter Julia
was, as wife successively of Marcellus, Agrippa and Tiberius and the
mother of Gaius and Lucius Caesar and of the more problematic
Agrippa Postumus, for more than a quarter of a century the trans-
mitter of the line of succession. Of the male members of the family,
Agrippa (his son-in-law from 21 BC), his stepsons Tiberius and
Drusus, and Drusus' son Germanicus all played major roles in the
foreign wars that resulted in the expansion of empire from the
20s BC down to AD 14; and it was they, along with his nephew
Marcellus (who died in 23 BC) and his grandsons and adoptive sons
Gaius and Lucius Caesar (who died in AD 4 and 2 respectively), from
whom Augustus selected and marked out his intended successors.

It was this creation of a family dynasty which showed most clearly
the change from a republican to a monarchical state. When Julius
Caesar made his will the year before he was assassinated he made the
young Gaius Octavius his main heir and gave him a new name, but
he did not make him, and could not have made him, his successor
to his position as dictator. Augustus was in an altogether different
position. His marking out of Marcellus, newly married to Augustus'
daughter Julia, by the grant of permission to hold the consulship ten
years earlier than normal in 24 BC, and the still greater and more
flamboyant privileges afforded to Gaius and Lucius Caesar in 5 and
2 BC, made it clear that these young men were meant in due course

---

80. For honours in 35 BC, see above, p. 64. On the influence of Livia and Octavia, see
N. Purcell, 'Livia and the womanhood of Rome', in Edmondson, *Augustus*, 165–94, and
other works cited there.

to succeed to his position.[81] Such honours were not official or constitutional announcements of their status as his successors but there is no doubt, from the reaction at the time and in the sources, that this is how they were regarded. Just as Augustus marked out those whom he chose as his closest collaborators in the work of ruling the empire and as potential *principes* with the grant of the *tribunicia potestas* to Agrippa in 18 and 13 BC and to Tiberius in 6 BC and then in AD 4 and 13, a power which was useful but hardly essential,[82] so the honours given to Marcellus and the brothers Gaius and Lucius effectively designated those who, while as yet too young to play as full a part in the business of government, were to be the rulers of the next generation.

The question of the succession shows more clearly than anything else the change to monarchy, and a glance at the different ways in which this was present at the three tell-tale dates of 44, 30 and 2 BC reveals much about the development of that change. If in 44 BC there was no possibility of a constitutional successor to Julius Caesar (as opposed to the inheritance of his wealth and, to an extent, of his political following), the position had not changed fundamentally by the time of the victory at Actium. Though Imperator Caesar, son of the divine Julius, as he then was, was the supreme leader and effectively monarch of Rome, there was no monarchy as such, nothing to pass to a successor; and in any case he was still a young man, in his early thirties. In the next decade, much changed. The effective monarch was named Augustus in 27 and in Egypt, for instance, was seen as the new king, in succession to the deceased Cleopatra.[83] By 23 BC, when Augustus nearly died, Marcellus was in place, married to Augustus' daughter Julia. Marcellus' death in the same year makes it impossible to know what might have happened thereafter had he survived and had he and Julia given Augustus grandsons, but the speed with which Augustus adopted Julia's sons Gaius and Lucius after her marriage to Agrippa, and the fact that Agrippa Postumus, born after his father's death in 12 BC, was not also adopted, suggest that his strategy with regard to the succession had developed: he was now looking for a closer link to his successor than

81. Marcellus: see above, p. 97; Gaius: see above, p. 151; Lucius: see above, p. 153.
82. Agrippa: see above, pp. 132–3. Tiberius was described by Velleius as made equal with Augustus by the sharing of the tribunician power (2.99.1). Tacitus famously called it *summi fastigii vocabulum* (the title of the highest eminence), mentioning the grants to Agrippa and Tiberius (*Ann.* 3.56.2).
83. See Millar, 'State and subject', 37–9.

might be achieved by a distant family connection, backed up by a marriage alliance, and the adoption of two grandsons provided him with a pair of sons, which should have proved sufficient for the purpose. So by 2 BC, with the coming of age of the younger brother, the scene appeared to be set. It should be noted, however, that, despite the change from the situation in 30 BC, in some ways the formal position had not changed. There was still no constitutional office of emperor: *princeps* was not the name of a magistrate and 'Augustus' was a cognomen voted to an individual by the senate. The functions of the emperor, for which later writers were to use the term *imperium*, which under the Republic had meant the power of a magistrate or pro-magistrate or of the Roman people as a whole, did not by this date have a single word to describe it.[84] By 2 BC, however, the transmission of the collection of powers and authority which lay at the base of Augustus' rule had become a matter of inheritance within the family, and in particular from father to son, irrespective of whether the son concerned was natural or adopted. So, after the death of Gaius in AD 4, Augustus adopted Tiberius, his stepson, and Agrippa Postumus, his grandson, whom he disowned shortly afterwards. In AD 14, after his own death, there were, according to Tacitus, other candidates whose names were considered, and had even allegedly been considered by Augustus, as possible successors, but no one but Tiberius emerged; and when in AD 41, after the assassination of the emperor Gaius Caligula, the senate met and debated the restoration of the old Republic and the abolition of the memory of the Caesars, the mass of the people stood outside, demanding Claudius, the last surviving son of Tiberius' younger brother Drusus.[85] For the next two centuries being the son, natural or adopted, of a former emperor was a crucial part of the establishment of legitimacy of a ruler. This undoubtedly monarchical structure was the direct result of the place that the imperial family had in Augustus' plans for the succession.

Imperium Romanum: *the new Roman Empire*

In the empire, outside Rome and the court of the emperor, the world had also changed in the years between the deaths of Julius Caesar

---

84. J. Richardson, *The Language of Empire: Rome and the Idea of Empire from the Third Century BC to the Second Century AD*, Cambridge: Cambridge University Press, 2008, 178–9.
85. Tacitus, *Ann.* 1.13.2; Suet. *Calig.* 60, *Claud.* 10.4.

and Augustus. The last decades of the Republic had seen a remarkable expansion of Rome's power with the conquests of Pompeius
in Asia Minor, Syria and the adjoining areas, and of Julius Caesar in
Gaul. What followed in the reign of Augustus outstripped even this.
By 30 BC he had (as he states in the *Res Gestae*) added Egypt to the
power of the Roman people;[86] between 26 and 19 BC the conquest
of Spain was completed with the subjection of the territories in the
north-west of the peninsula; in 16 and 15 BC the Alpine region
was subdued and subsequently Raetia and then Noricum, to the east
along the Danube, came under Roman military control; Illyricum
was the scene of Caesar's campaigns before he faced Antonius in
31 BC and was finally secured, along with Dalmatia, after the
suppression of the revolts of the Dalmatians and Pannonians by
Tiberius and Germanicus in AD 9; and Armenia, which Augustus
says he might have made into a province, was with difficulty secured
for a series of kings loyal to Rome.[87] A further immense extension of
Roman control into Germany came to an end with the disastrous
loss of three legions under Quinctilius Varus in AD 9, but even then
the appointment of Tiberius and Germanicus to commands there
probably was intended to show that a renewed securing of the area
was still a possibility.[88] The empire by the end of Augustus' reign
was quite different from what it had been in 44 BC or even in 30 BC,
and what is more it was seen quite differently by the Romans: it is
only then that *imperium* became the word for the geographical and
political entity which we call the Roman Empire, a change that
lasted throughout the rest of its history and beyond.[89] This was the
result of two factors: the expansion of the empire to cover so great
a part of what was to the Romans the known world; and the control
exercised over this vast area by one man, both in those provinces
('Caesar's provinces') which he controlled through his own *legati*
and in the rest of the empire through his power and authority in
Rome itself.

So far as the inhabitants of the provinces of the empire were
concerned there were also differences, though they varied substan-
tially depending on where they lived and (perhaps still more) on their
place in society. The empire was not only geographically immense
but also immensely varied. The eastern provinces were largely

86. Aug. *RG* 27.1.
87. Aug. *RG* 27.2.
88. See above, pp. 183–5 and 188–9.
89. See Richardson, *The Language of Empire*, ch. 4.

Greek-speaking; in the west the remark by the geographer Strabo, that the Turdetani in Baetica were so Romanised that they had entirely forgotten their own dialect and now spoke Latin, while perhaps exaggerated, shows both that the language of the Romans was being adopted and that this was not normal. The written languages in both east and west, Greek and Latin respectively, were used by officials and the upper classes, but also by others lower down the social scale; local indigenous languages were, however, still present and were probably the normal form of oral communication among the peasants who made up the bulk of the population, though the evidence is inevitably small.[90] The presence of Romans and Italians added to a linguistic shift towards Latin, aided by the number of the colonies of soldiers that Augustus established throughout the empire: he lists in the *Res Gestae* such colonies in Africa, Sicily, Macedonia, Spain, Achaea, Asia, Syria, Gallia Narbonensis and Pisidia, in addition to those in Italy.[91] For the upper classes living in the cities of the east or in the new foundations in the west, who controlled the areas in which they lived under the oversight of the local Roman governor, the establishment of the world-wide peace which was the result of Augustus' monarchy brought the benefits of stability. Tacitus states that the provinces welcomed the change, glad to be free of the struggles between powerful Romans and the greed of the magistrates which had marked the Republic, when little was to be gained from the Roman legal system, weakened by violence, politics and bribery. This may well have been a rhetorical exaggeration. The corruption and extortion of provincial governors still continued, but the absence of the civil wars which had wreaked havoc across so much of the empire can only have been appreciated by those who had suffered it.[92]

The cities themselves both in the east and in the west bore witness to the power of Rome, the *princeps* and his family in large-scale

---

90. Strabo, 3.2.15. For the partial survival of Punic in north Africa well into the imperial period see F. Millar, 'Local cultures in the Roman Empire: Libyan, Punic and Latin in Roman Africa', *Journal of Roman Studies* 58 (1968), 126–34; for Gaul, see G. Woolf, *Becoming Roman: The Origins of Provincial Civilization in Gaul*, Cambridge: Cambridge University Press, 1998, 91–105.

91. Aug. *RG* 28.

92. Tacitus, *Ann.* 1.2. On continuing extortion, see P. A. Brunt, 'Charges of provincial maladministration under the early principate', *Historia* 10 (1961), 189–227. On the impact on the cities of the Greek world of Augustus' regime, see G. Bowersock, *Augustus and the Greek World*, Oxford: Oxford University Press, 1965, 85–100 (= Edmondson, *Augustus*, 468–81).

building programmes, some in new foundations, such as the remark-able ensemble still to be seen at Emerita Augusta (modern Mérida), which became the capital city of Lusitania.[93] The increasing Roman-ness of such cities gave a fillip both to the sense of 'being Roman' within the cities themselves and to the regions surrounding them, and also to their economy. Long-distance trade had been developing, especially in the western Mediterranean, through the last century of the Republic but the Augustan period sees an increase, for example, in the amounts of wine and oil shipped from Spain, often through the dangerous strait of Bonifacio between Corsica and Sardinia.[94] Though there is no reason to believe that economic shifts of this sort were any part of the policy of Augustus, and the pattern of which they are a part had begun long before, the stability which resulted from the end of the civil wars encouraged and established these changes and contributed to the emergence of a different notion of what the empire was and the way in which both those at the centre and those in the provinces saw it.

Augustus and the new Rome

The changes that had taken place between the deaths of Julius Caesar and of Augustus, a period of some fifty-eight years, mark a major turning point in the history of Rome, both of the city, its population, its political structures and its physical appearance, and of the empire at whose head it stood. In part this was obviously the result of the emergence and establishment of the supremacy of one man, who became the predominant patron of the people who lived in Rome itself and the universally acknowledged ruler of the Roman world. There had of course been others in the previous half-century who had held immense power in Rome, notably Sulla, Pompeius and Julius Caesar, each of whom had for a brief time controlled the *res publica* and had been given extraordinary commands and offices and (especially in the case of Julius Caesar) honours within and beyond the constitutional structures; but none to the extent that Augustus held. One clear indication of this is the way in which he incorporated

93. W. Trillmich, 'Colonia Augusta Emerita, capital of Lusitania', in Edmondson, *Augustus*, 427–67.
94. G. Woolf, 'Provincial perspectives', in K. Galinsky (ed.), *The Cambridge Companion to the Age of Augustus*, Cambridge: Cambridge University Press, 2005, 106–29; A. Tchernia, *Le Vin de l'Italie Romaine*, Rome: École Francaise de Rome, 1986, 172–85; A. J. Parker, *Ancient Shipwrecks in the Mediterranean and the Roman Provinces*, BAR International Series 580, Oxford: BAR, 1992, 8–15.

his family into the public sphere, and in particular into his plans for the onward transmission of the role he had held. No previous Roman since the legendary time of the kings had been in a position to do such a thing, or even to have thought about doing it. The great figures of the Republic had promoted the interests of their families and of their associates, but there was no question of a succession of the sort that caused such problems for Augustus in the last twenty years of his rule.

The changes to the empire also can be linked directly to the position that Augustus achieved. Rome had over the previous three centuries grown to be the greatest power in the Mediterranean through the exercise of its military might, under the control of increasingly powerful individual commanders. The defeat of Marcus Antonius at Actium resulted in the military power being concentrated in the hands of one man; the allocation of a great swathe of provinces to Augustus in 27 BC and his effective control of the others gave a unity to the areas that were under the power of the Roman people (*imperium populi Romani*) so that by the latter years of his reign *imperium* became the word for the territory of the Roman Empire. The goddess Roma, which had been worshipped in the Greek east since the second century AD, was now associated with the name of Augustus and appeared on altars in the provinces of the west as well.[95] The world-wide empire became more than a series of areas under Roman control; the focus that Augustus and his successors provided was largely responsible for the change which might be characterised as being from the exercise of power by an imperial Republic into the Roman Empire under an emperor. In Rome itself the Porticus Vipsania, set up by Augustus in accordance with the will that Agrippa had left at his death in 12 BC, displayed the whole world, either as a map or as a listing of places, the details drawn from the results of the surveys undertaken by Agrippa himself; and in the Forum stood the golden milestone, recording the distances from the city to the major cities, either those in Italy or in the whole empire.[96] These monuments showed the place the city now

95. *Imperium*: Richardson, *The Language of Empire*, ch. 4. Rome and Augustus: Suet. *Aug.* 52.1 (see above, pp. 138 (Lugudunum) and 207–10).

96. Porticus Vipsania: Pliny, *HN* 3.16–17; 6.139–40. On the nature of the display, see C. Nicolet, *Space, Geography and Politics in the Early Roman Empire*, Ann Arbor: University of Michigan Press, 1991, 95–122; Kai Brodersen, *Terra Cognita: Studien zur römischen Raumerfassung*, *Spudasmata* 59, Hildesheim: Georg Olms, 1995. Golden milestone: Dio Cass. 54.8.4.

held as the capital of the world, and the same can be seen in the geographical work written in the reign of Augustus and the early years of Tiberius by Strabo. The effect was profound in Rome but even greater in the rest of the Roman world. When, in the reign of Nero, the Jewish Christian Paul of Tarsus was arrested by a Roman garrison commander in Jerusalem, he avoided being flogged by pointing out to his captor that not only was he a Roman citizen (like the Roman officer he was addressing) but he had been so since his birth.[97] He was born in south-east Asia Minor, probably in the reign of Augustus; the world in which he lived and through which he travelled was a Roman world and he was a Roman within it, though he was a Jew from a Greek-speaking province and did not set foot in Italy until his last journey to Rome. Ovid, writing his plea to Augustus to be allowed to return to Rome, describes the place of his exile in far-off Tomis as the last part of the coast of the Black Sea which is Roman, the furthest place under Roman law, a land barely clinging to the edge of Augustus' *imperium*.[98] Cities too marked the extent of that empire: Aphrodisias in Caria, in south-western Asia Minor, built in the mid-first century AD a great structure celebrating the imperial house which included a series of friezes depicting the peoples that Augustus had defeated or subdued across the world from the Arabs to the Callaeci in north-west Spain.[99] At a more mundane but no less important level, the Augustan period saw the listing by means of censuses of the details of people and property across the Roman world, which went to inform the account of the whole empire (*breviarium totius imperii*) which was brought before the senate along with Augustus' will in the days after his death.[100] As all this shows, 'Roman' was an epithet no longer relating only to a city but also to an empire and an emperor; and Rome itself had inevitably changed.

How much this was the result of Augustus' intentions, as opposed to the things he had done (a literal translation of *Res Gestae*), is

97. Acts 22.24–9. On Paul's citizenship and its probable origins, see A. N. Sherwin-White, *Roman Society and Roman Law in the New Testament*, Oxford: Oxford University Press, 1963, 144–62.

98. Ovid, *Tr.* 2.197–200.

99. J. M. Reynolds, 'New evidence for the imperial cult in Julio-Claudian Aphrodisias', *Zeitschrift für Papyrologie und Epigraphik* 43 (1981), 317–27, at 326–7; R. R. R. Smith, '*Simulacra gentium*: the *ethn* from the Sebasteion at Aphrodisias', *Journal of Roman Studies* 78 (1988), 50–77.

100. Suet. *Aug.* 101.5 (see above, p. 192). See Nicolet, *Space, Geography and Politics*, 121–83.

another matter. Scholars of an earlier generation were inclined
to believe that he had from early in his career a blue-print of an
imperial structure which he systematically and, for the most part,
successfully implemented through the period of his reign. The
historian T. Rice Holmes wrote in 1928 and 1931 a two-volume
work on the age of Augustus entitled *The Architect of the Roman
Empire*, still worth consulting for his detailed critique of the literary
sources; but the idea of Augustus as from the beginning a designer
of the empire he left at his death does not fit well with the changing
and sporadic fashion in which these changes actually occurred. More
recently historians have argued that even in so technical an issue as
the development of administrative posts under Augustus and his use
of members of the equestrian order in those posts, the process was
one of response to situations as they arose rather than any systematic policy.[101] The account that has taken up the greater part of this
book suggests the same picture of a willingness to revisit and to
adapt decisions previously made, whether on legislation on marriage
or on fire-fighting in Rome or on the problematic question of the
succession. The intentions of any figure from the ancient world are,
of course, notoriously difficult to identify, and in the case of
Augustus the difficulty is exacerbated by an apparent contradiction
between two notable characteristics of his rule. On the one hand, his
tenacious grip on the realities of power, both through his control
of the armies by his choice of commanders he could trust and his
rewarding of the soldiers who served in them, and through his
management of the political and constitutional structures in Rome,
shows him determined to maintain the monarchical power he had
won as victor in the civil wars; and his construction of an imperial
family and a series of dynastic successors makes clear that this
monarchy was to remain, and to remain within that family. On the
other hand, his repeated presentation of himself as a restorer of
things that had been lost in the years that preceded his victory seems
to portray him as a restorer rather than as a revolutionary. Already
in 29 and 28 BC he conducted the census for the first time in forty-
two years and announced the burning of records of debt to the
treasury and the annulment of decisions made improperly during
the triumvirate. This was a restitution of the rights and laws that the

---

101. W. Eck, 'The administrative reforms of Augustus: pragmatism or systematic planning?', in Edmondson, *Augustus*, 229–49.

Roman people had previously enjoyed.[102] The republican and constitutional tone of the *Res Gestae*, completed at the end of his reign,
has been noted already, and it is noticeable that Augustus prefaces
his account of the offices he held (*RG* 7) with two chapters on those
that he refused on the grounds that they were contrary to ancestral
custom (*RG* 5 and 6).

At first sight these two characteristics of his lengthy time in
power seem simply incompatible with one another, and various
explanations have been given. It is clear that when, as the final
confrontation with Marcus Antonius approached in the late 30s BC,
he presented himself as the leader of Italy and the champion of the
Roman world, he needed the support of as many members of the
senate and people, both in Rome and in the western provinces, as
he could get, and that for this purpose at least the appearance of
restoring and maintaining the old ways, as opposed to the exotic
Hellenistic kingship espoused by Antonius and Cleopatra, was
essential. Was he then trapped in the consequences of his own
propaganda, compelled to follow through the promises, implicit as
well as explicit, that he had made at a crucial moment in his career,
despite his own desire for monarchy? Was his 'Republican' stance
merely a sophisticated piece of 'spin', designed to disguise the reality
of his sole control and appease the senatorial classes, and especially
the nobility, who had lost the political power with which they had
been masters of Rome for the past centuries? If so, who was fooled
by this, and why did they allow themselves to be fooled, given the
blatant display of the realities of Augustus' position?

The first thing to note is that if the intention was to conceal
the actualities of the power of the new *princeps* it was a complete
failure. Already in the early 20s BC, Cornelius Nepos, in his biography of Cicero's friend and correspondent Titus Pomponius Atticus,
could describe the struggle between Caesar and Antonius as motiv-
ated by the desire of each to become the *princeps* not only of the city
of Rome but of the whole world; and the architectural writer Vitruvius, writing between 27 and 23 BC, composed a preface to the first
book of his work on buildings which addressed Augustus in fulsome
terms as the master of all nations, the director of the people and
senate of Rome and the recipient of the power which had been held
by his divine father, Julius Caesar.[103] These words could not have

---

102. See above, pp. 82–6.
103. Nepos, *Atticus* 20.5; Vitruvius, 1.*praef*.1–2.

been written if the intention and policy of Augustus had been to hide the fact that he was the master of Rome and the empire. The restoration of the *res publica* was evidently not incompatible with the presence of a sole ruler, and indeed the senate made a dedication in 29 BC in the Forum, in the context of the great triple triumph after the defeat of Antonius and Cleopatra, to 'Imperator Caesar, son of the divine Julius, consul for the fifth time, consul designate for the sixth time, acclaimed *imperator* (victorious general) for the seventh time, for the saving of the *res publica*'.[104] For the contemporaries of Augustus, *res publica* did not, or need not, mean the state of affairs in what we now refer to as the Late Republic, with the predominance of the great families in the politics of the city, but rather the proper life and business of the Roman state. Cicero, speaking in the senate in 46 BC about the decision of Julius Caesar to allow the return to Rome of Marcus Claudius Marcellus, the pro-Pompeian consul of 51, urged the dictator to undertake a number of measures to aid the *res publica*, which should live for ever even though Caesar himself was mortal. These were that the law courts be re-established, trust be brought back, licentiousness repressed, the birth of children encouraged and everything which had collapsed and become disordered be bound up with strict legislation. Admittedly Cicero was talking to someone he regarded as a tyrant, but what he describes as needed for the restoring of the *res publica* could stand as a description of the measures which Augustus, little by little over a long period, introduced to revive exemplary ancestral practices and introduce others for the imitation of posterity.[105]

This did not mean that Augustus faced no opposition, and the sources mention conspiracies against him. Of these, however, only three, those of Lepidus (the son of the former triumvir), of Caepio and Murena and of Marcus Egnatius, seem probable, and only the last a threat from someone with a political axe to grind.[106] These all come in the aftermath of Augustus' resignation from the consulship in 23 BC, when there was resulting uncertainty and turmoil. The

104. *EJ* 17.

105. Cic. *Pro Marcello* 23; Aug. *RG* 8.5. On the meaning of the restoration of the *res publica*, see F. Millar, 'Triumvirate and principate', *Journal of Roman Studies* 63 (1973), 50–67, esp. 63–7.

106. Lepidus: see above, p. 117; Caepio and Murena: see above, pp. 103–4; Egnatius: see above, pp. 109–10. On plots against and opposition to Augustus, see K. A. Raaflaub and L. J. Samons III, 'Opposition to Augustus', in K. A. Raaflaub and M. Toher (eds), *Between Republic and Empire: Interpretations of Augustus and his Principate*, Berkeley, Los Angeles and Oxford: University of California Press, 1990, 417–54.

problems he faced later in his reign, with Tiberius on his retreat to Rhodes in 6 BC, with his daughter Julia in 2 BC and with his grand-daughter Julia in AD 8 and his grandson Agrippa Postumus in the previous year, all derive from arguments within the imperial family, rather than from any antagonism with other members of the upper classes in Rome. By comparison with his successors, all of whom, down to and including the emperor Nero, faced conspiracy and the threat of armed revolt, his reign was remarkably free from violent conflict. Tacitus records that at his death there were those who spoke idly about the benefits of freedom and some hoped for war, though most dreaded it.[107] Since Actium there had been no likelihood of war and those who might have wished for the benefits of a free republic on the old style had been notably quiet.

Augustus, or Gaius Octavius as he had been then, was born into the political world of the late Republic, with its mixture of family-based oligarchic politics, the emergence of powerful military commanders, a growing world-wide dominance and a nostalgia (notable in Cicero) for the good old days of the second century BC, when morality was stern but respected and the populace listened to the voices of their leaders. He grew up in a context in which riot became common in the city and the laws were over-ridden by men with large armies. There is no reason to believe that the *res publica* which he claimed to be attempting to restore was other than that which those of his and his parents' generation had wanted to see. Rome, which, for the young Octavius in the years after the Social War of the early 80s BC, included Italy, was to be given back its rights and laws and brought back to the worship of the gods and a proper morality. The turmoil of the civil war between Pompeius and Julius Caesar, followed by the latter's assassination, had led to still more bloodshed and horror, in which Octavius, now called Caesar, had played his part; but it is worth remembering that the task that had been given to himself, Antonius and Lepidus in 43 BC, when the triumvirate was established by the law proposed by the tribune Publius Titius, was the reconstitution of the *res publica*. By the time of his death, he could claim to have carried that out.

Such a reconstitution, of course, is never a matter of turning the clock back. Young Caesar had, by the time he had removed Antonius at Actium, become the only player at the table, supported by a trusted group of friends and supporters. When he set about the

107. Tacitus, *Ann.*1.4.2.

process of restoring the *res publica* and its imperial glories, he might
(as he repeatedly insisted) have been acting on behalf of and with
the concordance of the senate and people, but even as first citizen,
princeps, he was doing so in a manner that was quite unlike that in
which the state of affairs he was restoring had come about. That he
was able to do so, and to produce what was in effect a *res publica*
which included a monarch, was made possible not least by the fact
that he lived to such a great age. From the defeat of Antonius to his
death, he was unquestionably the most powerful man in Rome for
forty-five years, by which time (as Tacitus again notes[108]) there was
almost no one alive who remembered how it had been before. One
of the greatest achievements of the divine Augustus, as he became
on 17 September AD 14, was to have lived so long. It is interesting
if fruitless to speculate what would have happened had he died in
23 BC when he was severely ill. It is certain, however, that the Roman
Empire would not have been the same. His successes and his failures,
which shaped the history of Rome for the next two centuries, were
the outcome of that long life, and made him the major figure in the
history of Europe that he undoubtedly is.

108. Tacitus, *Ann.* 1.3.7.

Chronology

	Political/Military	Religious/Cultural	Events elsewhere
BC			
44	(15 March) Assassination of Julius Caesar Gaius Octavius, heir to Julius Caesar and adopted under his will, takes name Gaius Julius Caesar		
43	(2 January) Caesar given *imperium pro praetore* and membership of senate (21 April) Battle of Mutina; death of Hirtius and Pansa (19 August) Caesar consul (27 November) *Lex Titia* establishes triumvirate		
42	(October) Battles of Philippi; suicides of Cassius and Brutus (16 November) Birth of Tiberius Claudius Nero, son of Tiberius Claudius Nero and Livia	Deification of Julius Julius Caesar	Sextus Pompeius controls Sicily
41	Caesar at war with consul Lucius Antonius		Antonius in Asia; meets Cleopatra in Tarsus (winter) and goes to Alexandria
40	Surrender of Perusia to Caesar by Lucius Antonius; death of Calenus in Gaul; Caesar marries Scribonia (September) pact of Brundisium		Parthian invasion of Syria (Pacorus and Quintus Labienus) (autumn) Herod granted throne of Judaea
39	(spring) Pact of Misenum Ventidius defeats Parthians; Agrippa campaigns in Gaul		(winter) Antonius and Octavia in Athens

	Political/Military	Religious/Cultural	Events elsewhere
38	(17 January) Marriage of Caesar and Livia Second victory of Ventidius against Parthians (death of Pacorus); Antonius captures Samosata; Sextus Pompeius' successes against Caesar off Cumae and in straits of Messina (27 November) triumph of Ventidius		
37	(summer) Pact of Tarentum; renewal of triumviral powers for five years (July) Capture of Jerusalem by Sosius; inauguration of Herod's reign		Appointment of client kings in Asia Minor by Antonius; 'marriage' of Antonius and Cleopatra
36	Removal of Lepidus from triumvirate; Caesar given *sacrosanctitas* of a tribune; honours for Livia and Octavia (3 September) Caesar defeats Sextus Pompeius at Naulochus Antonius' Parthian offensive, failure of siege of Phraaspa and retreat through Armenia		
35–33	Caesar campaigns in Illyricum		
35			Death of Sextus Pompeius in Asia
34	Antonius' invasion of Armenia and capture of Artavasdes; Antonius triumphs at Alexandria, followed by 'donations' to Cleopatra and her children		
33	Caesar's second consulship; Antonius remains in Armenia (year end) powers of triumvirate lapse		

	Political/Military	Religious/Cultural	Events elsewhere
32	Antonius divorces Octavia; Caesar publishes Antonius' will; oaths of loyalty to Caesar from Italy and the west		
31	Caesar's third consulship (2 September) Battle of Actium		
30	(1 August) Caesar captures Alexandria; suicide of Antonius (10 August) suicide of Cleopatra		
29	(13–15 August) Caesar's triple triumph Marcus Licinius Crassus pacifies Thrace and defeats Bastarnae; Caesar and Agrippa begin *lectio senatus* and census	(11 January) Doors of temple of Janus closed	
28	Caesar (for sixth time) and Agrippa consuls; return of control of *aerarium* to praetors; Caesar *princeps senatus*		
27	(13 and 15 January) Caesar in senate; grant of *provinciae* and right to use *legati* (16 January) Caesar named Augustus (4 July) Triumph of Marcus Licinius Crassus from Thrace Augustus in Gaul and Spain		
26–25	Augustus in Spain		
26	Dismissal and suicide of Cornelius Gallus (perhaps late 27); Aelius Gallus in Arabia Felix		
25	Marriage of Marcellus and Julia; Augustus ill; Marcus Terentius Varro campaigns in Val D'Aosta; Publius Petronius campaigns in Ethiopia	Doors of temple of Janus closed	Juba II made king of Mauretania; death of Amyntas and annexation of Galatia

	Political/Military	Religious/Cultural	Events elsewhere
24	Augustus returns to Rome from Spain, arriving after becoming consul for the tenth time		
23	Augustus ill; Agrippa given grant of *imperium pro consule*, sent to east; Augustus resigns consulship (1 July) Augustus receives *imperium maius* and *tribunicia potestas* for life Death of Marcellus		Phraates IV of Parthia sends embassy to Rome
22	Trial of Marcus Primus; conspiracy of Caepio and Murena; Augustus refuses dictatorship and life consulship, but accepts *cura annonae*; Augustus in Greece and Asia		
21– 20	Augustus in Greece and Asia		
21	Marriage of Agrippa and Julia		
20	Agrippa deals with trouble in Gaul; recovery of Parthian standards		Tiberius crowns Tigranes king of Armenia
19	Augustus returns to Rome, is given lifetime grant of consular *fasces* and seat between consuls in senate; Agrippa completes conquest of Spain; Lucius Cornelius Balbus campaigns against Garamantes in Africa and celebrates triumph	(21 September) Death of Vergil	
18	Renewal of Augustus' *provinciae*; Agrippa has *imperium* renewed and is given *tribunicia potestas* for five years; another *lectio senatus*; Augustus' moral and social legislation		

	Political/Military	Religious/Cultural	Events elsewhere
17	Augustus adopts Gaius and Lucius, sons of Agrippa and Julia; campaigns of Publius Silius Nerva in northern Italy and Alps (17–16); defeat of Marcus Lollius in Gaul (?16)	Celebration of *ludi saeculares*	
16–13	Augustus in Gaul; Agrippa in east		
15	Agrippa visits Jerusalem; Tiberius and Drusus invade Bavaria and reach Danube		
13	Augustus returns to Rome; Agrippa in east and Pannonia; Tiberius consul; Augustus' *imperium* renewed for five years; Agrippa's *tribunicia potestas* renewed, *imperium* renewed for five years and made *maius*; death of Lepidus the triumvir	(4 July) Ara Pacis in Campus Martius decreed	Troubles break out in Pannonia
12–9	Drusus in Germany; Tiberius in Balkans		
12	(March) Death of Agrippa	(6 March) Augustus elected *pontifex maximus*	
11	Tiberius divorces Vipsania and marries Julia; death of Octavia		Lucius Calpurnius Piso puts down rising in Thrace (11–9)
9	Drusus reaches Elbe but dies after accident (14 September)	(30 January) Ara Pacis consecrated	
8	Census held; Tiberius campaigns against Sugambri	Deaths of Maecenas and Horace; month of Sextilis renamed August by senatorial decree	
7	Recall of Tiberius to be consul for the second time; Tiberius' triumph over Sugambri; fourteen *regiones* of Rome established		

	Political/Military	Religious/Cultural	Events elsewhere
6	Tiberius granted *tribunicia potestas* for five years, retires to Rhodes		
5	Augustus consul; Gaius Caesar assumes *toga virilis* and is named *princeps iuventutis*; beginning of regular suffect consulships		
4			Death of Herod and division of Judaean kingdom
2	Augustus consul (5 February) Augustus named *pater patriae* Lucius Caesar assumes *toga virilis* and is named *princeps iuventutis*; Julia exiled; appointment of first praetorian prefects; *lex Fufia Caninia*	(12 May) Dedication of temple of Mars Ultor	Death of Phraates IV of Parthia; accession of Phraates V (Phraataces)
1	Gaius Caesar sent to east with *imperium*		
AD 2	(August) Death of Lucius Caesar at Massilia; return of Tiberius from Rhodes		Gaius Caesar makes agreement with Phraataces; Ariobarzanes installed as king of Armenia
4	(21 February) Death of Gaius Caesar (26 June) Augustus adopts Agrippa Postumus and Tiberius, who adopts Germanicus Tiberius given *tribunicia potestas* for ten years, invades Germany as far as river Weser; *lex Aelia Sentia*; another *lectio senatus*		
5	Tiberius reaches Elbe		
6	Establishment of *aerarium militare* and *vigiles*; outbreak of Pannonian and Illyrian revolt; revolt in Isauria		Judaea becomes a *provincia*, following banishment of Archelaus

	Political/Military	Religious/Cultural	Events elsewhere
7	Banishment of Agrippa Postumus to Planasia		
8	Banishment of Julia the Younger	Banishment of Ovid	
9	End of Pannonian revolt; defeat of Quinctilius Varus in Germany		
10	Tiberius on Rhine frontier	Dedication of temple of Concordia Augusta	
11	Tiberius and Germanicus in Germany		
12	Germanicus consul, takes command in Gaul and Germany (23 October) Tiberius' Illyrian triumph		
13	Tiberius given further ten years *tribunicia potestas* and *imperium maius*; Germanicus given *imperium*		
14	(11 May) *Lustrum* held (19 August) Augustus dies; Tiberius becomes *princeps* (early September) Augustus granted a public funeral (17 September) Augustus voted divine honours Death of Agrippa Postumus; army revolts in Pannonia and on Rhine, dealt with by Drusus and Germanicus respectively		

Guide to ancient authors

The main ancient sources for the period of Augustus are mostly writers who wrote long after the end of his reign, and both they and earlier writers have their own peculiarities which make the interpretation of their evidence problematic. The list that follows gives some help in identifying these crucial sources, and is arranged in roughly chronological order. The poets of the Augustan period are not included here, as they are more fully discussed in Chapter 6.

Cicero (or Marcus Tullius Cicero, to give him his full name) was the greatest orator of the last years of the Republic. A *novus homo* ('new man', who had no one in his family who had been a member of the senate), he was born in Arpinum in central Italy and rose to become consul in 63 BC, when he dealt with the uprising led by Lucius Sergius Catilina. As a consequence of his actions against Catilina and his associates, Cicero was sent into exile in 58 to 57 through a law proposed by his bitter enemy Publius Clodius, tribune of the plebs in 58. In the later 50s Cicero spent two years as governor of the province of Cilicia and returned to Rome as the struggle between Julius Caesar and Pompeius moved towards civil war, during which he was a somewhat half-hearted supporter of Pompeius. After Julius Caesar's victory Cicero returned to Rome but did not emerge into the political life of the city until after the assassination on the Ides of March 44 BC. What followed, including his enmity with Marcus Antonius, which led to his death in the proscriptions in December 43 BC, is told in Chapter 2. He was a prolific writer in prose, writing, in addition to the published versions of several of his speeches, on subjects including rhetoric and philosophy, and also a poet. For the period covered by this book the most important items are the large number of letters he wrote, both to his lifelong friend Titus Pomponius Atticus and to other important figures in the tumultuous years 44 and 43 BC; his virulent speeches against Marcus Antonius in late 44 and early 43, called the *Philippics* after the speeches that the Athenian orator Demosthenes made against King Philip II of Macedonia in the fourth century BC; and his philosophical work *De officiis* (On Duties), written in late 44 and addressed to his son, then studying in Athens, but clearly intended for a wider audience, in which he sets out his ideas on how a Roman of the upper classes should behave and of the importance of a public political career, and bitterly attacks the dictatorship of Julius Caesar. Cicero is the most approachable of all the individuals of the classical age of Rome because of the multitude and variety of his surviving writings; but he was a clever and a passionate man, deeply involved in the events about which he wrote, and in using his statements as evidence, care needs to be taken and attention paid not least to the audience he was addressing and his motives in writing.

Augustus himself provides the most significant and most elusive account of his activities in the *Res Gestae*, which is discussed in Chapter 6. Long before that was written he had also, in the 20s BC, produced an autobiography in which he defended himself and attacked his enemies in a style very different from that of the *Res Gestae*.[1] This has not survived, though it was used as a source by other authors. One of these was **Nicolaus of Damascus** (Nicolaus Damascenus), an almost exact contemporary of Augustus, a writer whose work included philosophical discussions on Aristotle and a large universal history containing a panegyrical account of Herod the Great, in whose court he spent much time, which was later used by the Jewish historian Josephus. Nicolaus wrote a life of Caesar (as he called him) from his boyhood which seems to have drawn heavily on Augustus' autobiography. The fragments which survive take the story down to Augustus' return to Italy from Apollonia and to his gathering troops in Campania in the autumn of 44 BC.[2] It is not known how far Nicolaus took his account or when he wrote it, but the tone of the work is, not surprisingly, strongly pro-Augustan. It is, however, by some distance the earliest surviving historical account of these years, with the exception of the *Res Gestae*.[3]

The historian **Livy** and the geographer **Strabo** were also contemporaries of Augustus, but, although Livy took his work down to the death of Drusus in Germany in 9 BC,[4] only brief summaries of the books covering our period survive. In the work as we have it there is little direct reference to Augustus and, although both men in their different ways clearly were interested in and respected the achievements of the Roman Republic, a comparison of their views on some of the great figures of the past reveals considerable differences.[5] Strabo's great survey of the world, written under Augustus and

1. See above, p. 201.
2. See above, p. 24.
3. An edition, commentary and translation of Nicolaus can be found in Jane Bellemore, *Nicolaus of Damascus: Life of Augustus*, Bristol: Bristol Classical Press, 1984.
4. See above, p. 118.
5. For Livy's reference to Augustus on the status of Aulus Cornelius Cossus, see above, p. 90. On the differences of their views of great men, see T. J. Luce, 'Livy, Augustus and the Forum Augustum', in K. Raaflaub and M. Toher (eds), *Between Republic and Empire: Interpretations of Augustus and his Principate*, Berkeley, Los Angeles and Oxford: University of California Press, 1990, 123–38 (and in J. Edmondson (ed.), *Augustus*, Edinburgh: Edinburgh University Press, 2009, 399–415).

in the early years of Tiberius, combines the disciplines of history and geography and gives not only an invaluable picture of the empire (though some of the details, often drawn from earlier writers, are not reliable) but also a contemporary Greek view of Rome and Augustus.

The earliest surviving historical work on the period is that of **Velleius Paterculus**, an Italian who was also a contemporary and one who was himself involved in the events of the latter part of Augustus' reign. He was a relatively junior member of the party which accompanied Gaius Caesar in his journey to the eastern provinces in AD 2 and was present at the great meeting with the Parthian king Phraataces on the river Euphrates;[6] later he served with Tiberius in Germany and Illyria. Velleius' history, dedicated to Marcus Vinicius, who was consul in AD 30, dealt with an immense period from Greek mythology to the year AD 29 in two books, an astounding coverage in so small a work. Almost all the first book is lost but the second book shows him writing with increasing fullness on Julius Caesar, Augustus and Tiberius. All this might suggest that Velleius would provide a prime source for Rome in the Augustan age, but his admiration for Augustus and especially for Tiberius has led many modern scholars to dismiss his work as mere panegyric or even downright falsity and by implication not worth reading.[7] This is too severe an assessment and, though Velleius' fawning on the two emperors may be distasteful to a modern audience, his account of the period, both as an eyewitness and not least as a faithful member of the imperial staff, deserves careful consideration.[8]

The next historian, in chronological order, whose work on this period is extant is very different from Velleius. **Tacitus** is one of the greatest historians of antiquity and in his *Annals*, to give it the name by which it has been known since the sixteenth century, he produced an extremely intelligent and highly critical account of the reigns of the Julio-Claudian emperors from Tiberius to Nero, probably written in the second and early third decades of the second century AD. Although much has been lost in the meagre manuscript tradition which survives, the first book of the *Annals*, which begins with the death of Augustus and the accession of Tiberius, is complete and paints a typically nuanced but essentially hostile picture of the two emperors, with Augustus in his last years as an enfeebled old man with a bloody and treacherous past and Tiberius as an embittered tyrant, concealing his true nature behind a Republican mask, while in the background Livia, Augustus' widow and Tiberius' mother, cunningly controls

---

6. See above, p. 163.
7. Notably Ronald Syme, 'Mendacity in Velleius', *American Journal of Philology* 99 (1978), 45–63 (= *Roman Papers*, Oxford: Oxford University Press, 1984, 1090–104).
8. For commentaries on the Latin text, see A. J. Woodman, *Velleius Paterculus: The Caesarian and Augustan Narrative (2.41–93)*, Cambridge: Cambridge University Press, 1983, and *Velleius Paterculus: The Tiberian Narrative (2.94–131)*, Cambridge: Cambridge University Press, 1977.

and dominates. This picture is a salutary corrective to the enthusiastic approval of Augustus in much Augustan literature and to the self-justifying presentation of the *Res Gestae*; but it must always be remembered that Tacitus is writing a century after the events he describes and is by no means a naïve and objective observer. He was a senator who had held the consulship in 97 AD and his suspicion of the emperors and of those of his own class who became their courtiers permeates all his work.

The biographer **Suetonius** was a younger contemporary of Tacitus, who served as an equestrian secretary in charge of libraries and later of imperial correspondence under the emperor Trajan and in the early years of the reign of the emperor Hadrian, before apparently being dismissed in the 120s on the fall from imperial favour of his patron, the praetorian prefect Septicius Clarus. Suetonius was a scholarly writer, with access, at least while he was a member of the imperial secretariat, to excellent sources. He wrote a set of twelve lives of the 'Caesars', beginning with Julius Caesar and ending with Domitian (complete except for the beginning of the first), as well as of literary men of note, most of which have not survived. Of those which relate to this period, those of Julius Caesar and Augustus contain more information and are more fully written than that of Tiberius (the life of Augustus is the longest of the twelve). Because he is writing biography and not history, much of Suetonius' account of each individual is arranged not chronologically but according to themes, showing his subjects' character or their actions with regard to particular topics, which sometimes cause problems for dating the events he describes; but his descriptions are, so far as can be told, mostly accurate and his style is economical and readable.[9]

Another biographer who deals with several individuals dealt with in this book is the Greek philosopher and essayist **Plutarch**, from the town of Chaeronea in Boeotia, who wrote in the last years of the first century AD and the beginning of the second. The biographies concerned are those of Julius Caesar, Cicero, Marcus Brutus and Marcus Antonius. They come from a series in which he pairs together lives of great Greek and Roman figures, so that the biography of Julius Caesar is paralleled by that of Alexander the Great, and that of Cicero by the life of Demosthenes, the great Athenian orator of the fourth century BC. As Plutarch explains in the opening of his life of Alexander, he is writing biography, not history, and so does not record all the great achievements of his subjects but rather those things which reveal their virtues and vices.[10] One result of this distinction, by which he defines himself as a philosopher rather than a historian, is that he is not always precise about the chronology of the events he narrates, but he is a scholar who has consulted a wide range of sources and has produced

---

9. For a useful commentary on the Latin text, see John Carter, *Suetonius: Divus Augustus*, Bristol: Bristol Classical Press, 1982.
10. Plut. *Alex.* 1.1.

a carefully composed and often dramatic account, notably in his life of Antonius.[11]

The two main narrative histories for the period from the death of Julius Caesar to the end of Augustus' reign are both Greek and written long after the events they describe. The first is by **Appian**, who came from Alexandria in Egypt. He was born probably in the last years of the first century AD, a member of the Greek upper class in the city, and practised as an advocate both there and in Rome, later holding an imperial appointment as a procurator. He wrote an immense work, the *Roman History*, probably in the mid-second century, which in twenty-four books sets out the growth of Rome's empire, first by narrating the wars and diplomatic exchanges with a series of foreign peoples (books 1 to 12), followed by five books covering the civil wars from the time of the Gracchi in the late second century BC down to the death of Sextus Pompeius in 35 BC, and four on the Egyptian wars, dealing with the struggle against Antonius and Cleopatra. The last three books seems to have covered the period from Augustus to Trajan, with the last two being about Trajan's campaigns in Dacia and the east. Though much of the *Roman History* has not survived (notably and regrettably, for the period dealt with in this book, the four books on the Egyptian wars and that on the early imperial age), the *Civil Wars* exists complete; and, since the first two of the five books are concerned with the hundred years down to the assassination of Julius Caesar while the last three are devoted to the decade that follows, it is clear that Appian is particularly interested in the aftermath of the Ides of March. Indeed his concentration on the period seems to have increased still further, given that it took him four books to deal with the Egyptian wars from 34 to 30 BC. His picture of the wars and their effect on Rome is bleak, especially in his graphic stories of the proscriptions,[12] and, although he assumes that the monarchy which resulted from them was inevitable and desirable (not surprisingly for a writer in the second century AD), he is far from being uncritical of those involved in the process which led to it. Rather he sees the wars between Romans, as opposed to those earlier conflicts with foreign peoples, as a potentially disastrous test from which the Romans emerged into unity and monarchy.[13] He is prone to errors from time to time and his treatment of the period immediately following the death of Julius Caesar is particularly confused, not least in the vagueness of its chronology, but for all that he gives a fair-minded and vivid account of the period.[14]

11. See the commentary on the Greek text by Christopher Pelling, *Plutarch: Life of Antony*, Cambridge: Cambridge University Press, 1988.
12. Appian, *B Civ*. 4.5–51.
13. Appian, *Praef.* 59; *B Civ*. 1.6.
14. An excellent recent translation with brief commentary is John Carter, *Appian: The Civil Wars*, London: Penguin, 1996.

The other Greek historian whose work on this period has survived is **Dio Cassius**, a Roman senator who reached the consulship in the early third century, probably under the emperor Septimius Severus, and was consul for a second time in 229 under Severus Alexander, but whose family came from Nicaea in the province of Bithynia in Asia Minor. Alongside a significant political and administrative career in what was for the senatorial class a troubled and sometimes dangerous period, he wrote his *Roman History* in eighty books, an account of the history of Rome from its origins down to his own time, intended (it would seem) for a Greek-speaking readership, consisting of those who, like himself, had been absorbed into the Roman imperial structure. He follows the pattern of annual sections, dated by the consuls of each year, which had been one of the main forms of history writing under the Republic and had last been used for a complete history of Rome by Livy, writing under Augustus, though it was also followed by Tacitus in his *Annals*, which dealt with a much shorter period. Of Dio's eighty books, those from book 36 to book 55, section 9, survive almost complete, covering the years 69 to 6 BC, with fragments and a much later abbreviation being all that is left of the rest. His great value for the period of Augustus lies in the fact that he alone provides a coherent narrative of the reign down to 6 BC, and much of our understanding of Augustus must at least begin with Dio's account, however much it is modified by evidence from other literary sources, from inscriptions and from archaeology. Like Appian he is of course dependent on earlier writers, now lost, for his information, and also like Appian his own views on monarchy are affected by the time in which he lived, which led him to believe that rule by a single emperor was inevitable. Discussing the assassination of Julius Caesar, he notes that the 'Liberators' proclaimed themselves as having destroyed Caesar and freed the people, but in reality they had plotted against him wickedly and thrown the city into chaos at a time when it had at last possessed a stable government. Dio sees Augustus as combining the freedom of democracy (the word he uses for the Republic) with monarchy and thus freedom with security and order.[15] Unsurprisingly he is very much in favour of Augustus, and this underlies his presentation of the changes Augustus introduced. Although he understandably regards Augustus as concealing his true intentions when in 27 BC he presented himself as unwilling to continue in control of the state, and is critical of the flattery which followed Augustus' allegedly reluctant decision to be persuaded otherwise, he puts this forward as a necessary manoeuvre by Augustus to show himself as 'democratic'.[16] Dio can be careless, sometimes when he is using more

---

15. Dio Cass. 44.2.2; 56.43.4. On Dio's political views, see F. Millar, *A Study of Cassius Dio*, Oxford: Oxford University Press, 1964, 74–7.
16. Dio Cass. 53.11–12 and 20.

than one source and does not notice contradictions and doublets, but he is mostly accurate and often inserts explanations for his Greek readership and comments of his own.[17]

17. See the text, translation and commentary by J. W. Rich, *Cassius Dio: The Augustan Settlement (Roman History 53–55.9)*, Warminster: Aris and Phillips, 1990; and the commentary on the Greek text by P. M. Swan, *The Augustan Succession: An Historical Commentary on Cassius Dio's Roman History, Books 55–56 (9 BC–AD 14)*, Oxford: Oxford University Press, 2004.

Guide to further reading

The Augustan age has been the subject of an immense amount of scholarly writing and the suggestions that follow are intended to do no more than to point the way to some of the more important and useful works in English for the further exploration of this fascinating period.

Histories of the Augustan period

Between the two world wars there appeared two very different accounts. The first was *The Architect of the Roman Empire*, 2 volumes, Oxford: Oxford University Press, 1928 and 1931, by T. Rice Holmes, a thorough if now very old-fashioned work, based on a scrupulous reading of the ancient sources, and still worth consulting on matters of detail. As its title suggests, it presents a favourable view of the emperor as the founder of an imperial system which endured for the next two centuries, though Rice Holmes was not blind to the horrors of the triumviral period. The second was Ronald Syme's *The Roman Revolution*, Oxford: Oxford University Press, 1939. This is a very different book, and one which shaped the study of Augustus and the change from Republic to empire for the rest of the twentieth century. Syme depicts Augustus as a dictator on the same pattern as Hitler and Mussolini, tracing the construction of a group of supporters which surrounded him and dismissing his claims to the restoration of the Republic as a screen, put in place to disguise his desire for power. It is a powerful and persuasive case, supported by Syme's formidable command of the evidence and presented with a literary flair and a bleak view of political operators, both of which resemble those of his favourite historian, Tacitus. Although his dominance of the field is no longer what it was, *The Roman Revolution* is an essential and exciting read.

By the time of the publication of the *Cambridge Ancient History*, 2nd edn, vol. X, *The Augustan Empire, 43 BC–AD 69*, Cambridge: Cambridge University Press, 1996, the fashion for general histories of a period had been replaced by more thematic treatments and so, as several reviewers noted, it seemed already outdated in style. It is nevertheless an important resource, containing a lively account of the triumviral period by Christopher Pelling and two admirably sane and humane chapters by John

Crook on the reign of Augustus. It also includes an overview of Augustan foreign policy by Erich Gruen, separate treatments of the various provinces of the empire and an excellent and innovative chapter by Andrew Wallace-Hadrill on the development of the court which surrounded the emperor. For all these reasons and many more, it is a volume that anyone interested in the world of Rome under Augustus will want to consult.

Specific themes and topics

The understanding of the interrelations of art and architecture with the history of the period covered by this book, and particularly Augustus' self-presentation, has been one of the major advances since the early 1980s. The classic work on this is Paul Zanker's *The Power of Images in the Age of Augustus*, Ann Arbor: University of Michigan Press, 1988, which is essential reading. Karl Galinsky, *Augustan Culture*, Princeton: Princeton University Press, 1996, brings together the visual and literary arts, religion, and political and social history in a broad thematic survey which explores the interaction of these elements in the creation of the Augustan age. Another fundamental book on the changed world that resulted from the events of this period is Claude Nicolet's *Space, Geography and Politics in the Early Roman Empire*, Ann Arbor: University of Michigan Press, 1991, which traces the growth in understanding of the physical and spatial environment which took place as a result of the need for the Augustan regime to extend control across the empire and of the measures which were put in place as a result.

On the period of the civil wars from 44 BC to the battle of Actium, Josiah Osgood's *Caesar's Legacy: Civil War and the Emergence of the Roman Empire*, Cambridge: Cambridge University Press, 2006, provides a vivid picture, concentrating on the effects on and notably the suffering of the people of Rome, Italy and the empire, and the ways in which this led to the establishment of the Augustan regime.

Collections of essays and articles

One of the results of the move away from general histories of the Augustan period to more limited and detailed study of particular aspects has been the appearance since the early 1980s of collections of shorter papers, some consisting of work specially written for the purpose and some gathering together important contributions which had previously appeared elsewhere. Of the first group, I would mention three. The book *Caesar Augustus: Seven Aspects*, Oxford: Oxford University Press, 1984, was edited by Fergus Millar and Erich Segal and emerged from a colloquium organised to celebrate Sir Ronald Syme's eightieth birthday. It contains contributions by major scholars of the time from Europe and the USA on different facets of Augustus and his impact, and includes important papers by Millar on the effects of the Augustan monarchy across the Mediterranean world, by Werner Eck on the self-representation of senators and by Jasper Griffin on the relations between Augustus and the poets. Published in 1990, *Between Republic and Empire: Interpretations of Augustus and his Principate*, Berkeley, Los Angeles and Oxford: University of California Press, edited by Kurt A. Raaflaub and Mark Toher, a collection of essays by nineteen scholars, was intended both to mark the fiftieth anniversary of Syme's *Roman Revolution* and to present a less bleak and more balanced portrait of the emperor than that of Syme.[18] The essays, though not providing an integrated picture, examine the historiography, poetry, art, religion and politics of the period, bringing together a series of analyses which certainly modify Syme's conclusions. More recently *The Cambridge Companion to the Age of Augustus*, Cambridge: Cambridge University Press, 2005, edited by Karl Galinsky, assembles sixteen chapters by scholars from Europe and the USA, which together give an overview of current work on many of the central issues.

In the second category, Jonathan Edmondson's *Augustus*, Edinburgh: Edinburgh University Press, 2009, collects fifteen major papers on the age of Augustus, including five very important contributions from Jean-Louis Ferrary (on the powers of Augustus), Werner Eck (on Augustus' administrative reforms), John Scheid (on cults in Augustan Rome), Tony Hölscher (on the Actium monuments) and Walter Trillmich (on Emerita, the capital of Roman Lusitania) which appear in English translation for the first time. These, and the other papers included, together with Edmondson's own lucid and perceptive introductions, make this an extremely useful volume.

---

1. The editors and contributors had intended to dedicate their book to Syme, who died just before it went to press.

Index